CORNISH STUDIES

Second Series

FOUR

INSTITUTE OF CORNISH STUDIES

Sardinia Pilchardus
(The Pilchard)

EDITOR'S NOTE

Cornish Studies is a fully refereed series which exists to reflect current research conducted internationally in the inter-disciplinary field of Cornish Studies. It is edited by Dr Philip Payton, Reader in Cornish Studies and Director of the Institute of Cornish Studies at the University of Exeter, and is published by the University of Exeter Press. The opinions expressed in *Cornish Studies* are those of individual authors and are not necessarily those of the editor or publisher. The support of Cornwall County Council is gratefully acknowledged.

CORNISH STUDIES

Second Series

FOUR

Edited by

Philip Payton

UNIVERSITY
of
EXETER
PRESS

First published in 1996 by
University of Exeter Press
Reed Hall, Streatham Drive
Exeter, Devon EX4 4QR
UK

British Library Cataloguing in Publication Data
A catalogue record of this book is
available from the British Library

ISBN 0 85989 523 8
ISSN 1352-271X

Typeset by Kestrel Data, Exeter, Devon

Printed and bound in Great Britain by
T.J. Press Ltd, Padstow, Cornwall

Contents

RESEARCH NOTES

REVIEW ARTICLES

INTRODUCTION

Much has been said and written, not least in the series *Cornish Studies*, about the 'new Cornish historiography', the 'new Cornish social science', and other manifestations of the general broadening that our subject has experienced in recent years. *Cornish Studies* itself has become an international medium for contact and interaction between scholars working in these areas (together with those engaged in more 'traditional' research), and the blend achieved shows the extent to which Cornish Studies as a discipline has been able to both penetrate and learn from the new discourses that characterize much mainstream academic activity today.

From postcolonial and postmodernist writings to gender studies and area studies (such as Australian, Canadian, Irish, and of course Cornish Studies), the 'grand narratives' of hitherto clearly delineated subjects such as 'History' and 'Politics' have experienced fragmentation and new re-alignment. Boundaries between disciplines and between 'Arts' and 'Sciences' are no longer clear (and, therefore, cannot be guarded jealously as they were in the past), while the distinction between 'past', 'present' and even 'future' has itself become blurred. The boundary between 'pure' and 'applied' research is similarly indistinct, not least in the context of the 'New' Cornish Studies that has emerged where—if there is a hint of a normative project or a not-so-hidden agenda—it is to marshal, synthesize and explain hitherto disparate knowledge so that we might better understand the nature and condition of Cornwall in its British, European and global contexts. This is not merely an academic exercise, for such a process cannot fail to inform, influence and guide planners and policymakers at every level—should they care to listen.

However, the process of re-alignment—in the academic world as a whole, and in Cornish Studies in particular—is not without pain, disunity, and uncertainty. Indeed, if we do live in 'postmodernist' times, how could it be otherwise?! For example, there are real difficulties in achieving the methodological links that will make for genuine cross-disciplinary transfer. Certainly, much that passes for interdisciplinary convergence (in the series *Cornish Studies* and elsewhere) is in fact only multi-disciplinary contact, the intimate juxtaposition of otherwise independent approaches. However, such contact should be welcomed as a prelude to cross-disciplinary transfer, a means (in the case of *Cornish Studies*) of introducing both contributors and readers to the opportunities that are opening up before us, a catalyst that will stimulate new thought and action.

The progress towards constructing a 'New' Cornish Studies has led, amongst other things, to the establishment of a New Cornish Studies Forum—an informal association of scholars from throughout the United Kingdom. However, the identification of a 'New' Cornish Studies does not imply easy definition (the process of construction is essentially evolutionary, with fits and starts and wrong turns), nor—emphatically—is it designed to be exclusive. In a very real sense, there is a home for everyone in Cornish Studies as an area of academic inquiry. The series *Cornish Studies*, for its part, will continue to reflect the latest movements in the field, and in so doing will demonstrate areas of genuine cross-disciplinary transfer as well as facilitating that more general juxtaposition of disparate and contrasting themes and approaches. *Cornish Studies: Four*, indeed, is an exemplar. Several articles demonstrate significant progress towards the cross-disciplinary transfer that will take our subject forward, while others, through their sheer erudition and depth, and the demonstrated capacity for micro-research, are a reminder that it is the excitement of new discovery that provides the stimulus for scholarly progress and inquiry in the first place.

To turn to individual themes, Alan Kent looks anew at that enigmatic exclamation 'Le Roy! a Cornish name: art thou of Cornish crew?' in Shakespeare's *Henry V*, suggesting that it tells us much about the specific relationship between the English and Cornish, colonizers and colonized, in that period. He concludes that, in contrast to the more easily explained and perhaps predictable portrayal of the Irish, Welsh and Scots in the play, the Cornish are afforded special treatment—an indication that for England, Cornwall had become a sort of manageable 'junior partner'.

Cornish 'particularism' in the early modern period is also Mark Stoyle's theme. In contrast to other historians of the Civil War, who have assumed that the Cornish army as a fighting force was finished after Lansdowne and the capture of Bristol, Stoyle investigates in detail the formation and exploits of the 'New Cornish Tertia'. He also examines the key role played by Sir Richard Grenville, another of history's enigmas, who increasingly saw his task as the preservation of Cornwall—a position that, as the Parliamentarian triumph in England began to seem inevitable, led him to argue that Cornwall should negotiate a separate peace as a semi-independent Royalist statelet.

Still in this early modern period, Brian Murdoch looks afresh at the well-known Cornish folktale *John of Chyanhor*, asking if it really is a 'Cornish *Ruodlieb*,' comparing the Bosons' seventeenth/ eighteenth-century Cornish language version of the story with the eleventh-century Latin poem *Ruodlieb* from southern Germany. Amongst other things, *John of Chyanhor* is set within a wider European literary context, not least with regard to cognate versions of the tale in other Celtic countries. And if, as is suggested, Nicholas Boson first heard the story in Cornish from his servants, then we have a picture of the last generations of Cornish-speakers which contrasts strongly with their conventional portrayal (even by some Cornish revivalists) as socially and culturally marginalized illiterates.

The activities of contemporary Cornish language revivalists are examined by both N. J. A. Williams and Bernard Deacon, albeit from radically different perspectives. Williams, as a Celticist and linguist with a particular expertise in the Cornish language, offers a detailed critique of Ken George's Kernewek Kemmyn ('Common' or 'phonemic' Cornish). He consideres that Unified Cornish remains the best version for language revival, although, recognizing (amongst other things) that Robert Morton Nance did not have the *Tregear Homilies* available to him when undertaking his reconstruction, he recommends significant 'improvements' to produce what is 'Unified Cornish Revised'— based on the 'Tudor Cornish' of the texts *Beunans Meriasek, The Creacion of the World*, and the *Tregear Homilies*. This is a view, incidently, with which Neil Kennedy expresses some sympathy in his review of N. J. A. Williams' book *Cornish Today*, although Kennedy's principal objective is to provide a critique of Williams' work from the perspective of a practising teacher of Modern Cornish.

Bernard Deacon, as a social scientist, steps back from the minutiae of linguistic dispute to suggest that the current Cornish language debate is best understood by recourse to social theory. Rather than a struggle between competing gurus, each with his own claim to 'superiority' and 'authenticity', Deacon argues that the debate is a response to postmodernist uncertainty. However, just as many revivalists are unaware of (or refuse to recognize) the ideological provenance of their particular paradigms, so many are also locked into a modernist 'scientific' project which prevents them from accepting or under-standing the plurality that has now emerged in the language movement. Indeed, as Professor Kenneth Mackinnon has remarked recently, perhaps now we should be referring not to 'Cornish' but to several 'Cornishes'. After all, we routinely recognize the existence of various 'Englishes'—Australian English, Jamaican English, even 'Celtic Englishes' (the title of a conference at the University of Potsdam in September 1995). In any event, as Deacon concludes, the Cornish language is too important to be left entirely in the hands of linguists.

If 'postmodernity' is a clue to the condition of contemporary Cornwall, then so to (if we may take an historical perspective) is the Great Emigration that characterized much of the nineteenth century (where the 'modernity' of industrialization came to any early and traumatic end) and whose legacy is still felt today. Philip Payton returns again to this theme, emphasizing that emigration was an integral part of Cornish life long before the copper crash of the 1860s. In focusing in part on the 'Hungry Forties', there is also a reminder that the potato was an important element of the Cornish diet, as it was in Ireland and the Highlands and Islands, and that the potato blight had serious consequences in Cornwall—especially in 1845–47. The point is made, however, that whilst considerable attention has been focused recently in both Ireland and Scotland on the potato famine (everything from scholarly books to television programmes and school and college projects), there has been an uncanny silence in Cornwall.

In a further demonstration of the importance of the link between historical and contemporary Cornwall, Rodd Sheaff addresses the hitherto long-neglected subject of Cornish health and healthcare, and comes up with some startling results, together with important observations in areas such as occupational and environmental health. His theme is centralization against the background of increasing peripherality, and he identifies the problems and difficulties that these trends have created. His provocative conclusion that, in theory, it would be quite possible for a Cornish local government (à la Malta) to undertake a healthcare purchasing function more or less independently, will provide much food for thought. So too will his observation that issues of Cornish 'nationality' cannot be ignored in a healthcare context.

An innovation in *Cornish Studies: Four* is the inclusion of Research Notes, shorter articles which discuss briefly relatively narrow issues, or which give brief synopses or overviews of work published elsewhere which might not be available to the general reader. Glanville Price's 'Negative Particles in Cornish' is an example of the former, a reassurring indication that the current revivalist debate has not discouraged wider comparative work by other linguists. Paul Thornton's 'Second Homes in Cornwall' describes a recent survey conducted by the Institute of Cornish Studies in co-operation with the Planning Department of Cornwall County Council, a study which—as well as examining the nature of second-home populations—throws up vital issues of 'territorial legitimacy' and 'moral geography'.

In a review article, Amy Hale presents a detailed critique of Malcolm Chapman's by now famous (or infamous) book, *The Celts: The Creation of a Myth*. While sharing many of the reservations expressed by other reviewers, she also insists that we should not dismiss Chapman without a careful consideration of the issues that he raises. This, in turn, becomes a plea for Celtic Studies as a discipline to acknowledge its intellectual and ideological origins, and to engage in the reassessment that is occurring elsewhere in the humanistic and social sciences. Here Hale is echoing a concern that has emerged elsewhere in the realms of Celtic Studies, and which has assisted the current broadening of 'New' Cornish Studies.

Indeed, in reminding us of Anthony P. Cohen's point that scholars, rather than casting academic aspersions, should seek to understand why certain groups adopt distinctive or oppositional identities, Amy Hale makes the bold pronouncement that 'It is this challenge that should engage us in the field of Cornish Studies'. She is probably right.

Philip Payton,
Reader in Cornish Studies and
Director,
Institute of Cornish Studies,
University of Exeter,
Redruth, Cornwall.

'ART THOU OF CORNISH CREW?' SHAKESPEARE, *HENRY V* AND CORNISH IDENTITY

Alan M. Kent

PISTOL: What is thy name?
KING HENRY (in disguise as a common soldier): Harry le Roy.
PISTOL: Le Roy! a Cornish name: art thou of Cornish crew?
    William Shakespeare, *King Henry V*, IV. i.

INTRODUCTION

'Beginnings', wrote Edward Said, 'have to be made for each project in such a way as to *enable* what follows from them'.[1] My project is located within the reality of the historic relationship of 'Cornwall' with 'England', the relationship of the 'colonized' and the 'colonizer' and the manner in which it has been reflected in literary expression. The project's beginning, the subject of this article, is an examination of the cultural engagements between the English and Cornish peoples in the sixteenth century, a crucial moment for both State and cultural formation in England. The roots of anglicization in Cornwall are, of course, much older, a process pre-dating as well as enshrined within the tenth-century Athelstan settlement; but it was in the Tudor period that the colonizing English State moved beyond its earlier accommodation of Cornwall to attempt full integration.

As Steven Ellis has argued, it was in the Tudor era that definitions of 'Englishness' became narrower and more insular: 'the loss of Calais [1558] finally ended the dreams entertained by Kings like Henry VIII to recreate Henry V's continental empire and forced the monarchy to concentrate on the British Isles'.[2] Simultaneously, attempts at conquering the 'Celtic fringes' of the British Isles were influential

. . . in shaping the characteristics of *English* nationality as it developed in Tudor times. Before the Reformation, the Tudor territories were united principally by a common allegiance to the English crown . . . a generally wide sense of 'Englishness' prevailed. After the breach with Catholicism, however, and the growing consciousness of differentiation from continental Europe which accompanied the Elizabethan idea of an elect nation, a narrower definition of Englishness emerged.[3]

Alongside this came another semantic shift, in the use of the word 'Briton'. The accession of James I as 'King of Great Britain', emphazised this shift and gave impetus to a renewed version of 'the British myth' which served to complement the narrower definition of 'Englishness'. This narrower Englishness may be traced not only to the loss of continental Europe, but also to the impact of the Reformation and to rapid overseas expansion. The fragmentation of Christendom, together with encounters with new civilisations, posed serious challenges to understanding for contemporary writers like William Shakespeare, Thomas More and Richard Carew, problems immeasurably compounded by those changes in the nature of language and representation to which Michel Foucault has drawn attention. Foucault has argued that, prior to the sixteenth century, the pre-classical *episteme*, or mode of acquiring knowledge, was based upon resemblance and finding affinities and similarities. He has suggested that 'the fundamental supposition was that of a total system of correspondence (earth and sky, planets and faces, microcosm and macrocosm) and each particular similitude was then lodged within the overall relation'.[4] In contrast, acquisition of knowledge within the classical *episteme* was based upon difference:

The activity of the mind . . . will . . . no longer consist in drawing things together, in setting out on a quest for everything that might reveal some sort of kinship, attraction of secretly shared nature within them, but, on the the contrary, in discriminating, that is in establishing their identities . . . In this sense, discrimination imposes upon comparison the primary and fundamental investigation of difference.[5]

In the case of later sixteenth- and seventeenth-century England, the conjunction of shifts in ways of acquiring knowledge with colonial expansion in Cornwall (and elsewhere) requires that we be aware that any writing by English people about Cornwall and the Cornish may not only have served to broaden English knowledge of the neighbouring land and its inhabitants, but also to define the qualities of 'Englishness' by simultaneously defining 'non-Englishness' or 'otherness'. In this case, that 'otherness' was Cornwall. A comparative Cornish example of this is to be found in *Beunans Meriasek* in Teudar's invocation of Mahound, where in the pre-Renaissance period that 'other' evoked would often have been the Jew or the Muslim.[6]

Michael T. Ryan has applied Foucault's postulation of pre-classical and classical *epistemes* in an examination of writings about the indigenous peoples of the Americas. He has shown that within the pre-classical *episteme* these 'new' peoples were assimilated into European frames of reference through the category of 'paganism'. What was specific in their practices, beliefs and appearance was seen as being of only minor significance in comparison to the similarities that could be discovered between their cultures and those of ancient and pagan civilizations and of the Eastern and Near Eastern world. In this way, the unknown became reassuringly familiar.[7] In the Tudor period it is this kind of 'familiarity' that the English felt for the Cornish. Cornwall was geographically close and smaller than the other 'Celtic nations'. It was also the first Celtic nation in Britain to experience the Anglo-colonization process. The completion of this process however, was to be more problematical.

CORNWALL AS 'JUNIOR PARTNER'

The process of describing the colonized and inscribing them in discourse as 'second-order citizens' in comparison with the colonizers commences with the invocation of the judicial and military power of the State. Subsequently, however, the colonizers attempt to convince the colonized themselves of their irremovable 'deficiencies' and the consequent 'naturalness' and 'permanence' of their subordination. Thus Cornwall became a sort of manageable 'junior partner', but not a slave or automaton. Evidence for this ambiguous status is to be found in the constitutional accommodation of Cornwall (from the re-establishment of the Stannaries in 1508 to the creation of new Parliamentary boroughs) as well as in the co-option by the English State of elements of the Cornish gentry (for example, the high position achieved by families such as the Godolphins).[8]

The wish of the colonizer that subjection should be willingly accepted, rather than require constant recourse to coercion, can be seen in *Henry V*, the culmination of Shakespeare's second historical tetralogy, itself a dramatization of the process involved in the creation of the unified nation. In particular, this is expressed in the constitution of the unified and ordered subject who, to emphazise the power of the process, is the monarch himself.[9] The transformation of 'Hal' to 'Henry', particularly through the rejection of Falstaff, is a highly charged realization of the denial and repression of the 'other' attendant upon the constitution of the ordered subject and nation. What Shakespeare dramatizes is the originating moment of nationhood when the nation 'becomes conscious of itself, when it creates a model of itself. [This] model defines the unified, the artificially schematized image, that is raised to the level of structural unity.'[10]

We may go as far as to argue that the 'nation' Cornwall is largely a fiction created by the rulers of England in response to specific needs at a precise moment in British history. We can identify the position of superiority from which the colonizer speaks, a position so entrenched that no aspect of the identity of the colonized can safely be assumed to be inherent. A number of recent analyses of the reciprocity between colonizer and colonized have concluded that colonial discourse establishes the colonized as the repressed and rejected 'other' against which the coloniser defines an ordered self and onto which all potentially disruptive psycho-sexual impulses can be projected.[11] The colonized are thus constrained to assert a dignified self-identity in opposition to discourse which defines them as, variously, barbarian (Cornwall was 'West Barbary'), pagan, uncultured, backward, ape-like, female, on the fringe; but always subordinate and inferior.[12] Hence 'positional superiority' puts the colonizer in a whole series of possible relationships with the colonized 'without ever losing him the relative upper hand'.[13] With specific regard to the historic image of 'barbarism' in Cornwall, we may also argue that since the phrase has its originary moment in indiginously Cornish sources, it was used by Cornish writers to demonstrate the transformation wrought by Methodism.

However, as Uri Lothman has argued, 'Culture requires unity'; a unity acquired by the introduction of order and the elimination of contradictions.[14] And yet, though often attempted, this unity is rarely achieved and, as Stephen Greenblatt has argued, the goal of unity itself requires a periodic re-definition which only the presence of an excluded (rather than eliminated) 'other' can provide.[15] This formulation may be clarified by reference to those of Shakespeare's history plays which were themselves the final manifestation of a new form of English historical writing; a form distinguished by being 'intensely nationalistic' and 'deliberately propagandistic'.[16]

Henry V (1599) dramatized the might and mercy of the English Nation State. The action is resolved as the victory at Agincourt is crowned by Henry's kissing the French Princess in recognition that she is his 'sovereign queen'. The result of this betrothal, it is hoped, will be that the contending kingdoms should share an equal unity and 'Christian-like accord' (Act V, Scene ii).[17] One may argue that the resolution of this imperial war is a piece of dramatic wish-fulfilment:

that the contemporary discord between England and her Celtic nations should come to a similarly satisfactory conclusion. And behind the marriage which binds Henry to France, just as behind the mercy dispensed to Harfleur, there lies the reality of the sword and colonization. Unity of the Nation State will be achieved either by incorporation of the discordant elements or by their elimination. The play shows a direct engagement with the problems of 'internal colonialism'. The famous scene at the English camp, when English, Welsh, Scots and Irish captains meet in an encounter whose main function is to dramatize their united presence in an army constantly referred to as 'English' (Act III, Scene ii), reveals that (just as in the marriage which unites England and France) so in the union which produces the English Nation State, there is a relationship which is 'structured in dominance'. These Celts are united in their service to the English crown. Their use of the English language, however, reveals that 'service' is the operative word, for in rank, in dramatic importance, and in linguisitc competence, they are comical second-order citizens.

The role of the Cornish contingent in the army facing France is altogether different, however. The moment appears incidental: the audience has already seen Pistol and knows him to be an 'ancient' (i.e. an ensign or second officer) and that he is a mountebank, a swashbuckler who wields words as if they were cutlasses. His dramatic style is is that of a medieval braggart or the boastful soldier of Roman comedy. Being an ancient, Pistol presumably knew most of the differing contingents or 'nations' within the 'English' army. He is certainly projected as having liaisons and comradeship with the Cornish. This is suggested in the scene where he encounters the disguised King Henry, who is assessing the mood of his soldiers before the battle by wandering around the camp. 'What is thy name?' Pistol asks. 'Harry le Roy', replies the King, giving a pun on his name which the English audience, would have understood well. Pistol instantly recognizes that the name is an 'other'; it is strange and odd sounding, like no 'English' name he has encountered—or even that of one of the other Celtic nations. This demarcation of 'otherness' is instant and confident on Pistol's part; his response is brief, but significant: 'Le Roy! a Cornish name: art thou of Cornish crew?'

These three lines tell us a great deal. Firstly, in terms of nomenclature, the Cornish were different from the English (to Pistol their names sounded funny) and there were other such names in the camp which Pistol has already come across. Secondly, Shakespeare, significantly, uses the word 'crew', suggesting fondness, familiarity and respect—a group working together in a gang. Since no other Celtic group is delineated in quite the same manner in the play, it becomes clear that Shakespeare chooses not to make the Cornish a 'nation' in the way that he does the Welsh, Irish and Scots. This knowledge is significant.

Taylor, in his 1982 edition of *Henry V*, argues that to retain the Folio spelling 'Roy' is misleading since it suggests a mispronunciation of the French. He notes that 'Shakespeare always spells the word "roy" as he spells "moy" for "moi", and can 'find no evidence that Leroi is, or would have been considered, Cornish.'[18] Taylor misses the point here. It does not matter that Leroi is not Cornish—it is *obviously* French—but because Pistol is 'simple' he does not recognize the joke that the audience hear. To him, the name is still strange, of another land, and therefore seems 'Cornish'. We should remember that the projected character of Pistol has already encountered expert 'Celtic' opinion on the direction and 'concavities' of the mines outside the town of Harfleur and it is likely the Cornish had something to say there as well.

In his forward to G. Pawley White's *A Handbook of Cornish Surnames*, A.L. Rowse states that Shakespeare thought 'Leroy' was a Cornish name, but 'he was wrong'. Rowse does however, justify the 'otherness' of Cornish names:

> Many people have been struck by the individuality, to them the strangeness, sometimes the beauty of Cornish names—and this goes for surnames as well as those of the places from which they often come. There is the old rhyme, known to Walter Scott:
> By Tre—, Pol—, Pen—
> Ye may know most Cornish men.[19]

Evidence of the role of the Earl of Cornwall from *King Lear* (Kent comments 'Goose, I had you upon Sarum Plain, I'd drive ye cackling home to Camelot' [Act ii, Scene ii]) suggests that Shakespeare was not altogether ignorant of the significance of Cornwall either. We may attribute the distinctive treatment he gives the Cornish in *Henry V* (compared to the Welsh, Scots and Irish) to several possible reasons. By the time Shakespeare was writing, the question of Cornwall's allegiance to the Nation State may already have been established, at least in the estimation of the English elite. Or, it may well be that the English had a greater fondness and respect for the Cornish contingent in their army and that, writing retrospectively, for Shakespeare the 'differences' expressed in the Cornish rebellions of 1497 and 1549 were thus negated. Another reason was that Cornwall was of immense strategic important to the English Nation State, particularly when we consider its proximity to Spain and the position of Fowey and later Falmouth as important trading ports.

The Spanish attack on Mousehole in 1595 was a salutary reminder of both strategic significance and vulnerability. The English knew well that they should guard their territorial 'backdoor' and so gave the Cornish both respect and status. It was only with the military and political breakdown of the Civil War, half a century after Shakespeare's death, that the English response to the Cornish became more complex. Whilst the Royalists continued publicly to offer status and respect, deferring to the martial qualities that the Cornish had so loyally deployed in the King's cause, privately there was concern amongst the King's advisors that arming the Cornish might not be a good idea. More significantly, the Parliamentarians (in an echo of 1497 and 1549) reverted to descriptions of the Cornish as 'rebels', 'heathen pagans' and kleptomaniac 'Cornish Choughs', evolving an imagery that was entirely reminiscent of English descriptions of Irish Catholic rebels in 1641.[20]

MICHAEL WILLIAMS AS CORNISHMAN

When *Henry V* was written, however, the Cornish were no longer (or rather, were not yet) a threat to the English State. Significantly, the enduring influence of the Shakespearian perspective offered by Pistol was demonstrated in a strikingly similar piece of modern dialogue, in Kevin Reynolds' stylish 1991 film *Robin Hood: Prince of Thieves*, where there is what is effectively a reinterpretation of the scene. Upon their return to Britain from the Crusades, Robin Hood (played by Kevin Costner) and his Muslim colleague Azeem (Morgan Freeman) call at the castle of Peter Dubois (a knight who was killed in the escape from the dungeons of Jerusalem) to inquire after the Lady Marian. They are accompanied by Duncan, Robin's father's old retainer, who has been blinded by the Sheriff of Nottingham. Duncan is unable to see Azeem and fails to realize that he is both a Muslim and Black. 'A curse on Moors and Saracens,' says the old retainer. He then faces Azeem. 'What manner of name is *Azeem*? Irish? Cornish?' Duncan, like Pistol, finds the name strange. It has an 'otherness' and he can only relate to names of a Celtic origin. Irish is offered initially, but he feels the need to be more outlandish: thus, Cornish is the second nationality offered. Azzeem's eventual rhyming reply is all the more humorous in this context: 'Moorish!' comes his answer. The ideology in both Duncan's and Pistol's questioning is identical.

A further piece of evidence for the curious politico-cultural situation in which the 'Cornish crew' found itself at Agincourt lies in the couplet that once accompanied a portrait of Henry V over the south gate in Launceston:

He that will do aught for mee
Let him love well Sir John Tirlawnee.[21]

Sir John Trelawny fought at Agincourt under Henry V, and again an enduring memory of a distinctive Cornish presence in that battle is displayed in modern performances of *Henry V*. In the 1989 film version of the play, directed by Kenneth Brannagh, for example, a black and white flag can be seen clearly, an echo perhaps of the popular myth that St Piran's Cross (the Cornish flag) was flown at Agincourt. More radically, the 1985 English Shakespeare Company's version of the entire sequence of English History plays, directed by Michael Bogdanov and Michael Pennington as *The Wars of the Roses*, decided that the Cornish contingent should be reassessed within the play, and so made the doubting common soldier Michael Williams a Cornishman. Williams is often and inappropriately played as Welsh (there is no hint of 'Welshness' in his dialogue when compared to that of Fluellen), but his non-conformity and his desire for the King to understand how the ordinary soldiers feel, smacks of the traits of Cornishness: 'If the cause be not good, the King himself hath a heavy reckoning to make, when all those legs and arms and heads chopped off in a battle, shall join together at the latter day and cry all "We died at such a place" . . .' (Act IV, Scene i, Lines 123–126). The identification of 'traits' may appear subjective , but the oral myth of the 'archtetypal Cornishman' continues to exist and is routinely portrayed in contemporary journalism and literature: for example, with Roger Nowle as television's *The Skipper* and in the charactérization of the Cornish-based detective series *Wycliffe*.[22] Typically, like Williams, the Cornishman is presented as disruptional and often as confrontational. A number of scholars has aimed to define these 'traits', while the recent articulation of a 'Cornish identity theory' offers a credible explanation for their origins and persistence over time.[23]

To suggest that Williams is Welsh is (despite the name) wrong-headed. Later in the act in which Williams appears, the soldier John Bates is revealed as the lone character pleading for unity: 'Be friends, you English fools, be friends! We have French quarrels enough if you could tell how to reckon.' This is addressed to Williams as it is to other soldiers. As a Cornishman, Williams might be accommodated as an 'English fool', but as a 'stage Welshman' he could never be. As Moseley notes, and as *Henry V* attests, there were stage Welshmen, Irishmen and Scotsmen in the Elizabethan theatre, as there are in our own. He views their role as positive: 'Their disputes are comic and long-winded, but they are about the art of war and the serious matter in hand.'[24] The Cornish did not have a stage persona in this way, and their skills in the arts of war need not be discussed—they are taken for granted. Even today the name Williams may be considered Cornish—it is the most common surname to be found in the British Telecom telephone directory for Cornwall and the Isles of Scilly.

As Hazlitt recognized in relation to *Henry V*, 'Poetry is right-royal' and 'The language of poetry naturally falls in with the language of power'.[25] Nowhere is this better reflected than in the pre-Agincourt scenes. In conversation with the disguised King, Michael Williams, John Bates and Alexander Court ask him what the stranger (Henry in disguise) thinks his commander, Sir Thomas Erpingham, feels about their position or 'estate' against the French. Henry's response is interesting, since (if he noticed that the men were Cornish) the metaphor chosen in his response is most appropriate: 'Even as men wrecked upon a sand, that look to be washed off the next tide.' Such a response may allow us to think of the Cornish crew beyond just a collection of brothers in arms, but rather a real naval-based crew who presumably sailed with the King from Southampton. The sea imagery for this 'crew' is continued by Henry some forty lines later in an effort to convince them that they, not the King, are responsible for their souls: 'So if a son that is by his father is sent about merchandise do sinfully miscarry upon the sea, the imputation of his wickedness, by your rule, should be imposed upon his father that sent him.' (Act IV, Scene i, Lines 134–137). Henry is presented as a clever military leader; the imagery chosen is of the kind that his soldiers recognize—thus they are more likely to understand him and eventually fight well for him. Indeed, the maritime imagery would have had a particular resonance for the Cornish, maritime terminology finding its way into most aspects of Cornish life (for example, tin mine depths were measured in 'fathoms', mine managers were 'captains').

AGINCOURT

Another intriguing reference to the Cornish involvement at Agincourt is made in the work of the poet Michael Drayton (1563-1631), author of the narrative poem *The Battaile of Agincourt* and the great topographical poem on England *Poly-Olbion*. In the latter work, Drayton asserts that Cornish soldiers fought at Agincourt beneath a banner depicting two wrestlers. Similarly, several commentators have indicated that many (most?) of the 'Welsh' archers within the 'English' army were in fact Cornish, first at Poitiers and then later at Crécy and Agincourt. As Halliday reminds us, in 1415

Cornish ships were in the fleet, 'a city on the inconstant billows dancing', which sailed from Southampton to Harfleur, and a contingent of Cornishmen fought at Agincourt under a banner bearing a device of two wrestlers. Sir John Cornwall and Sir John Trelawny lived to feast their neighbours on the anniversary of Saint Crispin's Day, but the body of Sir John Colshull was brought home to rest in Duloe church. . . Three years later another Cornish Sir John, Sir John Arundell of Lanherne, contracted to supply the king's uncle, the Duke of Exeter, with 364 men-at-arms and 770 archers for service in France . . .[26]

Additionally, Richard Carew tells us in his *Survey of Cornwall* of 1602 that archery was still a popular pastime in Cornwall and that the Cornish were accomplished at the skill. Indeed, Carew directly alludes to Agincourt and also lifts a phrase from Shakespeare's version of Henry V's famous Harfleur speech ['which I doubt not' (Act III, Scene 1, Line 28)]. This stands as remarkable evidence of the Cornish connection:

Amongst bodily pastimes, shooting carrieth the preeminence; to which in mine younger years I carried such affection, as I induced Archery, persuading others to the liking, by this ensuing prosopopeia:

'My dear friends, I come to complain upon you, but to yourselves; to blame you, but for your good; to expostulate with you, but in the way of reconciliation. Alas, what my desert can justify your abandoning my fellowship, and hanging me thus up, to be smoke-starved over your chimneys? I am no stranger unto you, but by birth your countrywoman, by dwelling your neighbour, by education your familiar. Neither is my company shameful, for I haunt the light and open fields, nor my conversation dangerous: nay, it shields you from dangers, and those not the least, but of greatest consequence, the dangers of war. And as in fight, I give you protection, so in peace I supply you pastime; and both in war and peace, to your limbs I yield active pliantness, and to your bodies healthful exercise; yea, I provide you food when you are hungry, and help digestion when you are full. Whence then proceedeth this unkind and unusual strangeness? Am I heavy for burden? Forsooth, a few light sticks of wood. Am I cumbrous for carriage? I couch a part of myself close under your girdle, and the other part serveth as a walking-staff in your hand. Am I unhandsome in your sight? Every piece of me is comely, and the whole keepeth an harmonical proportion. Lastly, am I costly to be provided, or hard to be maintained? No, cheapness is my purveyor, easiness my preserver; neither do I make you blow away your charges with

my breath, or taint your nose with my scent, nor defile your face
and fingers with my colour, like that hell-born murderer, whom
you accept before me. I appeal then to your valiant princes,
Edwards and Henries; to the battles of Cressy, Poitiers, Agincourt,
and Flodden; to the regions of Scotland, France, Spain, Italy,
Cyprus, yea, and Jewry, to be umpires of this controversy; all which
(I doubt not) will with their evidence plainly prove, that when
mine adverse party was yet scarcely born, or lay in her swathling
clouts, through me only, your ancestors defended their country,
vanquished their enemies, succoured their friends, enlarged their
dominions, advanced their religion, and made their names fearful
to the present age, and their fame everlasting to those that ensue.
Wherefore, my dear friends, seeing I have so substantially evicted
the right of my cause, conform your wills to reason, conform your
reason to practice, and convert your practice to the good of
yourselves and your country. If I be praiseworthy, esteem me; if
necessary admit me; if profitable, employ me; so shall you revoke
my death to life, and show yourselves no degenerate issue of such
honourable progenitors' And thus much for Archery, whose tale,
if it be disordered, you must bear withal, for she is a woman, and
her mind is passionate'.

And to give you some taste of the Cornishmen's former suf-
ficiency that way, for long shooting, their shaft was a cloth yard,
their pricks twenty-four score; for strength they could pierce any
ordinary armour, and one Master Robert Arundell (whom I well
knew) could shoot twelve score, with his right hand, with his left,
and from behind his head.[27]

We know that at Agincourt it was the archers who largely
determined the outcome of the fight. One French Chronicler tells us
that the arrows 'were like hail'. Another describes them as a 'snowstorm
or thick fog obscuring the sky'.[28] The longbowmen were reckoned to
have made up about three-quarters of Henry's army. The longbow itself
was as tall as a man. It took great strength and constant practice to
shoot; hence the respect that the Cornish earned. The bowstring was
pulled right back behind the ear. An archer could fire twelve arrows
per minute and was deadly accurate up to at least 250 metres. At close
range an arrow could penetrate plate-metal armour. At Agincourt, the
Cornish thus equipped were in the thick of it. Years later Thomas
Hostell (or Ostell, or Austell even?), an archer who was wounded at
Harfleur and at Agincourt, hit by a 'springbolt through his head, losing
one eye and his cheek bone broken', petitioned Henry VI for aid. He
was 'sore feebled and debruised, now fallen to a great age and poverty,
greatly inbedted, and may not help himself . . .'.[29]

It is certainly feasible that Williams and his company were

envisaged by Shakespeare as part of this force of accomplished archers. Williams' broader dramatic purpose is to teach Henry a lesson in humility, and to lead up to the great soliloquy before the battle ('What have Kings that privates have not too, Save ceremony, save general ceremony . . . ?' (Act IV, Scene i. Lines 211–213)). Williams is sometimes presented as one of the cheerfully cynical cockneys who man the lower decks in those stiff-upper-lip films of the Second World War, but logic suggests that more than likely he was Cornish. If Cornwall has a claim in any Shakespearean character aside from the Earl of Cornwall in *King Lear*, then it is with Michael Williams. Interestingly, even though Cornwall's part in *King Lear* is small, similar 'traits' to those of Williams' are shown. Even in the sequence where he demonstrates his high-handedness towards Kent, there is that wish for clarity and 'plainness':

> An honest mind and plain, he must speak truth!
> And they will take it, so; if not he's plain.
> These kind of knaves I know, which in this plainness
> Harbour more craft and more corrupter ends
> Then twenty silly ducking observants
> That stretch their duties nicely.
> (Act ii, Scene ii, Lines 93–99.)

Henry V, then, in its fleeting allusions to the Cornish tells us much about the relationship between Cornwall and England. Whilst the Irishman Macmorris questions 'What ish my nation?' (Act III, Scene ii), the position with regard to the Cornish is clearer; they already know their colonial fate. Macmorris' outburst is a denial of such separate status and is therefore only a rhetorical question to which the answer is supplied by his service—and possible conscription, in view of his reluctance to fight—in the English army. The status of the Cornish is entirely different; the sense of 'otherness' is expressed in the linguistic demarcation of 'crew', and yet not presented in terms of comedy. Thus, though Macmorris and the other captains are fashioned into goodly and biddable second-order citizens, perhaps because of temperament, already established suppression, military skill or innovation, the Cornish are *integrated*, yet are still perceived as retaining 'otherness'. Within this, there remains the process of self-fashioning. The continual presence of an 'other' allows the maintainance of subtle points of differentiation from the colonizer which would continue to reproduce not only the subordination of the colonized, but the superordination of the colonizer.

ENGLISH CULTURE AND THE DRIVE FOR UNITY

Whilst on the one hand Cornwall can celebrate its inclusion in such a significant text as *Henry V*, critics may object that Shakespeare continues to represent the peak of English cultural and literary achievement—and so his work has actively, if unknowingly, placed Cornish literature in submission. The problem, however, is not only 'literary colonialism', but that the English have always acclaimed Shakespeare as their greatest and most characteristic genius. Taylor, for example, argues that England's cultural legacy (of which Shakespeare is a crucial part) is one which has actively suppressed other peoples. He asserts that:

> Most of the political revolutions of the later eighteenth century were attempts by disenfranchised peoples—American colonists, native Irishmen, colonized Italians, Haitian slaves, the French third estate—to claim for themselves liberties like those which native Englishmen already enjoyed. One of those enviable English liberties was a right, and a determination, to celebrate their native literature, in defiance of the fact that it did not conform to the prevailing international aesthetic system.[30]

This function of dramatizing the internal relations between the various peoples who together constituted the emergent 'English' Empire may readily be grasped, and is vital to any complete understanding of Cornish literature. The ramifications will be widespread and significant, and it is this author's intention to pursue them at length elsewhere. As Hayden White has argued: 'A given culture is only as strong as its power to convince its least dedicated members that its fictions are truths.'[31] White's use of the term 'fictions' in this context seems to be derived from that of Frank Kermode when he argued that 'Fictions can degenerate into myths whenever they are not consciously held to be fictive.'[32] The distinction that Kermode draws between the two terms is that fictions are a means of finding things out and are consequently open to change, while myths 'are the agents of stability'.[33] The Shakespearean 'fiction' and consequent English fiction of *Henry V* is, then, the expression of a politically advantageous 'myth' and indeed is expressed in terms which are themselves subsequently utilized for overtly political purposes.

James I of England (and VI of Scots), whose accession to the throne came only four years after the completion of *Henry V*, expressed the indissolubility of 'the Nation' in terms of marriage: 'I am the husband, and the whole isle is my lawful wife'.[34] This merging of the marginal with the mighty or rather the 'fringe' nation with the composite state is equated by James with the fate of the brook which flows into a river which, in turn, flows into an ocean: 'so by the conjunction of divers little kingdoms in one are all these private differences and questions swallowed up',[35] connecting exactly with the metaphor of the final Act of *Henry V* ('God, the best maker of all marriages, Combine your hearts in one, your realms in one.' (Act v, Scene iii, Lines 322–323)).

'English' culture, then, requires the drive toward—if not the achievement of—unity. But the contradictions that are necessarily played down as a means of its achievement are quite literally those elements which contradict, speak against and speak otherwise than the dominant group. While Henry can be seen to court the French Princess in her own tongue and she replies in English, the same degree of linguistic parity is not extended to the Celtic characters of the play, for their position in the contemporary world of Elizabethan England was potentially, and actually, far more disruptive than that of a nation whose separate status was now an acknowledged if not welcome fact of political life. For the Cornish, what cannot be explicitly acknowledged is their possession of an alternative language, literature and culture, for to do so would be to stage the presence of the very contradictions which the play denies in its attempt to stage the ideal of a unified English Nation State. The resolution in the play is seen to be achieved by marriage rather than massacre, by incorporation rather than exclusion, but the inclusion of the Cornish with the English State, of which the army is a paradigm, is a result of an equally devastating act of cultural elision. The victims in the process of the march towards unity are those who contradict, and so implicitly question the dominance of the incorporating power. Shakespeare's work engages with the process of colonial discourse in Cornwall at the moment of its mobilization, but the position of the colonized—namely the 'Cornish crew'—is seen as being one of proud inclusion.

COLONIZED AND COLONIZER

In this sense of 'otherness', the play is an idealization of an actuality which stubbornly refused to conform. In the relationship of colonizer and colonized, inclusion is available at the cost of de-culturation. This issue is crucial as far as Cornwall is concerned: distinctiveness is only possible at the risk of cultural genocide. The implied superior role of the English language over Cornish, supported by the threat of physical power in colonial relations, finds even clearer expression in *The Tempest* (1611), the Shakespearean play which, more than any other, has been read in the context of colonial discourse.[36] The English language is indeed revealed to be the 'perfect instrument of empire', as Antonio de Rebrija stated in 1492;[37] through his knowledge of Prospero's tongue Caliban is not only capable of being commanded to fetch in fuel, but also capable of comprehending the physical consequences of disobeying. The only resistance that Caliban can muster is to curse Prospero, but the very curse itself is a confirmation of his subjection: 'The red plague on you/For learning me your language!' (Act I, Scene ii). Imprisoned by language and power, Caliban in his 'uncultured' form is the paradigm of the colonial subject in colonial discourse: a 'monster' (an ape-like barbarian) who both threatens the virginity of Miranda and through his abortive rebellion, the life of Prospero. The conclusion to be drawn from such a presentation is the necessity of Caliban's subjection to the self-protective power of Prospero who must be constantly alert to the threat of treachery on the part of his slave. The similarity between this and the Tudor context of Cornwall and other Celtic nations is startling.

Shakespeare's presentation of Caliban as possessing a consciousness chafing under the restraints and injustices of his position has marked similarity to the view of Franz Fanon, that the independent consciousness of the colonized maintains its discrete existence within the subjugated body: 'he is overpowered but not tamed; he is treated as an inferior but not convinced of his inferiority'.[38] The position implicit in Fanon's formulation is that, just as the colonized are subjected by force, so will a superior force lead to liberation. While the reality of force in colonial relations can never be denied, the problem in Fanon's analysis resides in his assertion that the colonized are 'not convinced' of their inferiority: this amounts to a reduction of the colonial enterprise to might alone and a failure to engage with the role of culture in forming consciousness.

Louis Althusser, for example, has argued that the failing of traditional Marxism, such as that adapted to the colonial situation by Fanon, was that it reduced the power of the State to that of its repressive force alone. The reality, he argued, was that power could not be maintained without control over what he termed 'Ideological State Apparatuses': those social institutions which embrace the domains of religion, culture, education and familial relations and are distinguished from 'Repressive State Apparatuses' in that they 'function "by ideology" '.[39] Just as there is a need for the productive skills of (capitalist) society to be maintained, so (argues Althusser) is there a need for the working class to be confirmed in the 'naturalness' of its subordinate status—exactly the position Cornwall found itself in after the Tudor rebellions of 1497 and 1549. In other words, there must be an ideological extension of the subordinate class' submission to the rules of the established order. This 'misrecognition' which then occurs is consequent upon the subordinate class' (or people's) acceptance and adoption of the image proffered by the dominant group.

The issue, then, is consciousness—in this case the consciousness of the cultural position in Cornwall and its relationship to England, its colonizer. Althusser, like Antonio Gramsci before him, recognized that, far from being merely the object which responded to changes in the means of production, 'Man is above all else mind, consciousness'.[40] Gramsci considered that, in the consciousness of the colonized, recognition of the *possibility* of freedom was not enough. There had to be a defining moment, and this would be created through the construction of a 'counter-hegemony' to confront the 'hegemonic' or ideological control of the colonizers. This 'counter-hegemony', argued Gramsci, would be constructed by a coalescence of like-minded intellectuals. Intriguingly, some observers of contemporary Cornish life would argue that this is precisely what is beginning to happen in late twentieth-century Cornwall. As Michel Foucault puts it, 'discourse is the power which is to be seized',[41] and there is evidence that, by engaging in a range of new discourses, Cornish intellectuals are responding to Foucault's challenging question: 'How does the struggle for the taking over of the discourse take place between classes, nations, linguistic, cultural or ethnic collectivities?'[42]

CONCLUSION
However, this is not to herald that 'Cornish freedom' is now at hand but rather to argue that it is only now that Cornish intellectuals (and sympathetic colleagues elsewhere) are equipped to fully understand, contextualize and explain the cultural history of Cornwall. For example, recent insights into cultural formation in early modern Cornwall have come from the drama of the period, which has been read 'against the grain' to supply an understanding of the forces at play in a time of rapid internally and externally generated economic, political and social change. Thus Payton and others have demonstrated that *Beunans Meriasek* is actually a subversive document, rather than just a pre-Reformation saint's play.[43] In the process, historians have suggested that, as well as achieving qualatively high levels of artistic achievement, the poets, monks and dramatists who constructed the early modern Cornish literature were also on occasions conscious of the magnitude of the changes that were occurring around them, and sought to respond to them.

The Tudor period was a time of rebellion and upheaval in Cornwall, resulting in the rapid decline thereafter of the Cornish language and literature. In 1549 the Cornish may have declared that 'We the Cornishmen, whereof certain of us understand no English, utterly refuse this new English'[44] but in reality, in the aftermath of rebellion, they were to choose collusion rather than collision in defining their relationship with the English State. Collision having already failed twice, in 1497 and 1549, collusion was their only option. By the time *Henry V* was written, this collusion was accepted; the 'blip' against the Nation State, if not forgotten, at least forgiven.

Put another way, the colonizer had gone a significant way in persuading the colonized to accept their subordinate status. But in such circumstances, as Fanon noted, the colonized are 'overpowered but not tamed' (*vide* Cornish behaviour in the Civil War). Indeed, in the longer term, especially in the nineteenth century when industrial prowess brought a new confidence to the Cornish identity, writers from Cornwall sought to produce forms of connection which would make it possible for 'the intellectuals' to assume cultural leadership of the people. This dynamic process may be reaching a high-point in the closing years of the twentieth century where a coalescence of intellectuals engaging in a range of new discourses is facilitating both the articulation of the Cornish identity with a renewed self-confidence *and* a fuller understanding of Cornwall's cultural history. At last, we can begin to make sense of *Henry V's* 'Cornish crew'.

NOTES AND REFERENCES

1. Edward Said, *Orientalism*, London, 1985, p. 16.
2. Steven G.Ellis, *Tudor Ireland: Crown, Community and the Conflict of Cultures*, London, 1985, p. 15.
3. Ellis, 1985, p. 319.
4. Michel Foucault, *The Order of Things*, London, 1970, p. 55.
5. Foucault, 1970, p. 55.
6. Myrna Combellack, *The Camborne Play: A Verse Translation of Beunans Meriasek*, Redruth, 1988, pp. 45–47.
7. Michael T.Ryan, 'Assimilating New Worlds in the Sixteenth and Seventeenth Centuries', *Comparative Studies in Society and History*, 23, 4, 1981.
8. A.L. Rowse, *Tudor Cornwall*, London, 1941, repub. Redruth, 1990, pp. 54–55 and pp. 92–93.
9. E.M.W. Tillyard, *Shakespeare's History Plays*, London, 1944, pp. 304–314.
10. Uri. M. Lotman, 'On the Semiotic Mechanism of Culture', *New Literary History*, IX, 2, 1978.
11. Homi K. Bhabha, 'The Other Question', *Screen*, 24, 6, 1983; Homi K. Bhabha, 'Of Mimicry and Man: The Ambivalence of Colonial Discourse', *October*, No. 28, 1984; Ashis Nandy, *At the Edge of Psychology: Essays in Politics and Culture*, Delhi, 1980; Ashis Nandy, *The Intimate Enemy: Loss and Recovery of Self Under Colonialism*, Delhi, 1983.

12. Such images are reported almost routinely in Cornish literature; for example, see Jack Clemo, *The Shadowed Bed*, Tring, 1986, p. 21; Alan M. Kent, Pol Hodge and Bert Biscoe, *Berdh Arnowydh Kernewek/Modern Cornish Poets*, St Austell, 1995, pp. 4, 115–116; Allen M. Ivey and Philip Payton, 'Towards a Cornish Identity Theory', in Philip Payton (ed.), *Cornish Studies: Two*, Exeter, 1994, p. 156; Daphne Du Maurier, *Jamaica Inn*, London, 1936, p. 36; Michael Williams (ed.), *My Cornwall*, St Teath, 1973, p. 1; Denys Val Baker, *A View From Land's End: Writers Against a Cornish Background*, London, 1982, p. 11.
13. Said, 1985, p. 7.
14. Lotman, 1978, p. 227.
15. Stephen Greenblatt, *Renaissance Self-Fashioning: From More to Shakespeare*, London, 1980.
16. Irving Ribner, *The English Play in the Age of Shakespeare*, New York, 1979, p. 2.
17. See Peter Saccio, *Shakespeare's English Kings: History, Chronicle and Drama*, London, 1977, pp. 65–89.
18. Gary Taylor (ed.), *Henry V*, Oxford, 1982.
19. G. Pawley White, *A Handbook of Cornish Surnames*, Penzance, 1972, p. 6.
20. Mark Stoyle, ' "Pagans or Paragons?": Images of the Cornish During the English Civil War', *English Historical Review*, CXI, 441, April 1996.
21. A.L. Rowse (ed.), *A Cornish Anthology*, London, 1968, p. 114.
22. Geoff Tibbals, *The Wycliffe File: The Story of the ITV Detective Series*, London, 1995.
23. Ivey and Payton, 1994; Bernard Deacon and Philip Payton, 'Re-inventing Cornwall: Culture Change on the European Periphery' in Philip Payton (ed.), *Cornish Studies: One*, Exeter, 1993; Bernard Deacon, 'And Shall Trelawny Die?' in Philip Payton (ed.), *Cornwall Since the War: The Contemporary History of a European Region*, Redruth, 1993.
24. C.W.R.D. Moseley, *Shakespeare's History Plays: Richard III to Henry V, the Making of a King*, London, 1988, p. 156.
25. William Hazlitt, *Characters of Shakespeare's Plays*, London, 1906, p. 214.
26. F.E. Halliday, *A History of Cornwall*, London, 1959, p. 148.
27. Richard Carew, *Survey of Cornwall*, ed. F.E. Halliday, London, 1953, pp. 145–147.
28. Marilyn Bell, Elizabeth Dane and John Dane (eds), *Shakespeare: King Henry V*, Cambridge, 1993, p. 233.
29. Bell, Dane and Dane, 1993, p. 235.
30. Gary Taylor, *Reinventing Shakespeare: A Cultural History from the Restoration to the Present*, London, 1990, pp. 122–123.
31. Hayden White, 'The Forms of Wildness: Archaeology of an Idea' in Edward Dudley and Maximilian E. Novak (eds), *The Wild Man Within: An Image in Western Thought from the Renaissance to Romanticism*, Pittsburg, 1972, p. 6.
32. Frank Kermode, *The Sense of an Ending*, London, 1966, p. 39.

33. Kermode, 1966, p. 39.
34. Philip Edwards, *Threshold of a Nation*, Cambridge, 1979, p. 84.
35. Edwards, 1979, p. 84.
36. Francis Barker and Peter Hulme, 'Nymphs and Reapers Heavily Vanish: The Discursive Con-texts of The Tempest', in John Drakakis (ed.), *Alternative Shakespeares*, London, 1985; Paul Brown, 'The Thing of Darkness I Acknowledge Mine: The Tempest and the Discourse of Colonialism', in Jonathon Dollimore and Alan Sinfield (eds), *Political Shakespeare: New Essays in Cultural Materialism*, Manchester, 1985; Trevor R. Griffiths, 'This Island's Mine: Caliban and Colonialism', *The Yearbook of English Studies*, 13, 1983.
37. Barker and Hulme, 1985, p. 197.
38. Franz Fanon, *The Wretched of the Earth*, London, 1965, p. 42.
39. Louis Althusser, *For Marx*, trans. B. Brewster, London, 1979, p. 145.
40. Carl Boggs, *Gramsci's Marxism*, London, 1976, p. 59.
41. Michel Foucault, *Power/Knowledge: Selected Interviews and Other Writings*, ed. Colin Gordon, Brighton, 1980, p. 531.
42. Michel Foucault, 'Politics and the Study of Discourses', *Ideology and Consciousness*, Vol. 3, 1978.
43. Philip Payton, ' "a . . . concealed envy against the English": A Note on the Aftermath of the 1497 Rebellions in Cornwall', in Philip Payton (ed.), *Cornish Studies: One*, Exeter, 1993.
44. Rowse, 1941 and 1990, p. 271.

'SIR RICHARD GRENVILLE'S CREATURES': THE NEW CORNISH TERTIA, 1644–46

Mark Stoyle

INTRODUCTION

The exploits of the five Cornish infantry regiments which held Cornwall and captured the South West of England for King Charles I during the first year of the Civil War are justly famous. Under the command of Sir Ralph Hopton, Sir Bevill Grenville, Sir Nicholas Slanning and other Royalist champions, the Cornishmen seized control of the two great counties of Devon and Somerset, trounced the Parliamentarians at the battles of Stratton and Roundaway Down, and finally crowned their success by taking part in the storm and capture of Bristol— the second city of the kingdom. Scholars all agree that the Cornish soldiers exhibited quite unusual valour and enthusiasm during the period 1642–43. But they also agree that the storming of Bristol brought this golden age to an end; that after Bristol, as C.V. Wedgwood once expressed it, 'the splendid Cornish infantry went to pieces'.[1]

The terrible casualties inflicted at Bristol and Lansdowne certainly had an enormous impact on the Cornishmen's morale. Yet to argue from this—as Wedgwood and so many other writers have done—that the Cornish army was a broken sword after July 1643, a force which had 'withdrawn from operations', is quite simply wrong.[2] It is too often forgotten that the five Cornish infantry regiments which suffered so badly at Bristol later went on to reduce the whole of Dorset to the Royal allegiance, as well as storming the Parliamentary strongholds of Dartmouth, Exeter and Mount Stamford.[3] Thereafter, the 'Old Cornish' (as these regiments came to be known) went on to participate in the siege of Plymouth (1643), the siege of Lyme (1644), the

Lostwithiel campaign, the Newbury campaign, the siege of Taunton (1645), the Langport campaign and the investment of Exeter (1645–46). Throughout this period the Cornish infantry regiments continued to fight stoutly. Yet, chiefly because there was no one to chronicle the later campaigns as Hopton himself had chronicled the campaigns of 1642–43, the service which the Old Cornish soldiers performed for the King during the latter stages of the Civil War has gone largely unrecognized.[4]

If the later history of the Old Cornish regiments has been neglected, that of the King's other Cornish infantry units has been virtually ignored.[5] Many of these units were as tough and determined as those which Hopton had led to victory in 1643, however, and without them the Royalist war effort in the West could not have been sustained for as long as it was. This article gives an account of the most important of these forgotten infantry formations: the 'New Cornish Tertia' of 1644–46. At the same time, it casts some fresh light on the tertia's commander, Sir Richard Grenville, and on the way in which his military activities were misrepresented by Edward Hyde, Earl of Clarendon, in his *History of the Great Rebellion*.[6] In addition, the paper makes one or two preliminary comments about the fierce devotion which Grenville inspired in his troops, a subject which I hope to explore in detail elsewhere.

GENESIS

The story of the New Cornish Tertia began in the aftermath of the Lostwithiel campaign of 1644, as Charles I, fresh from his victory in Cornwall, prepared to return to the main theatre of war in the east. The King planned to take with him not only his own main field army, but also that of Prince Maurice, which included the Cornish regiments raised in 1642. The removal of these units would leave Cornwall and the West extremely vulnerable to attack from the Roundhead garrison at Plymouth and it was therefore decided that the town should be blockaded by Royalist troops. This task was entrusted to Sir Richard Grenville, a Cornish gentleman and professional soldier, who had already conducted an unsuccessful siege of Plymouth earlier in the year.[7] Grenville is an intriguing figure. A deserter from the Parliamentary ranks, he was vilified by the London pamphleteers, whilst many on the King's side disliked him for his vindictiveness and his quarrelsome nature. As a result Grenville has received perhaps the worst 'press' of any Civil War general. Yet Sir Richard was a tough, resourceful commander.[8]

Grenville took command of the blockading forces at Plymouth in

September 1644. According to his own account he possessed only 300 soldiers at this time.[9] Other commentators put the figure a little higher, but agreed that Grenville's forces were comparatively small: the King having left him with 'not above 500 foot and 300 horse'.[10] A month later Grenville still had only 700 men under his command.[11] Yet between October and December his forces grew very quickly indeed. Grenville himself later claimed that 'in a short time' he had 'increased his forces to . . . above 5,000 foot and 1000 horse', while Sir Edward Walker agreed, stating that Grenville had 'so actively pursued both the levying forces [and] keeping them in good order . . . as that his strength . . . increased into an army' by the end of the year.[12] Sources hostile to Grenville told the same story; Roundhead newsbooks acknowledged that he had gathered together an army of 5–6,000 men.[13] Even the Earl of Clarendon, who hated Grenville and took every opportunity to do him down, was forced to admit that Sir Richard's forces had 'suddenly increased' during late 1644.[14]

The Royalists were perennially short of foot soldiers and Grenville's success in raising 4–5,000 infantrymen in just three months (this at a time when the King's own field army contained 6,500 foot 'at most') is remarkable.[15] How had he managed to do it? The family name undoubtedly helped. Many must have followed Sir Richard in the hope that he would emulate the successes of his dead brother, Sir Bevill: the man who had led the Cornish army to victory in 1643.[16] It is clear, too, that Grenville's ranks were swelled by many hundreds of Cornish soldiers who had deserted from Prince Maurice's army in order to escape being marched off to the east.[17] Grenville's military experience and undoubted organizational ability were also important. As A.C. Miller has observed, the fact that so many deserters were prepared to serve under him 'is a tribute to his qualities of leadership'.[18] But most important of all may well have been the fact that Grenville himself was a Cornishman. Seventeenth-century Cornwall was a fiercely particularist society: a territory whose inhabitants saw themselves as set-apart, distinct.[19] And while space forbids detailed discussion of the evidence here, there are good grounds for thinking that Grenville's success in recruiting men during 1644 partly reflected the skill with which he now began to present himself as a specifically 'Cornish' leader, as a man who was primarily concerned with the welfare of this particular county and its inhabitants.[20]

THE TERTIA

The infantry force which Grenville had amassed by Christmas 1644 had three main component parts. First there were the Cornish trained-bands, or county militia. It was with Cornish militia regiments that Grenville threw the Parliamentarians out of Saltash in October 1644, and these units continued to guard the western bank of the Tamar throughout the rest of the war.[21] On the other side of the Tamar, the Devon trained-bands played a similar role. Assisted by a volunteer regiment under Colonel Champernowne, the Devon militia blocked up the Plymouth garrison as best they could and garrisoned the various forts and strongpoints which Grenville had erected around the town.[22] At the core of Sir Richard's army, however, lay a completely new infantry formation, one which he had recruited from the surrounding countryside during October–December 1644 whilst the militia kept the Plymouth garrison in check. This formation was the New Cornish Tertia.

The tertia (or division) was divided into four regiments: those of Grenville himself, John Arundell, Richard Arundell and Lewis Tremaine. All four of the regimental commanders were Cornish, and all four had enjoyed considerable military experience, despite their relative youth (both the Arundells had served as field officers in the King's Western Army during 1642–44, while Tremaine had been Bevill Grenville's ensign at Stratton).[23] The two Arundells' regiments were made up exclusively of Cornishmen, but Tremaine's unit contained many Devonians as well.[24] A list survives, in Tremaine's own hand, of 'the names of the p[ar]ishes I have sent for to clothe their men, and the time of their appearance and how many of each p[ar]ishe'.[25] This document probably dates to September 1644 and shows that Tremaine was hoping to recruit around 500 men from West Devon at this time. The rest of Tremaine's soldiers probably came from north-east Cornwall where he himself and many of his officers dwelt. Recruitment on a similar scale presumably took place all over Cornwall during late 1644 as the commanders of the New Cornish Tertia struggled to bring their units up to strength.

Quite how long it took to raise the soldiers is unclear. The private papers of George Yeo, of Huish in North Devon, who served as a captain in Richard Arundell's regiment, reveal that he did not arrive at the Royalist headquarters at Plympton until 23 October.[26] The officers and men of the other regiments may well have taken even longer to come up: Grenville's forces were still reported to be 'inconsiderable' three weeks later.[27] By early December, however, soldiers were pouring into the Royalist camp and Sir Richard was said to have gathered 'an armie'.[28] Roundhead propagandists claimed that Grenville's officers had used great cruelty in raising the men and this was almost certainly true.[29] Yet once the soldiers had arrived in Sir Richard's quarters they found themselves unusually well looked after.

Grenville provided his troops with comfortable, well-fortified billets.[30] He also made sure that they were paid. All sources agree on this. Thus the Royalist newspamphlet *Mercurius Aulicus* observed that Grenville's troops were 'constantly paid by the poll', whilst a Parliamentarian journal acknowledged that 'he pays every soldier his pay every Saturday night, and each foot soldier duly receives 3s 6d'.[31] Grenville himself once observed that 'he neither would nor could command men who were not paid' and the point is constantly reiterated in his surviving correspondence.[32] Having been assigned a large proportion of the weekly contribution of Devon and Cornwall towards the maintenance of his army, Sir Richard was determined to collect the money in full. He was constantly aware of 'the hazard of the disbanding of the forces under my charge if they fail of their pay' and he strained every nerve to prevent this from happening.[33] If Grenville was unusual amongst Royalist commanders in the care which he took to ensure that his soldiers were paid, he was also unusual in the concern which he evinced for civilians. Grenville did not allow his men to plunder and even Clarendon acknowledged that 'the discipline he exercised over his men at Plymouth, in keeping them from committing any disorder or offering the least prejudice to any man . . . raised him much credit amongst the country people'.[34]

There is a familiar ring to all this. In its discipline, its regular pay, and its care of civilians, Grenville's New Cornish Tertia was strikingly reminiscent of Parliament's contemporaneous New Model Army. To draw too close a parallel between the New Cornish and the New Model would obviously be unwise. Yet it is hard to avoid the conclusion that, of all the Royalist commanders during the latter stages of the Civil War, it was Grenville who came the closest to building an effective, well-balanced and potentially sustainable infantry force.

INTO BATTLE

By 8 January 1645 Grenville felt confident enough of his men to unleash them upon Plymouth. The events of the next three days were to prove a terrible baptism of fire for the New Cornish. Having advanced from the Royalist fort at Penny Cross Hill, just to the north of the town, Grenville's men built a series of temporary breastworks in the no-man's land between the Cavalier and Roundhead lines.[35] From here a major assault was launched against the Parliamentarians' northern outworks on the night of 9–10 January. According to one report, Grenville's forces attacked in three divisions: a forlorn hope of 2,000 men and two supporting brigades of 1,500 men apiece.[36] Almost certainly it was the New Cornish who formed the advance brigade, whilst the militia regiments made up the other two formations. The attack failed, and the Royalists lost several hundred slain and at least seventy captured. Amongst the latter was 'Colonel Arundell'—probably one of the regimental commanders of the New Cornish—whose troops had initially managed to capture Little Penny Come Quick Fort but had later been driven out again by the Parliamentarians.[37] That Arundell got as far as he did indicates that the New Cornish had performed well in the assault. Grenville later claimed that Plymouth would have been won 'had my seconds performed their parts', suggesting that it was the failure of the support brigades to back up the New Cornish which had caused the attack to fail.[38] This was certainly the inference of a Roundhead report, which claimed that Arundell's men had been abandoned by the rest of Grenville's forces.[39]

Whoever was to blame for the defeat of 10 January, the scale of the Royalist casualties ensured that there would be no more attacks on Plymouth for some time—and when Grenville did resume offensive operations, things again went badly wrong. On 18 February Colonel Champernowne's regiment was attacked and mauled by Roundhead units to the south of Plymouth whilst the bulk of Grenville's forces were away to the north.[40] Soon afterwards Grenville received word that he and his men were needed in Somerset, where Royalist forces were besieging Taunton. Sir Richard was unwilling to relinquish command of the blockade at Plymouth and he prevaricated for as long as he could. At the beginning of March, however, the King himself ordered Grenville to go to Taunton.[41] Sir Richard had little choice but to obey.

Over the next couple of weeks Grenville made his dispositions. During his absence the blockade of Plymouth was to be maintained by the local militia. They would be assisted by several cavalry regiments, and by the shattered remains of Champernowne's foot.[42] The New Cornish and the bulk of the cavalry, meanwhile, would accompany Grenville on his march to the east. By 15 March all was in readiness. On that day the Royalist forces 'withdrewe [themselves] from off their works and line; and the greatest part of them went to the east, the rest to [the forts at] Hopton's Worke, Penny Cross . . . and Plympton'.[43] Grenville that he left 2,000 foot and 400 horse before Plymouth, well supplied with 'armes and municion, and strong workes'.[44] These were mostly second-rate troops, of course. It was amongst the 2–3,000 foot and 800 horse whom Grenville took with him to Taunton that his 'best officers and souldiers' were to be found.[45]

Clarendon gives a very different picture of events in his *History*, claiming that Grenville:

had never maintained or raised near half the number of men to
which he was obliged till the week before he was required to march
to Taunton, when he called up the posse comitatus [a gathering
of the able-bodied men of the county] and thence forced almost
the whole number of foot which marched with him thither, bringing
them with him to Exciter unarmed, and there compelled the
commissioners to supply him with arms and ammunition.[46]

Scholars have long been aware that Clarendon's *History* is unreliable
as far as Grenville is concerned, however, and the more closely one
examines the evidence, the more obvious this unreliability becomes.[47]
As the following pages will show, Clarendon not only misrepresented
Sir Richard's military activities, but also downplayed the importance
of the forces under his command. This is well illustrated by the way in
which Clarendon progressively reduced his estimate of the number of
men whom Grenville had left at Plymouth; initially stating that these
troops had numbered 2,000 foot and 400 horse but later scaling this
figure down to 1,500 foot and 400 horse and later still to 'but 1,500
foot and 300 horse'.[48]

If Clarendon was curiously inconsistent in this respect, his claim
that newly-raised posse men made up 'almost the whole' of the force
which Grenville led to Taunton in March 1645 seems at best a gross
exaggeration, at worst a downright lie. Whilst other sources show that
Grenville did indeed summon the posse before he left Plymouth, this
was done to reinforce his existing strength, rather than to create a
completely new army.[49] Sir Richard already possessed some 5,000 men
by January 1645 and—even allowing for the losses sustained in the
attack of 9–10 January—this force was quite large enough to recruit
both the Taunton expedition and the Plymouth blockade. The force
which Grenville led into Exeter in March 1645 was no mere rabble; it
was a well-paid, experienced infantry division, one which he had been
building up since September 1644. That Grenville requested arms and
ammunition for his troops once he had arrived in Exeter is hardly
suprising: the city was the administrative capital of South-West England
and Royalist commanders regularly tried to obtain supplies here
throughout the period 1643–46.[50]

The New Cornish and the cavalry regiments which accompanied
them finally arrived before Taunton around 2 April.[51] The tertia was
now at the peak of its strength, all sources acknowledging that Grenville
possessed some 2–3,000 infantrymen.[52] The general demeanour of
these troops continued to be quite unusually good. One Royalist officer
informed a friend at this time that 'Grenvile keeps his soldiers in that
discipline they dare not plunder nor wrong any person', ruefully adding

'[I] would ours were so'.[53] Having settled these paragons of military virtue in their quarters around Taunton, Grenville made at least one unsuccessful attempt to storm the town, then ordered his men to move in as close as possible for a major assault. Yet before this attack could be launched, Grenville was shot in the groin by a sniper while viewing the Parliamentary garrison at Wellington House. Seriously wounded, he was carried back to Exeter in a horse-litter: leaving his Cornish soldiers leaderless and demoralized.[54]

DECLINE

With Grenville out of action the governor of Exeter, Sir John Berkeley, assumed temporary command of the New Cornish. According to Clarendon, Grenville publicly agreed to this arrangement but secretly encouraged resentment amongst his officers, so that 'neither officer nor soldier did his duty after he was gone'.[55] There is no way of knowing if this charge is true. But whether or not Grenville was stirring the pot, the men of the New Cornish Tertia had every reason to feel bitter and aggrieved in the wake of his departure. The Cornish soldiers' preference for serving under their own commanders is well attested, and Berkeley can have been but a poor substitute. Worse still, with Sir Richard gone, the regular pay which his soldiers had been accustomed to receiving quickly dried up.[56] Simultaneously, the hazards which they were expected to face became greater than ever before. Throughout April-May 1645 the New Cornish were exposed to constant heavy fighting at Taunton. Grenville's men suffered terribly in a whole series of frontal assaults. The surgeon Richard Wiseman later recalled seeing a soldier of Colonel Arundell's regiment horribly mangled in the aftermath of one such attack.[57] More direct evidence comes from the petition of Griffin Morgan—a husbandman of Molland, in Devon—who also served in Arundell's regiment. Long after the war, Morgan remembered how:

> at the siege of . . . Taunton, after many and dangerous assaults, [he] was thrust through with a halberd in his thigh and shott throughe the other thigh with a bullet . . . and yet was not himself taken, but took some of the enemies [prisoner] and brought them away.[58]

Despite such acts of individual heroism, spring 1645 saw death, disease and above all desertion taking a terrible toll of the New Cornish. According to Clarendon, Berkeley was soon complaining that 'those soldiers brought to Taunton by Greenevill every day mouldered away, and he had reason to believe it was by his [Grenville's] direction'. Grenville strongly denied that 'the soldiers left the leaguer . . . by any direction of his' but, for whatever reason, the desertions continued.[59] In May Lord George Goring assumed command of the forces before Taunton, thus making matters even worse. Goring not only 'discouraged his own foot so much that they ran away faster than they could be sent up to him', he also seems to have gone out of his way to antagonise the Cornish soldiers.[60] By mid-June only 600 of the New Cornish were left.[61]

Anxious to stem this tide of desertion, the Prince of Wales— who had recently been appointed titular commander of the Royalist forces in the South West—invited Grenville to resume command of his old brigade. Sir Richard, by now recovered from his wounds, had already requested 'that he might be re-established in the command of those men he had formerly levied' and he accepted the Prince's offer with alacrity.[62] At the same time, he agreed to take up a commission as Field-Marshal and to proceed to Lyme, in Dorset, in order to institute a blockade of the Parliamentary garrison there. Grenville's cheerful acceptance of this comparatively minor role has surprised his latest biographer.[63] Yet it was clearly the prospect of regaining control of the New Cornish Tertia which persuaded Grenville to take up the post. Late in June he made his way to Lyme with a small body of horse and foot, confident that the New Cornish—together with other Royalist troops—would shortly be joining him.[64] Yet these men never arrived.

Early in July Roundhead troops marched into Somerset, forcing Goring to abandon the siege of Taunton. Already short of men, Goring could no longer afford to send the New Cornish to Grenville and he kept them with his own army instead. Meanwhile, most of the other troops whom Grenville had been promised were diverted to protect the Prince.[65] Sir Richard was now further away than ever from regaining control of his old tertia: indeed he was placed in the supremely humiliating position of being a Field-Marshal with no soldiers. Complaining that he had no 'men fit for service', Grenville threw up his commission in disgust.[66] A few days later, Goring's army was decisively beaten by the New Model Army at Langport, an engagement which saw the New Cornish suffering still further losses. Roundhead newsbooks recorded the capture of five of Grenville's officers, and no doubt the tertia lost many common soldiers as well.[67]

In the wake of what George Yeo—by now Lieutenant-Colonel of Arundell's regiment—referred to as 'the rout at Langport', Goring's army fled westwards. Yeo arrived back home at Huish in North Devon on 12 July, just two days after the battle.[68] Over the next week what was left of the Royalist infantry slowly regrouped around Bideford.

The shattering defeat at Langport had clearly hastened the dis-integration of the New Cornish Tertia, and Goring informed a correspondent that 'Colonell [Richard] Arundell is goeing into Corne-wall to recover his men, most of his regiment being runn home'.[69] Arundell's was not the only regiment to have suffered through massive desertion at this time: Goring went on to confess that 'most of the Newe Cornish' had run away.[70] The Prince and his advisers—who had by now retired into Cornwall—did what they could to round up these deserters and return them to the front. On 22 July Lord Culpepper wrote to Goring, informing him that 'his highnes hath taken the most effectual course in his power for getting up of the foure Cornish regiments dispersed from you'.[71] Goring was at first unwilling to credit these assurances but by 1 August he had been persuaded that a vigorous campaign of impressment might yet bring the tertia back up to strength.[72]

Goring's optimism was probably encouraged by the fact that the New Model Army had temporarily halted its advance to the West. Emboldened by this, his forces began to drift back towards Exeter during August, eventually establishing themselves at Crediton.[73] The New Cornish were still there on 6 September when Yeo left the town to go home on leave, but by the time that he rejoined his unit on 25 September the tertia had moved still further east, to Tiverton.[74] During Yeo's absence a major reorganization had taken place. Richard Arundell had now been absent from the formation for almost two months, so he was relieved of his command and his regiment was merged with that of Colonel Tremaine.[75] Henceforth the New Cornish Tertia was to consist of just three regiments: Grenville's, Tremaine's and Jonathan Arundell's.[76]

By this time the strength of the formation had reached an all-time low: on 28 September it was reported that only 200 of the New Cornish were left.[77] In despair, the Prince's Council once again turned to Sir Richard Grenville, who had already been appointed overall com-mander of the Cornish trained-bands, and was now restored to command of 'his own three regiments' as well.[78] It took Grenville some time to get his old soldiers back, however, for—in the face of a renewed Parlia-mentary advance—Goring had drawn his infantry units into Exeter. Not until mid-October was Colonel Tremaine able to lead the battered remains of the New Cornish Tertia out of the city towards the West.[79]

RECOVERY

Tremaine's destination was originally said to be Newton Abbot. Yet, within days of his departure, Goring's entire cavalry force had begun

to move into the countryside to the south-west of Exeter. As a result
billets in this area must have become extremely scarce and Tremaine
eventually took up quarters further south, at Totnes. Here Grenville
—who had recently advanced into Devon with the Cornish trained-
bands—at last rejoined his loyal officers. The occasion was marked
by considerable celebration; the Mayor of Totnes providing a 'feast'
for 'Sir Richard Grenville with all his Cornish Commanders'.[80]
Grenville could not afford to relax his vigilance, however, for Parliamentary troops had by now occupied much of East Devon and the
Royalists to the west of Exeter feared an imminent attack. On 21
October the town authorities purchased '86 candles . . . for the watch
at [the] bridge for the Cornish Guards . . . by Sir Richard Grenville's
command'.[81]

Towards the end of October Grenville and the New Cornish left
Totnes and marched away to Okehampton, where Sir Richard clearly
planned to concentrate all his forces in order to resist any further
Roundhead advance.[82] Cornish trained-band units were already
billeted in Okehampton and they and the New Cornish were soon
working together to build defences: a townsman later recalled that 'in
Oct. and Nov. [1645], Sir Richard Grenville did raise barricadoes and
other works and made this town a garrison'.[83] Meanwhile Guy Molesworth, whom Grenville had recently appointed Major General of the
tertia, was procuring badly-needed supplies: an ammunition train under
his command passed through Chudleigh, some miles north of Totnes,
on 5 November, presumably on its way to the Cornish troops at
Okehampton.[84]

Clarendon gives an unusually detailed account of the events of the
next few weeks. Throughout most of November, he observes, 'Sir
Richard Greeneville stayed still at Okington, with his three regiments
of old soldiers'. Towards the end of that month, however, Grenville
'retired with his three regiments from Okington into Cornwall', despite
having received express instructions not to do so. As a result,
Clarendon claims, a gap was created in the Royalist line and the New
Model Army encouraged to advance. Clarendon then goes on to relate
how Grenville 'quartered his men upon the River Tamar, that divides
Cornwall from Devon, with express command to guard the passes, and
not to suffer any of Lord Goring's men . . . to come into Cornwall'. By
these 'unheard of and unwarrantable means', Clarendon concludes,
Grenville 'prepar[ed] the country to . . . a hatred of the Lord Goring's
forces' and 'alienated all men's spirits' from the service.[85] Clarendon's
description of the New Cornish Tertia's movements during late 1645
is broadly accurate. George Yeo's accounts show that Tremaine's
regiment—and presumably the rest of the New Cornish as well—did

indeed leave Okehampton on 20 November, whilst Grenville's own letters make it clear that the New Cornish were quartered on the west bank of the Tamar by early December.[86] The interpretation which Clarendon puts upon these manoeuvres is much more doubtful, however.

Clarendon suggests that Grenville had abandoned an important strategic position for no good reason, weakening the Royalist position and encouraging the Parliamentarians to advance. What has hitherto been overlooked is the fact that, around 14 November, 600 veteran soldiers were sent out of the Royalist garrison at Exeter and ordered to quarter themselves in the countryside to the west. Crucially, these troops were reported to be heading for Okehampton.[87] In the light of this, it is hard to believe that Grenville's departure from the town a few days later was really as illogical as Clarendon suggests. Far from abandoning Okehampton to the enemy, Grenville had left it in the hands of 600 battle-hardened Royalist troops. Nor is this all. As we have seen, Clarendon alleged that Grenville's withdrawal had had disastrous strategic consequences. He backed this up by claiming that, on or shortly before 26 November, the Prince of Wales received letters from Exeter which lamented 'the extreme ill consequence of . . . Greenevill's drawing off from Okington, upon encouragement whereof a strong party of the enemy was come to [Crediton]'.[88] Here again, Clarendon has deliberately falsified his evidence. A Parliamentary advance to Crediton did indeed occur, but not until 7 December, at least two weeks after Grenville had left Okehampton.[89] Sir Richard can be entirely exonerated of Clarendon's charge that he precipitated a major Parliamentary advance by his withdrawal to the Tamar.

If the New Cornish Tertia's evacuation of Okehampton was not, after all, the result of some mental aberration on the part of its commander, then how can the manoeuvre be explained? Almost certainly Grenville's march to the west was prompted by a popular insurrection: one which Clarendon typically fails to mention. Parliamentary pamphlets make it clear that, in late November 1645, the inhabitants of the upper Tamar valley rose up in revolt against Goring's plundering cavalry.[90] The actions which Grenville subsequently took —leaving Okehampton, marching back to Stratton, and posting his troops along the west bank of the Tamar—were surely designed to deal with this potentially very serious problem. Once arrived on the scene, Grenville allied himself with the countrymen and posted guards on the Tamar bridges in order to keep Goring's plunderers out.[91] The disturbances were thus brought to an end. Sir Richard had acted quickly and effectively in difficult circumstances. Yet Clarendon, by suppressing any reference to the original revolt, makes it appear that it was

Grenville who had been responsible for whipping up popular feeling against Goring's men in the first place. Once again the truth has been seriously distorted.

Clarendon's account of events is not completely without foundation, however. Grenville may not have initiated the trouble between the country folk and Goring's men, but there can be little doubt that he later took advantage of the bitter hatred which existed between the two groups in order to strengthen his own position as the champion of the 'Cornish interest'. Throughout the first half of December, Grenville's troops remained stationed along the west bank of the Tamar, effectively protecting Cornwall from any incursion by Goring's cavalry. At the same time, Sir Richard himself—apparently realizing that the war was lost—attempted to persuade Prince Charles to sign a separate peace with the Parliamentarians. Significantly, Grenville couched his proposals in specifically Cornish terms, urging the Prince to withdraw from the war and to set up a neutral, semi-independent statelet in West Devon and Cornwall. It is easy to see how such a scheme might have appealed to Cornish particularist sentiment—and boosted Sir Richard's credit among ordinary Cornish people.[92]

Yet Grenville's efforts were to no avail: the Prince was determined to fight on and Sir Richard had little choice but to obey. On 14 December he wrote to Colonel Tremaine, warning him to gather his men together for an immediate advance into Devon and a week later the New Cornish re-occupied Okehampton, the troops who had previously been stationed there having returned to Exeter.[93] By the end of December the New Cornish were firmly established in Okehampton. Clarendon states that the tertia was 800 strong at this time: a Parliamentarian report of 1 January 1646 put the figure a little higher, at 1,000 men.[94] The speed with which the formation had grown since it came back under Grenville's command in October is striking, especially when one considers that almost all the other Royalist infantry units in the West were now shrinking fast.

December 1645 had seen the King's commanders in the South West making frantic efforts to raise an army capable of dislodging the New Model Army from its positions around Exeter. Yet in the end it was to be the Roundheads who struck first. On 8 January 1646 Molesworth's guards at Okehampton were 'advanced upon' by Parliamentary units.[95] Badly outnumbered, Molesworth had little alternative but to retreat. By the end of that day the New Cornish had abandoned Okehampton, probably falling back on Tavistock where Grenville himself was quartered.[96] Yet there was to be little respite here, for the Royalist position was now crumbling across the whole of South Devon. Within the week Tavistock, too, had been evacuated, as the Royalist infantry fled back across the Tamar. Many desertions took place during this panic-stricken flight. According to Clarendon, the strength of the New Cornish Tertia fell from 800 to 600 men within a week—and worse was still to come.[97]

On 19 January Grenville himself—whose ambitions had now come to be seen as positively dangerous by the Prince's councillors —was imprisoned at Launceston, on a charge of insubordination.[98] Next day he was cashiered from his various regiments, 'all which were then disposed of to others commands in the market-place at Launceston'.[99] (Command of Grenville's foot regiment devolved on his former Lieutenant-Colonel, George Collins).[100] Sir Richard's arrest was greeted with shock and disbelief by the soldiers under his command and they petitioned for his release.[101] Yet these efforts all failed. Grenville remained in gaol, while Lord Hopton assumed overall command of the New Cornish. The transfer of command was not altogether smooth. Although Cornish soldiers had been willing to work with Hopton in the past, the New Cornish were very much Grenville's regiments, and the officers, in particular, were said to be 'entirely his creatures'.[102] It was noted by one Roundhead pamphleteer that 'those foot which Sir Richard Grenville hath got together do refuse to obey either the Lord Hopton or any other save Sir Richard himself' and, whilst this may have been an exaggeration, it does convey the deep sense of loyalty which the New Cornish felt towards their original commander.[103]

DEFEAT

Following his arrest, Grenville was sent to St Michael's Mount in the far west of Cornwall. Here he remained a prisoner while his men prepared to take part in a last, desperate, Royalist offensive. In February Hopton led the Prince's army to Torrington in North Devon, and it was here that the New Cornish Tertia clashed with the New Model Army for the last time. Accounts of the Cornishmen's performance in the ensuing battle varied: Hopton claimed that after a brief struggle the Royalist foot 'quitted their posts', but Roundhead sources painted a very different picture, stating that the King's foot had stood to it 'manfully'.[104] Whatever the case, Torrington was a shattering defeat for the Royalists and the New Cornish suffered heavy losses. Fourteen of Tremaine's soldiers were captured, along with eight of Collins's and five of Arundell's.[105] Major Frayne, of Tremaine's regiment, was killed, whilst George Yeo, realizing that the war was now lost to the King, finally laid down his arms and went home.[106]

Despite the crushing nature of this defeat, many of Grenville's old soldiers managed to make it back across the Tamar: 500 of them were reported to be gathered at Launceston on 25 February.[107] But soon afterwards the advance of the victorious Roundhead army forced the tattered remnants of the New Cornish to evacuate the town and join the rest of the King's broken forces in a long, slow, retreat down the Cornish peninsula. On 28 February the Royalist foot were at Bodmin, on 2 March at Probus and on 9 March at Truro.[108] The Royalist army was now beginning to disintegrate, but Hopton still hoped to salvage something from the wreckage. On 9 March he ordered Colonel Collins and his men to march into garrison at St Michael's Mount.[109] Did the men of Grenville's old regiment hope that their former commander still lay immured within the castle walls? If so, they were to be disappointed, for Sir Richard had managed to escape to France just a few days before.[110] On the same day that Collins's soldiers marched into the Mount 'the remainder of Colonel John Arundell's and Colonel Tremayne's regiments, being about 200 men' marched in to join the Royalist garrison at Pendennis.[111] As the castle gates slammed shut behind them, the field career of the New Cornish Tertia came to an end.

Even so, much hard fighting remained ahead, for—although the bulk of the King's Western Army surrendered to Fairfax on 14 March—the troops who had retired into Pendennis and the Mount were Royalist diehards ('excellent good foot, and as good officers as any' Hopton termed them)[112] and they would not give up without a struggle. Collins's men held out on the Mount until 16 April and Pendennis resisted even longer. The garrison's resolve may well have been strengthened by the fact that three out of four of the New Cornish Tertia's original commanders were present in Pendennis, Richard Arundell having rejoined his old comrades at the last minute by marching into the castle with 'the remainder of his train-bands'.[113] Bolstered by the presence of officers like these, the garrison refused to surrender until 17 August, by which time they were the very last body of soldiers 'in England' still holding out for the King. The 'stoute Cornish men', as even their enemies admiringly termed them,[114] could scarcely have done more—and it seems fitting that it should be in 1996, exactly 350 years after the surrender at Pendennis took place, that the military service of the New Cornish regiments should at last be commemorated, in a series dedicated to the Cornwall in whose defence they fought.

NOTES AND REFERENCES

1. C.V. Wedgwood, *History and Hope*, London, 1987, p. 280.
2. C.V. Wedgwood, *The King's War*, London, 1958, p. 249; see also Mary

Coate, *Cornwall in the Great Civil War and Interregnum 1642–1660*, Truro, 1963, p. 100

3. For the events of July-October 1643, see R. Hutton, 'Clarendon's History of the Rebellion', *English Historical Review*, 97, 1982, pp. 76–78. For Mount Stamford, see Mark Stoyle, *Loyalty and Locality: Popular Allegiance in Devon during the English Civil War*, Exeter, 1994, p. 68; and Todd Gray and Mark Stoyle, 'A Cavalier Cartographer', *History Today*, Vol. 44, No. 3, March 1994.

4. For Hopton's account of the earlier campaigns, see C.E. Chadwyck Healey (ed), *Bellum Civile: Hopton's Narrative of his Campaign in the West (1642-44)*, Somerset Record Society, 18, 1902. For the one reliable account of the later service of the Old Cornish regiments, see M.D.G. Wanklyn's excellent MA thesis, 'The King's Armies in the West of England, 1642–46', University of Manchester, 1966.

5. The honourable exception is again Wanklyn, 1966.

6. Historians have long been aware that Clarendon's *History* is not to be trusted as far as Grenville is concerned. For detailed discussion, see Amos C. Miller, *Sir Richard Grenville of the Civil War*, London, 1979, pp. 1, 61–62, 70, 98–99, 119–20, 130, 132–33, 138, 165–76; and Hutton, 1982, pp. 85, 87.

7. For Grenville's earlier career, see R. Granville, *The King's General in the West: The Life of Sir Richard Granville*, London, 1908, pp. 1–58; and Miller, 1979, pp. 1–74.

8. For favourable assessments of Grenville's military capabilities, see Coate, 1963, p. 177; Hutton, 1982, p. 85; Miller, 1979, pp. 165–66; and Wanklyn, 1966, p. 123.

9. T.E. Carte (ed.), *A Collection of Original Letters and Papers . . . found among the Duke of Ormonde's Papers*, London, 1739, p. 97.

10. E. Walker, *Historical Discourses upon Several Occasions*, 1705, p. 85.

11. Walker, 1705, p. 105.

12. Carte, 1793 p. 97; and Walker, 1705, p. 85.

13. See, for example, E.21 (6) and E.24 (23).

14. Edward Hyde, Earl of Clarendon, *The History of the Rebellion and Civil Wars in England*, ed. W.D. Macray, Oxford, 1888, Book 8, p. 145; see also Amos C. Miller 'Joseph Jane's Account of Cornwall during the Civil War', *English Historical Review*, 90, 1975; and Miller, 1979, pp. 93–94.

15. J.L. Malcolm, *Caesar's Due: Loyalty and King Charles, 1642–46*, London, 1983), p. 203.

16. Miller, 1979, p. 71; see also Coate, 1963, p. 164.

17. Miller, 1979, p. 94.

18. Miller, 1979, p. 94.

19. See Mark Stoyle, ' "Pagans or Paragons"?: Images of the Cornish During the English Civil War', *English Historical Review*, CXI, 441, April 1995.

20. I hope to examine this subject in a forthcoming article.

21. Bodleian Library, Oxford [hereafter: Bod.], 4.M.68.art, *Mercurius Aulicus*, 13–19 October 1644; and E.266 (37).

22. For Phillip Champernowne, see P.R. Newman, *Royalist Officers in England and Wales, 1642–60: A Biographical Dictionary*, 1981, p. 67.
23. See Devon Record Office [hereafter: DRO], Seymour MSS, 44/50–51; and Bod., Wood Pamphlets, 376, *Sergeant Major James Chudleigh: His Declaration to his Countrymen*, Oxford, 1643, p. 2. For brief accounts of Tremaine and the two Arundells, see Newman, 1981, pp. 6–7, 377.
24. For the exclusively Cornish nature of the two Arundells' regiments, see S. Reid, *Officers and Regiments of the Royalist Army*, four volumes, Leigh on Sea, n.d., I, pp. 3–4.
25. Cornwall Record Office [hereafter: CRO], Tremaine MSS, DDT, 1756.
26. R.W. Cotton, 'A North Devon Cavalier's Expenses', *Devon and Cornwall Notes and Gleanings*, III, 1890, p. 70.
27. E.18 (7).
28. E.21 (13).
29. See Miller, 1979, p. 103.
30. E.18 (5).
31. E.270 (14); and Miller, 1979, p. 113.
32. Miller, 1979, p. 111; see also Granville, 1908, p. 116; and Bod., Clarendon MSS, 25, 1911, 1933.
33. Granville, 1979, p. 116.
34. Clarendon, 1888, Book 9, p. 54. See also Hutton, 1982, p. 85.
35. E.270 (14).
36. E.25 (10).
37. For the capture of Arundell, see T.W. Birch (ed.), *The Military Memoirs of Colonel John Birch*, Camden Society, New Series, 7, 1873, pp. 14–15.
38. Granville, 1908, p. 108.
39. E.25 (13); for a general account of this engagement, see Miller, 1979, pp. 99–10.
40. E.258 (28); see also Miller, 1979, pp. 101–02; and BM, Add. MSS 35297, f.62.
41. Miller, 1979, p. 102.
42. For the summoning of local militiamen and James Smith's cavalry regiment to replace Grenville's foot, see PRO, SP/19/149/70.
43. BM., Add. MSS 35297, f.62.
44. Granville, 1908, pp. 115–16.
45. E.260 (16).
46. Clarendon, 1888, Book 9, p. 22.
47. See Note 6.
48. Clarendon, 1888, Book 9, pp. 22, 26, 27.
49. See DRO, Seymour MSS, 1392/L/1645/3.
50. See Mark Stoyle, *From Deliverance to Destruction: Rebellion and Civil War in an English City*, Exeter, 1996.
51. E. Green, 'The Siege and Defence of Taunton, 1644–45', *Somerset Archaeological Society Proceedings*, 25, part 2, 1879, p. 39.
52. See E.260 (16); William Salt Library, Stafford [hereafter: WSL], Salt MS 45 (Lord Clarendon's book of memoranda, unpaginated), entry for 6

April 1645; Clarendon, 1888, Book 9, p. 56; Granville, 1908, p. 117; Wanklyn, 1966, p. 220.

53. R.N. Dore (ed.), *The Letter Books of Sir William Brereton: Volume I*, Gloucester, 1984, p. 207.

54. WSL, Salt MS, 45, entry for 11 April 1645; Miller, 1979, p. 108.

55. Clarendon, 1888, Book 9, p. 15.

56. See Carte, 1739, p. 99; and Clarendon, 1888, Book 9, pp. 22, 27 n.2, 52.

57. C. Carlton, *Going to the Wars: The Experience of the British Civil Wars, 1638–51*, 1992, p. 226.

58. DRO, Maimed Soldiers' Petitions, 85/3.

59. Clarendon, 1888, Book 9, pp. 24–25.

60. Clarendon, 1888, Book 9, p. 47.

61. Clarendon, 1888, Book 9, p. 56.

62. Clarendon, 1888, Book 9, p. 56; Carte, 1739, p. 98.

63. Miller, 1979, p. 116.

64. Carte, 1739, p. 99.

65. Clarendon, 1888, Book 9, p. 59.

66. Bod., Clarendon MSS, 25, 1911.

67. *A Letter . . . concerning the Routing of Col. Goring's Army neer Bridgewater*, London, 22 July 1645.

68. Cotton, 1890, p. 70.

69. Bod., Clarendon MSS, 25, 1920.

70. Bod., Clarendon MSS, 25, 1920.

71. Bod., Clarendon MSS, 25, 1921.

72. Bod., Clarendon MSS, 1925, 1928 and 1933.

73. Bod., Clarendon MSS, 1922; and Cotton, 1890, p. 70.

74. Cotton, 1890, p. 70; see also E.303 (26).

75. See Bod, Clarendon MSS, 25, 1920–21 (for Arundell's initial departure), 1963 (for his assignment to new duties in Cornwall and his removal from command of his regiment) and West Country Studies Library, Exeter [hereafter: WCSL], O.M. Moger (ed), 'Devonshire Quarter Sessions Petitions, 1642–85', p. 254 (for the eventual merger).

76. See Clarendon, 1888, Book 9, p. 92, for a reference to Grenville's 'three regiments'.

77. Bod., Clarendon MSS, 25, 1975.

78. Clarendon, 1888, Book 9, p. 92. The statement in the *History* that Grenville was appointed commander of the Cornish trained-bands 'about the middle of September', is contradicted by one of Clarendon's own letters, which shows that Grenville had already been appointed to this position by 6 August (see CSPD, 1645–47, p. 46). Once again, this discrepancy does not seem to have arisen as the result of a simple mistake on Clarendon's part. Instead, the later date would appear to have been substituted on purpose, in order to lend weight to Clarendon's claim that Grenville had 'commanded absolutely without any commission' in Cornwall throughout August and early September 1645 (see Clarendon, 1888, Book 9, p. 76).

79. Bod., Clarendon MSS, 25, 1993.
80. DRO, 1597, 7/48A (Totnes Mayoral Accounts).
81. DRO, 1579, 7/48A (Totnes Mayoral Accounts).
82. DRO, 1579, 7/48A; and J. Sprigg, *Anglia Rediviva: England's Recovery*, Oxford, 1854 ed., p. 163.
83. W.H.K. Wright, *Some Account of the Barony and Town of Okehampton*, Tiverton, 1889, p. 96.
84. R.M. Ellis and M.A. Pulbrooke (eds), 'Chudleigh Parish Records', (1938, unpaginated, copy kept in WCSL), part 14.
85. Clarendon, 1888, Book 9, p. 103.
86. Cotton, 1890, p. 70; and CRO, Tremaine MSS, DDT, 1618/1.
87. E.266 (22).
88. Clarendon, 1888, Book 9, p. 104.
89. Sprigg, 1854, pp. 170–71.
90. See E.266 (23); E.266 (24); E.266 (27). The first report to mention the disturbances is dated 19 November.
91. CRO, Tremaine MSS, DDT, 1619–1620.
92. I hope to examine this episode in more detail elsewhere.
93. CRO, Tremaine MSS, DDT, 1620; Bod., Clarendon MSS, 26, 2056, and Stoyle, 1996.
94. Clarendon, 1888, Book 9, pp. 108, 117; and E.315 (4).
95. Bod., Clarendon MSS, 26, 2086.
96. Bod., Clarendon MSS, 26, 2086.
97. Clarendon, 1888, Book 9, pp. 117, 135; see also Carte, 1739, p. 109.
98. See Clarendon, 1888, Book 9, p. 138; Carte, 1739, p. 107; and E.319 (22).
99. Carte, 1739, p. 107.
100. For Collins, see Newman, 1981, p. 77; and Bod., Clarendon MSS, 25, 1924.
101. Clarendon, 1888, Book 9, p. 141; and Carte, 1739, p. 108.
102. Clarendon, 1888, Book 9, p. 135.
103. E.327 (2).
104. See Carte, 1739, p. 113; E.323 (8); and Sprigg, 1854, p. 196.
105. WCSL, *A More Full Relation of the Continued Successes of His Excellency Sir Thomas Fairfax*, London, 1646, pp. 5–6.
106. There is a memorial to Frayne in Langtree church. See also Reid, n.d., p. 174 and Sprigg, 1854, p. 204 (where Frayne is mistakenly referred to as 'Major Threave'). For Yeo, see Cotton, 1890, p. 70.
107. Sprigg, 1854, p. 207.
108. Carte, 1739, pp. 116, 123.
109. Carte, 1739, p. 123.
110. See Miller, 1979, pp. 139–40.
111. Carte, 1739, p. 124.
112. Carte, 1739, p. 124.
113. Carte, 1739, p. 125
114. E.325 (11).

IS *JOHN OF CHYANHOR* REALLY A 'CORNISH *RUODLIEB*'?

Brian Murdoch

JOHN OF CHYANHOR AND *RUODLIEB*

The link between the sole story recorded in late Cornish, Nicholas
Boson's tale of *John of Chyanhor*,[1] and the eleventh-century Latin
poem in Leonine hexameters, *Ruodlieb*, probably from Tegernsee in
Southern Germany, has been noted at various intervals, from Johann
Andreas Schmeller in the 1840s to Fritz Peter Knapp in a recent edition
(with German translation), where reference is made to the *engste
Übereinstimmung*, the 'closest of connections' between the works.[2] Such
references, whilst numerous, are usually fairly brief, and the most
sustained comparison appeared in 1978 as a paper in an American
Festschrift by Robert Fowkes, who used not only the phrase the
'Cornish *Ruodlieb*', but also the somewhat recherché but in fact entirely
appropriate word 'congener' to express the connexion between the two
texts.[3] Their relationship is, it must be said, a distant one. Much of
Fowkes' paper had to do with the motif of the 'red-haired man' in
Ruodlieb, which has no relevance to the Cornish tale, and beyond
documenting the widespread nature of some other elements in the
Cornish tale, the paper adds little to the study of *John of Chyanhor* as
such. Fowkes concludes with the very tentative suggestion that the
Cornish story and its later Irish analogues might provide evidence of
an ultimate insular shared provenance for *Ruodlieb* itself, via Irish
monks in medieval Germany; but he is not really convinced of the point
himself, and the paper ends with the somewhat forlorn hope that
'perhaps folklore scholarship may come to our rescue' in drawing a
closer comparison. It is not easy to see how it might do so, and the
best that has been done thus far is the topological identification of both
works as belonging to Category 910B in the list of folktale types

categorized by Aarne and Thompson, the type tagged as 'the servant's wise counsels'.[4] This approach focuses, of course, upon similarities rather than on differences, even though the latter may be in terms not only of individual motifs, but of structure, intent or reception. Even in thematic terms, and in spite of Knapp, there are very considerable differences, as well there might be, between a lengthy Latin poem composed in Germany in the eleventh century and a brief prose story composed, translated, adapted or recorded (it is impossible to specify the genesis of the Cornish piece more closely) in Cornwall in the later part of the seventeenth. Whether there is any genuine *relationship* in a closer sense at all is indeed, *pace* Fowkes, highly improbable. The comparison as such continues to exercise a fascination, however, for all that the Latin text, with its somewhat unfamiliar diphthongs, suffers regular misspelling outside German studies.[5]

RUODLIEB

In fact it is only the framework, in its broadest sense, and the basic form of two of the three precepts in the Cornish tale that constitute the similarity. The young hero, Ruodlieb, seeking to better his own position, although he is himself of gentle birth and has an inborn nobility (*ingenitatem... nobilitatem*, I, 2), works as a hunter and warrior for a king (the 'greater king' in the story), and on leaving his service is given wisdom instead of money after he claims:

> non uolo peccuniam, sitio.gustare sophiam (V, 445)

> It is not gold I crave; wisdom I'd rather have.

As in the Cornish tale, however, he is given gold as well, baked into loaves of bread rather than into a cake. The first three maxims in the Latin poem, however, are: not to trust a redheaded man (because such men are of uncertain temper); not to leave a road to cross a ploughed field (since that will anger the owner of the field); and not to stay where a young wife has an old husband. These three are then exemplified, and only the narrative associated with the last is particularly close to the Cornish, for all that the Latin is incomplete. The converse situation is also commended in the Latin poem: that one might well lodge in the house of a young husband who has married an old widow, and who will therefore pose *no* sexual threat. The question of quickness to anger, the final precept in *John of Chyanhor*, is one of the many other maxims—there are twelve in all—given to *Ruodlieb*, but there is no context, and it is not exemplified.

The *Ruodlieb* is a literary work with entertainment as the principal element, the first 'courtly romance'. It is true that the eponymous hero serves a king and receives concealed payment and an amount of advice, but he also arranges the marriage of his cousin, and at the end of the fragmentary work attempts to find a wife. The central figure is directly affected by the points of wisdom in the first part, however, and has to act upon some of them, even though in *Ruodlieb* many of the points of wisdom are either practical and general (on how to treat your servants, on not forgetting to go to mass), sometimes to the point of obviousness, or they are text-specific, such as the injunction never to trust a redheaded man. The large number of maxims, the verse form, and the extent of the work makes it differ radically from the folktale conciseness of *John of Chyanhor*, and both smaller circumstantial elements—such as the localization—and also major episodes—the child in the bed, for example— are different or absent.

THE *GESTA ROMANORUM*

It is not only the *Ruodlieb* that provides a medieval parallel for the tale of *John of Chyanhor*. There is a version of the story that is in some (but only in some) ways closer to the Cornish story in the thirteenth-century collection of moral tales known as the *Gesta Romanorum*, and critics have drawn attention to this parallel with the Cornish piece on an equally regular basis. But although the succinctness of the narrative on the one hand and the restriction to three pieces of advice in story CIII of the *Gesta Romanorum* matches that of the Cornish tale rather better than does *Ruodlieb*, the differences of context and structure are as striking.

The actual engagement of the central figure with the moral precepts as part of an individual learning process is a feature shared fairly closely by *Ruodlieb* and *John of Chyanhor,* but less so with the *Gesta Romanorum*, in which the central role is played not by a servant in any sense, but by the Roman emperor Domitian himself, who is described, in defiance of history, as a 'wise and just prince'. He buys three points of wisdom from a passing merchant, all of which save his life, although not all of them involve action (or more accurately, avoidance of action) on his part. The first precept is, however, the injunction not to act unreflectively, which is the final maxim in the Cornish work, although it is far from prominent in *Ruodlieb*. But it saves Domitian only in a passive sense, in that he has the maxim written out as an inscription, where it is read by a barber who has been charged by conspirators to cut Domitian's throat; influenced by reading the maxim, the barber decides against committing murder. The central

figure, therefore, whilst much approving the advice and indeed saved
by it, is not *himself* faced with a situation in which he has to behave in
accordance with it. The person who actually takes the advice is indeed
a servant, however, and he does avoid an action that he would regret
in moral terms at least. The other two maxims do involve the emperor
himself, but again not as closely as is the case with *John of Chyanhor*.
By not leaving a highway for a byway he avoids robbers, and he escapes
from a conspiracy of assassins in the last incident too, by avoiding the
house with the young wife, again a somewhat fortuitous use of the
precept. In a sense, all three pieces of advice (which are all essentially
warnings) serve here rather as talismans by which Domitian is able to
avoid assassination. They are more or less coincidental aids against
specific acts aimed at him, rather than general points of wisdom for the
individual. The moral element of the story in the *Gesta Romanorum* is
accordingly rather different, and does not come from within. Taking
the narrative unit as an exemplum, a moral, or more properly a
sequence of morals, is then attached as a separate and tropological
interpretation of that narrative as a whole unit, rather than emerging
from the text and deriving its effect from audience response to the acts
and subsequent salvation of main character. Here it is the passive *fate*
of Domitian that is interpreted. The 'application' appended to the text,
the *declaracio*, takes the emperor as any good Christian, the merchant
who gives him the wisdom as Christ, and the florins with which he pays
for it as the virtues. The maxims are the grace of God, and on the
specific points, the highway is the road of the commandments, the
byway a bad life, on which one can be ambushed by heretics. The old
man is the world, his young wife vanity, and the conspirators trying so
very hard to kill Domitian are the ever-present forces of evil, the devils.
In comparison with the Cornish, too, there are differences not only in
the framework (as in the absence of any idea of a quest, or of working
for another man, which *is* present in *Ruodlieb*), but again in the details;
the notion of the stranger in the bed is significantly absent, and the old
man/young wife passage is different in its implications. Finally, although
the variation in the setting from Cornwall to Rome is not of particular
importance, the shift in the central figure from a poor serving-man to
an emperor cannot but be significant. It is of interest to note, finally,
that in the various early English versions of the *Gesta Romanorum* this
tale is not present, although the larger Latin collection was known. The
Cornish *John of Chyanhor* is a folktale, where *Ruodlieb* is a large-scale
narrative about the doings of a courtier, even if we cannot necessarily
call it an early courtly romance, and the tale in the *Gesta Romanorum*
is an exemplum which gains its real effect from the independent
interpretation. This in its turn is augmented by the fact that the story

here is not isolated, but is one of a large collection of similar tales, all interpreted in the same fashion.

THE THREE (LITERARY) VERSIONS AND THEIR INTENT

The three texts representing early recorded forms can, of course, be compared with one another, and there is clearly a thematic relationship at one level. The overall sense in all cases is the value of wisdom, chosen above gold in the first instance, with the wisdom-seeker rewarded for that choice in various ways, most basically in the preservation of his life. He may also be rewarded by the provider of the maxims with the (earned) gold as well, as a secret gift (which is therefore protected during the hazardous journey home), so that the poor man who gains wisdom is seen also to become rich. Additional money is provided in some versions, indeed, when the central figure receives incidental rewards. The framework concept of the itinerant and initially indigent but worthy worker setting out to earn wealth, but acquiring wisdom as well, is shared by *Ruodlieb* and *John of Chyanhor*, though not by the most objectively moralized version in the *Gesta Romanorum*, in which the central figure is already rich. The idea of the poor man's quest is familiarly found in, and indeed is a determinative element of the folktale. It reflects the human quest for wisdom, of course, offering a reflection in story of the acquisition of experience, and this much is immanent in the structure of the tale, whatever the specific elements may be.[7] The maxims themselves constitute the next essential element. Three is, of course, a familiar number, and the fact that in the oldest of our written texts, the *Ruodlieb*, there are twelve argues against, rather than indicates that this was the original. As noted, the additional points of wisdom adduced in that text are often relatively trivial. In one of the printed versions based on *John of Chyanhor*—as we shall see—there are apparently four points of wisdom, but in that case the extra maxim has plainly been added in, and is done awkwardly.

The three pieces of advice in *John of Chyanhor*, in the *Gesta Romanorum* and in later analogues (precepts which are all present, at least, if not given the same prominence in *Ruodlieb*) have in common that they are essentially prohibitions, advice *not* to do something: not to leave a highway, not to lodge in a particular place, not to act in anger. They are, however, rather different from each other. The first and the last are very similar to each other, practical notions with general applications, and each of these two is tested in action, saving the central figure from external danger or from incurring moral and legal guilt. The central episode is a little different, however; the advice on the avoidance of a house with an old husband and young wife, although broadly concerned with the avoidance of risks once more and hence plausibly linked with the others, is nevertheless a restricted situational one which contrasts contextually with the others. Of the latter the most general, that of being slow to anger, is echoed in a number of biblical passages, notably in the wisdom books (such as Prov. 16: 32). It is the presence of the two general precepts beside the situational one which raises the Cornish tale above the level of what Jacobs referred to as a droll, a humorous anecdote.

That middle maxim—involving the old man and the young wife—has the most complex tradition, and the situation as such (with embellishments) is found not only in the folktale, but more prominently in learned satirical tales in prose or verse, such as in the medieval *fabliau* or *Schwank*. The tradition of the *senex stultus* in this situation goes back to antiquity, and variations on the theme have been noted in a variety of cultures. W. A. Coupe has shown further, for example, how widely it was used in iconography, too, in the sixteenth century, with as an example a picture attributed to Dürer of an old man with his young wife, who is taking money from him and giving it to her younger lover.[8] The sexual implications for the would-be-lodger himself (of which there is an element in *Ruodlieb*) or the possible danger for any casual observers that they might be used as scapegoats for the wife's wickedness (as with the merchants in *John of Chyanhor*) are patent. That the Cornish story involves a monk, however, ties in particularly well with the medieval comic tale, examples of which are known in a wide and perhaps predominantly Continental tradition.[9]

As far as the *intent* of the three early versions of the narrative is concerned, all three were written (down) for a literary/learned purpose. The oral tradition may, for the moment at least, be regarded as separate. *Ruodlieb* is a poem of entertainment, sometimes seen as the first courtly poem in Germany, in spite of its language, a learned piece in Latin hexameters. The *Gesta Romanorum* is a collection of moralizing anecdotes in prose, hung sometimes precariously onto the supposed historical authority of different emperors, but with a very clear, though independently tropological moral spelt out at the end. *John of Chyanhor* was written down in the form we have it by John Boson to help William Gwavas learn Cornish, and printed in full by Lhuyd as a linguistic illustration. If Nicholas Boson did indeed—as is generally thought—write it down originally, we do not know why, unless it was part of the programmatic attempt to save the scraps of Cornish. The purpose of its survival, then, was either linguistic–pedagogic or (as perhaps with Nicholas Boson and certainly with Lhuyd and, later on, Pryce) philological and antiquarian, rather than for moral purposes.[10] It is not clear, of course, where Nicholas Boson heard the story, and whether he had heard it in Cornish perhaps from servants, as might be suggested by his *Nebbaz Gerriau dro tho Carnoack.* It may thus be cognate with other Celtic versions, of which oral versions were collected far later, and as such a genuine representative of the oral tradition, or it may have been adapted at some stage from English or Latin (just possibly even from the *Gesta Romanorum,* though the differences are so significant that one would need to postulate a considerable remove and/or extensive adaptation). The two alternatives—that *John of Chyanhor* came directly from the oral tradition, or that it was influenced by or derived from a written version of some sort—are not, of course, mutually exclusive, and the possible cross-influence of the oral and the written tradition needs to be borne in mind, since these traditions clearly existed side-by-side for some centuries.

THE NARRATIVE AS FOLKTALE

The simple structure of the Cornish text has a number of features that are familiar in the folktale and which distinguish it from the deliberately literary and far more diffuse verse *Ruodlieb* and also, in terms of context, from the imperially located tale in the *Gesta Romanorum.* The style is clearly that of an orally transmitted folktale, too, with specific localization,[11] a formulaic introduction ('once upon a time'), and the paratactic linking of narrative units—exactly half of the forty-six paragraphs begin with '*Ha. . .*'. The framework of need on the part of John himself, leaving to undertake a quest, the quest for (self-)knowledge, which leads to the unnamed master, and then home, allowing him to resume his earlier life with the addition of wisdom is encountered regularly in the folktale, and it contrasts with the *Gesta Romanorum* version, in which the entry of the merchant is somewhat unprovoked. The parallelism and formulaic numbers of the three years work, each for three pounds, is significant, and the three episodes demonstrating the efficacy of the wisdom whilst the money is safely preserved are in simple form. This is true even of the central episode with the old man and the young wife, which is actually divided into separate and more complex elements in some folktale versions. It is true, of course, that John's quest wins him no princess, and indeed he gains nothing beyond what he has earned; so, too, the narrative lacks a specific magical element, and even the action of the work-provider, in concealing the payment for the hazardous journey home, is practical rather than magical. But it is not a mere anecdote, not a droll: the time-reference, the variable localization, the quest-framework and the acquisition of wisdom, and then the direct presentation of the three illustrative episodes, the last of which returns us to the starting-point

of the quest, has an archetypal quality.[12] It is a story of the questing
hero of the fairy-tale set firmly in the real world, and it is easy to see
how this could have been adapted into the moral exemplum of the
Gesta Romanorum, or indeed expanded into the developed medieval
Latin narrative poetry of *Ruodlieb*; it is less likely that the process
could have worked the other way. It is more logical to think of a shared
source for three ultimately fixed but different literary strands, a source
which led to a folktale collected in Cornish as well as a secular poem
in Latin and one of a set of theological Latin exempla.

SOME FURTHER VERSIONS

Later versions—by which is meant versions collected and put into
written form at a later date than those so far examined—of the story
may be grouped into different categories. The continuing oral tradition may be represented by the two Irish narratives translated by
Mühlhausen.[13] These versions, which appeared in the proceedings of
the Gaelic League (*Imtheachta an Oireachtais*) and in the journal
Béaloideas in 1901 and 1930 respectively, were, of course, collected far
more recently than *John of Chyanhor* and thus stand more than two
centuries further along in the tradition as a whole. The first version is
from Ballingeary, in Co. Cork, the second from Galway, and in each
case the story has again been localized, the first specifically, the second
more generally as 'in this country'. In the first, a poor man works for
an unspecified time for another (slightly mysterious) man, and takes
three pieces of wisdom instead of the three guineas he is owed; he is
also given three cakes for his journey home. The points of wisdom are
the same: to keep to the direct road, not to sleep in the house with a
young wife and old husband, and not to do in the evening what he
might regret in the morning. The formulations are slightly different but
the essence remains. There are also variations in the demonstration of
the precepts. The poor man actually takes a new road for a short time,
but then goes back to the original path, while his companion at that
point—who does *not* turn back—is killed rather than merely attacked.
The second part of the narrative is split—three men murder the old
husband with the connivance of the wife, but no blame is yet placed
on anyone, and the traveller takes a label or mark from the coat of
one of the killers. He then returns home, and we have the 'son in the
bed' episode. Following this and the discovery of the money we return
to the young wife element, which is now given a new twist. The division
of the episode and the return to it later (in both Irish versions, though
they are not identical in detail) looks like a consciously literary
development, and it contrasts with the linear simplicity of the Cornish

version. It has in the meantime been discovered that the old man was strangled—a forensic detail that also points to more recent construction —and a reward is offered for the capture of the villains. The poor man produces his evidence, and the culprits are apprehended and executed, whilst the poor man receives a reward. A final localization in place and time is given in that the man's grandson is claimed still to live in the associated district, another regular feature of the authentication of such tales. Bottrell's version—commented upon below—adds that the central figure's descendants 'may still be flourishing in St Levan'. We are not told how long the man was away, but his son has grown to unrecognized manhood in the interim and his presence in the bed is explained, though awkwardly; however, that scene is equally in need of interpretation in the Cornish, where one might well wonder how is it clear that the wife is talking to a man.

In the second Irish tale the length of service is twenty-one years, although the precepts are the same; once more an initial travelling companion is killed, and in the third episode the son has gained a beard. The divided second episode is somewhat differently presented, however, and is provided with more suspense when the principal character is himself arrested for murdering the old man. This has some similarities with the Cornish version, of course, although here he has no companions. He is able to prove his own innocence, however, in the usual manner, by showing his hard evidence, so that the second precept has on this occasion saved his life as well.

The age of the collected folktale versions, in Ireland or Scotland, or, for that matter, in Cornwall, is difficult to determine, and only Nicholas Boson provides a *terminus ante quem* for the Cornish version. There are various printed versions of the story in English, and even though the Cornish tale was (via Lhuyd) the direct source in some cases, this does not of course mean that there was not an ongoing English-language oral tradition (which could have derived from the *Gesta Romanorum*) and which could in its turn have influenced and been influenced by printed versions at any stage. Lhuyd's text seems, at all events, to have been instrumental in the dissemination of the story. When the tale has appeared in English—usually within a larger collection of folktales—it is sometimes set in Cornwall, and equally often provided with new localizations; sometimes, too, there are deliberate variations, as when Jacobs amended the final scene with the 'strange man in the bed' in his tale of 'Ivan' because it was not suitable for his target audience of girls and boys.[14] Jacobs does retain the second episode, of course, and one supposes that the more alert *virgines* and *pueri* might have asked precisely *why* the woman and the monk wanted the old husband out of the way. William Bottrell's version, from the

Hearthside Stories, in which the central figure is called Tom, from 'a little out-of-the-way place called Chyannor', and which appeared in a collection the contents of which were claimed as having been collected from oral tradition, adds a clearly intrusive extra piece of advice —'never swear to any body or thing seen through glass'—which is awkwardly incorporated into the narrative with a new episode involving the central figure's daughter as a developed (and indeed distracting) figure. The addition of this extra piece of wisdom—which is bracketed together with the third piece of wisdom in the Cornish version—might be seen as bringing the text closer to *Ruodlieb*, where there are twelve pieces of advice, although it is of course *not* one of the pieces of advice in the Latin text. Rather, it has a fortuitous air; it is far more likely to have been added as a literary extra, and it does little more than gild the lily in the last part of the tale. It also detracts from the essential triad of precepts by adding a highly specific instance to what is otherwise general. If on the other hand the sense is simply that one should not act until one is sure of the circumstances, then this overlaps completely with the third precept in any case. Such adaptations constitute a tradition in their own right, of course, and the addition may perhaps be compared with the quasi-learned adaptations in the Irish versions of the tale. Whether—or more plausibly, to what extent—the oral tradition in the late nineteenth century was already influenced by the printed versions which had appeared before that time is, of course, difficult to determine.[15] That the story regularly appears in collections of folktales (in Jacobs, Bottrell and elsewhere) will have an effect, too, upon both presentation and reception, since the reading of other similar works might well affect the reading of this.

The tradition of which *Ruodlieb* and *John of Chyanhor* form a part, then, is a complex one, a stem of narrative from which versions have been written down at various points. The initial stage may have been an oral tradition, but this is not certain, and *Ruodlieb* certainly provides evidence of a literary tradition of some antiquity. The narrative might well have moved, so to speak, fairly freely between the oral and literary tradition from the earliest period. The central episode —especially if the miscreant lover is a monk—may have begun as a literary motif in any case; the expressed fear of the redhaired man sounds like an oral proverb, is given literary form in the Latin poem, and then more or less disappears altogether. The Irish versions and indeed that of Bottrell—albeit certainly or possibly collected from the oral tradition—seem to have undergone a quasi-literary adaptation in the division of the central episode (which may in any case originally have been literary), or in the addition of extra material. What is special about the Cornish tale is its narrative completeness and satisfactory simplicity in comparison with the earlier literary-theological analogues and indeed with collected or adapted later versions, even when Nicholas Boson's version was the source of such versions.

RUODLIEB REVISITED—THE CORNISH *CHARTER FRAGMENT*

Whatever the precise relationship between Boson's *John of Chyanhor* and the *Ruodlieb*, there is clearly some kind of link between the works. The medieval Latin poem can perhaps be used, however, in a rather different comparative context to throw light on another Cornish work, namely the so-called *Charter Fragment*. It is not suggested, of course, that the enigmatic handful of lines from the back of BL Add. Ch. 19491, dated to 1340 and relating to St Stephen-in-Brannel, might have any direct connexion with *Ruodlieb*. The Latin poem might, however, help to provide a possible parallel for the work. Since Jenner's discovery of the Cornish fragment, the genre to which it belongs has been a matter of debate; Jenner (and many of those after him) wanted it to be part of a play, and as Lauran Toorians has pointed out in his sober *Forschungsbericht*, 'this wishful thinking of Jenner soon began to lead a life of its own'.[16] There is, of course, no hard evidence that this is part of a play at all, and if it is, one of the supplementary problems is what kind of a play it would be. Indeed most surviving early Cornish literature is dramatic, but is also religious. The theme of the fragment seems to be matchmaking, but there *are* elements in the major plays which are less than spiritual. One such is the scene with King David's butler in the *Origo Mundi*, who offers to procure a girl for his companion, and which uses vocabulary not dissimilar to that of the fragment.[17] As Toorians concludes, we simply do not have a context, and his description of it as part of a poem about marriage—since it is poetic in form and its theme is clearly marriage—must suffice. Tenuous or not, however, it is this aspect which invites comparison with *Ruodlieb*, which is also a medieval poem about marriage and which might therefore offer a potential context type. Towards the end of the *Ruodlieb*, when the hero has decided to seek a wife—a standard situation in many early medieval works—a (male) friend approaches him with advice:

> Vnus at exsurgens, cui notae sunt regiones
> Et noti domini bene, qui fuerant ibi summi,
> Is 'dominam' dixit 'unam scio, quae tibi par fit
> Moris honestate uirtute et nobilitate.

Hanc uellem uideas, cum uideris ut fatearis,
In mundo nullam quod uidisses dominellam
Omnem uirtutem tam strennuiter facientem,
Talis quae fuerit, ut quemque uirum decusisset'.
(XVII, 65–70)

[Then one of those around, a man to whom was known
the land and gentry there came forward to declare:
'One lady I can tell would really suit you well
Known for her probity and great nobility.
I'd much like you to see her, and then you'll agree
that no young woman here on earth is quite as fair,
who has all the virtues that anyone would choose,
such that she can be an adornment for a man.']

The *Charter Fragment* speaker addresses a companion (*cowez*), possibly during a chance encounter,[18] and refers to a young lady (*mowes*) who is known to him and is the most beautiful in the district (*an parz ma ze pons tamar*), and indeed without equal (*nag vs y far*). Toorians has discussed convincingly the word *far* as a mutation of *par* against other editors. Again with the prefatory caution that it is not being presented as a possible source, the *Ruodlieb* has a companion of the hero who knows the district referring to a young lady (*dominella*) that he knows, who *tibi par fit*—'is your peer'. Small verbal parallels are not meant to imply real connexions, and of course the match is not exact; nor would one expect it to be. Besides, even the text of *Ruodlieb* is not entirely clear: there has been discussion, for example, of whether one adjective applied to the *dominella* is to be read as *formosa* or *morosa*, 'beautiful' or 'sulky'.[19]

What does emerge is that the *Ruodlieb* might be compared in very general terms with the fragment, and the parallelism with *Ruodlieb* at this point could suggest that there is no absolute necessity for this to be a female matchmaker, something which has been assumed, although this sometimes goes hand-in-hand with the assumption that the first person speaking in each part of the fragment is the same. There are plenty of male matchmakers in medieval writing— Pandarus, for example—and even in Cornish the similar comments of the Butler in the *Origo Mundi* argue against assuming this matchmaker to be a woman.[20] As far as the *dominella* in *Ruodlieb* goes, the lady in question is discovered by Ruodlieb himself to have been having an affair with a cleric; when he reveals his knowledge to her by a stratagem, she refuses to marry him, as he had known she must. There is a section missing from the Latin poem at this point, so that we do not see the initial matchmaking from the side of the *dominella*, and hence can make no judgements on it. Having caught her out, Ruodlieb exclaims (and we may note the dramatic character of the text in the passage concerned):

Ruo: 'Nunc opus est aliam, reor ut, mihi poscere sponsam,
Quae non furtiue quem suescat amare super me.' (XVII, 83f.)

Ruodlieb: 'Well, now it's up to me to find a bride-to-be
who'll marry me and not seek others furtively'.

In the second part of the *Charter Fragment* we may have the same initial speaker, but—in spite of Occam's razor—this need not be the case. A woman is being given advice about dominating a man, but we have no idea why, or by whom she is given the advice, and nor, since we have no idea how the fragment ends, of whether the man ever discovers the stratagem. The proposed behaviour might even be a subterfuge, with the speaker as the woman's lover plotting against a cuckold husband (Ovid's *Amores* I, v provides the *locus classicus* here, perhaps, although it is more erotic). At risk of too much speculation (but at the same time to illustrate how many possibilities are offered by the fragment), the noun *meystres* in line 32 might even not imply a wife at all, but mistress of the house. In *Ruodlieb* again, one of the pieces of advice given to the young man is that he should not elevate his maidservant to that level:

Ancillam propriam quamuis nimium speciosam
Non uelut uxorem facias tibi consocialem
Ne contemnat te tibi respondendo superbe
Neue reatur, se domui debere prae esse
Si pernoctabit ad mensam siue sedebit
Tecum manducans pernox tecum ue repausans
Continuo domina cunctorum uult fore summa
Talia famosum faciunt ignominiosum. (V, 476–83)

You should never treat your maid, however sweet,
as if she were your wife and your equal in life,
or she'll despise you and talk back at you, too,
and come to be so bold and rule the whole household.
If she should share your food and spend the night with you
sit at the table's head and then should share your bed
she'll always want to be mistress of all she sees,
and that's the kind of fame that leads only to shame.

The Cornish fragment does appear to offer a description of a potentially manipulative woman (whether or not this represents either 'a male nightmare' or 'the realities of life for women in the middle ages'—Newlyn offers both as possible readings), and this could place the work into the extensive medieval tradition of the duplicitous wife. Innumerable examples might be adduced from Ovid, and later from Chaucer and, on the continent, from the *fabliau*, the *Schwank* or indeed the *Fastnachtspiel*. The presentation of women in positions of power over the man is also encountered, finally, in medieval—and notably in Celtic—writing,[21] but usually in serious contexts, and the tone here seems at least to speak against that kind of work.

A CAUTIONARY CONCLUSION

Beyond this we cannot—or rather, should not—go. As far as the *Charter Fragment* is concerned, we are quite unable to point to actual relationships in literary terms, however distant, and any comparison with a work like *Ruodlieb* can lead only to negative assumptions, indicating that the fragment need not be dramatic, nor anything to do with a 'wooing play' involving a 'female bawd' (if there is indeed such a genre in broad terms). The intention here has been, however, simply to use the *Ruodlieb* to draw attention to a *type* of work that might provide a non-dramatic analogue to the *Charter Fragment*.

The connexion between *Ruodlieb* and the tale of *John of Chyanhor* is rather different and far firmer, of course, but two lines of literary approach need to be borne in mind: the comparative and the contrastive. It may be admitted, of course, that a fairly strictly literary approach to the problem of textual relationships here avoids some issues of importance. In fact, the evidence provided by these texts seems to support a transmission on the template model (and any model depends upon extant texts), with a certain flexibility in each realization, which might be oral or indeed in a learned genre such as *Ruodlieb*. Far less clear is the question of interaction between written and oral forms; widespread knowledge of *Ruodlieb* seems unlikely, but the *Gesta Romanorum* was indeed a very widely read (and heard) text and might well have influenced later structuring of the tale when retold. *Ruodlieb* and the other close 'congener', the tale in the *Gesta Romanorum*, are different in detail, context and intent, while what we may call the 'collected folktale' versions (which are usually later) sometimes show literary adaptations, which are foreign both thematically and stylistically to the Cornish version. It is important not simply to juxtapose the various versions, nor to select similar elements, but to assess each on its merits, as far as possible within its own context. We know why John Boson used the Cornish text, if not why Nicholas recorded it in the first place, but this folktale, clearly 'caught early and fixed in print,' has a satisfactory and individual simplicity not shared by the lengthy Latin poem and the over-moralized prose of the *Gesta Romanorum*, nor indeed by the later collected versions, whether they were printed separately or as part of collections.

NOTES AND REFERENCES

1. The standard text is that by Oliver J.Padel, *The Writings of the Boson Family*, Redruth, 1975, pp. 14–23. Padel discusses the dates and putative origins of the tale in Cornish. The first fourteen sections are preserved in the Gwavas papers in the hand of John Boson, but the final thirty-two are known only from the text printed by Lhuyd in 1707 in his own orthography, with a Welsh and English translation. I have noted editions in my *Cornish Literature*, Cambridge, 1993, p. 133, n.6, referring to those by Lhuyd and William Pryce at either end of the eighteenth century, then by Davies Gilbert in the nineteenth, plus that in the 1930s by Ludwig Muhlhausen; it was used (as John Boson had done for Gwavas) for pedagogic reasons by R. Morton Nance from the 1920s onwards, and later by John Page, whose *Jowan Chy an Horth Examined*, Redruth, rev. ed. 1982, is extremely detailed.

2. *Ruodlieb* is here cited from the Latin text in the parallel edition and translation by Edwin H. Zeydel, *Ruodlieb: The Earliest Courtly Novel (after 1050)*, Chapel Hill, 1959, repub. New York, 1969, although the translations (which attempt to match the original Leonines) given are my own. However, there are various other editions and translations, sometimes with significant text variants. See for a brief but exemplary recent survey of the editions (and of the work itself) the essay by Dennis M. Kratz in Will Hasty and James Hardin (eds), *German Writers and Works of the Early Middle Ages, 800–1170*, Detroit, 1995. There is a Latin edition by Gordon B. Ford, and Kratz himself has edited and translated the work. The most recent major texts are those by C.W. Grocock, *The Ruodlieb*, Oak Park, 1985, and the facsimile edition by Benedikt Konrad Vollman, *Ruodlieb: Faksimile-Ausgabe*, Wiesbaden, 1985. For a discussion of textual variations, see the review of Grocock by Haijo J.Westra in *Speculum*, 65, 1990, and note also the recent book by Vollman in the Darmstadt *Ertage der Forschung* series, *Ruodlieb*, Darmstadt, 1993, which has a useful text outline, pp. 21–23. The parallel Latin/German edition for Reclam's pocket library by Fritz Peter Knapp, *Ruodlieb*, Stuttgart, 1977, is also convenient and has a useful afterword and bibliography. The poem was probably composed (it is unclear whether by a cleric or a layman) around the middle of the eleventh century, and consists of eighteen fragments of varying size, with a total of just over 2300 lines. Two manuscripts are known, and the work seems not to have been finished; the text is notoriously difficult in places.

3. Robert A.Fowkes, 'Some Thoughts on the "Cornish *Ruodlieb*" and its Congeners', in Stephen J. Kaplowitt (ed.), *Germanic Studies in Honor of Otto Springer*, Pittsburgh, 1978. This has now been reprinted in the *Cornish Banner*, 83, February 1996.

4. A. Aarne, *The Types of the Folk-Tale*, tr. and rev. Stith Thompson, Helsinki, 1929, 910B; see also Stith Thompson's *Motif Index of Folk Literature*, Bloomington, 1966, categories J21.2-J21.5.1.

5. An interesting paper by Jan Gendall, 'John of Chyanhor and the Oral Tradition', *The Celtic Pen*, 1/4, Summer 1994, unfortunately suffered badly from printer's gremlins.

6. The Latin text was edited by Herman Oesterly, *Gesta Romanorum*, Berlin, 1872; see now on this still relatively neglected but important late thirteenth-century text the two-volume study by Brigitte Weiske, *Gesta Romanorum*, Tubingen, 1992. There is an older English translation with a significant subtitle by Charles Swan, *Gesta Romanorum, or Entertaining Moral Stories*, rev. by Wynnard Hooper, London, 1877, in the Bohn Library. Story CIII is on pp. 177–180. This particular story is not present in the earliest English translations of the collection: see Sidney J. Herrtage, *The Early English Versions of the Gesta Romanorum*, London, 1879. However, Fowkes, 1978, p.135, notes that the *Gesta Romanorum* is one of the best known collections of Latin stories, and that it has a large number of manuscripts, also in Britain; he draws attention, too, to the Oriental origins of some of the tales, and our story has been included in this category. See further on the point Wynnard's notes to the Swan translation, pp. 386–388, n.9. I have myself referred to the Latin collection in this context in *Cornish Literature*, 1993, p. 133; the *Gesta Romanorum* tale has occasionally been claimed as the source of the Cornish tale.

7. The model of the quest as a life-symbol in the folktale is well known, of course; see such works as C.G. Jung (ed.), *Man and His Symbols*, New York, 1968, on transcendence and individualism. A study pertinent to the first precept tested by John of Chyanhor is that by Wolfgang Harms, *Homo viator in bivio*, Munich, 1970.

8. W.A. Coupe, 'Ungleiche Liebe—A Sixteenth-century Topos', *Modern Language Review*, 62, 1967.

9. Stanley J. Kahrl, *Traditions of Medieval English Drama*, London, 1974, p. 120 refers to the relative paucity in Britain of tales in which 'lecherous priests . . . find their ways into the beds of the willing wives of aged husbands'. But the plot is a well-known one in European terms, even if here it takes a particularly sinister turn.

10. There are few analogues of the use of the story within other literary works; Fowkes, 1978, p. 135 discusses the Old French *Joseph d'Arimathie*, which resembles all three versions in quite separate respects: the *Gesta Romanorum*, in that the pieces of advice save the life of the character involved more or less accidently; *John of Chyanhor* in the incident with the young wife; and *Ruodlieb* in that although the warnings about the main road and about the young wife, are present, the middle piece of advice is

on avoiding redheaded men. That against impetuosity (however it is worked out) is absent, as is the payment motif; the advice comes from a hermit. For other parallels with elements of *Ruodlieb* (and notably with Aarne/Thompson 910A rather than the closest category, 910B) see Werner Braun, *Studien zum Ruodlieb*, Berlin, 1962, p. 11 and Knapp, *Ruodlieb*, p. 239 (with reference to sermon exempla).

11. On the identification of Chyanhor, see Padel, 1975, p. 22, n.1; Padel refers to P.A.S. Pool, *The Place-Names of West Penwith*, Penzance, 1973, 2nd ed. 1985, p. 46.

12. See V. Propp, *The Morphology of the Folktale*, trs. Laurence Scott, 2nd ed., Austin and London, 1968, for a basic structural analysis. It is interesting to consider the discussion on the nature of the folktale/fairy-tale, the *Marchen*, by Andres Jolles, *Einfache Formen*, Tubingen, 1930, pp. 218–246, with reference to the immanence of *das Wunderbare*, to the naivety of situational simplification and to the difference between the enclosed world of the *Marchen* and that of the (Tuscan) novella. See also Elizabeth Cook, *The Ordinary and the Fabulous*, Cambridge, 1969, and such celebrated works as J.R.R. Tolkien's paper 'On Fairy- Stories' in *Tree and Leaf*, London, 1964. As it stands, *John of Chyanhor* is not a fairy-story in that sense, but were some of the encounters more magical, or the giver of the maxims more mysterious (as he almost is in an Irish version) it could well have become one.

13. Ludwig Mühlhausen, *Die kornische Geschichte von den drei guten Ratschlagen, nebst Ubersetzung und Glossar und zwei irischen Versionen Ubersetzung*, Berlin, 1938; the Irish texts are in German translation on pp. 34–40, and Muhlhausen refers to the originals on p.7f. He also discusses in his introduction other Irish, Scots and Nordic versions. See Note 14 below for further references via Jacob's *Celtic Fairy Tales*.

14. Mühlhausen, 1938, p. 6. refers to a German-language collection of Irish tales where there is a version of the third episode which matches that used by Jacobs to replace the 'man in the bed'—a new episode illustrating that 'honesty is the best policy'. Mühlhausen also comments on Jacob's motivation for making the change and notes a parallel in K. von K[illinger], *Erin. Auswahl vorzuglicher irischer Erzahlungen VI. Sagen und Marchen*, Stuttgart and Tubingen, 1849.

15. The principal versions are in W.Bottrell, *Traditions and Hearthside Stories of West Cornwall*, partial facsimile, Llanerch, 1989, pp. 51–67 (as 'Tom of Chyannor, the Tin-Steamer') and Joseph Jacobs, *Celtic Fairy tales and More Celtic Fairy Tales*, 1892–94, repub. London, 1985, pp. 125–135. Jacobs, whose tale of 'Ivan' is taken from Lhuyd and adapted, as indicated, *virginibus puerisque*, lists a wide range of parallels, including English versions in journals in the early nineteenth century, plus the versions printed by Bottrell, and in Hunt's *Popular Romances* and Campbell's *Popular Tales of the West Highlands*. He considers the ultimate source to be the *Gesta Romanorum*, however, and refers to Irish versions. On the Bottrell version, see Gendall, 1994.

16. Lauran Toorians, *The Middle Cornish Charter Endorsement. The Making of a Marriage in Medieval Cornwall*, Innsbruck, 1991, p. 19. Wishful thinking, moreover, may not only make the fragment into a play, but may also lead to assumptions about the work that take on a life of *their* own in secondary literature; *vide* the way the fragment is sometimes used precisely in secondary studies of the medieval drama. The fragment is here cited from Toorians' 1991 edition, of which see pp. 1–3 on the earlier editions by Jenner, Stokes, Nance, Ellis and Campanile; that by the last-named is of some interest and rather different from that by Toorians in some respects. There are occasionally some fairly radical difference of opinion about the meaning of individual passages, most notably in line 33, in the reading *cas* (Toorians) against *ras* (most other versions). As Toorians points out, there is no reason for the lenition which has to be supposed for a reading based on the word *gras*, 'grace'; but his reading has an awkward tense and is difficult to put into the context. It is doubtful that the passage will ever be clarified satisfactorily.

17. I have made this point in Murdoch, 1993, p. 55.

18. The context for the conversation in the *Charter Fragment* is not entirely clear, since the person addressed is apparently invited to 'alight and rest'. The rhyme *powers* is a convenient one, however, and the line may just be formulaic.

19. References are in the *Speculum* review by Westra of Grocock's *Ruodlieb* edition, p. 164.

20. See Evelyn S.Newlyn, 'Between the Pit and the Pedestal: Images of Eve and Mary in Medieval Cornish Drama', in Edelgard DuBruck, *New Images of Medieval Women*, Lampeter, 1989, pp. 142–143. Newlyn is persuaded on account of the dramatic tradition of the 'wooing play' and cites Richard Axton, *European Drama of the early Middle Ages*, London, 1974, p. 21; however, Axton cites the Cornish fragment as part of his evidence that there *is* such a thing, and since this may not be a play at all, and other evidence for the figure is fairly limited, the whole becomes rather circular. Axton does refer on more than one occasion, incidently, to *Ruodlieb* as having parallels in the drama. Newlyn notes that Nance had seen the matchmaker as a greybeard, and that, too, is an interpretation which has little substance. Toorians, p. 26, would like the fragment to be from a lost saint's play, but admits this is a personal preference only.

21. See most recently, David Gabriel, 'The Power of the Woman over the Man in Medieval Irish Prose Tales', *Studia Celtica Japonica*, 7, April 1995. On medieval marriage and the notion of the (happily) unconsummated marriage, see Jean Leclerq, *Monks and Marriage: A Twelfth-Century View*, New York, 1982, pp. 43–48, and (with the literary aspects taken into account), the standard work by Christopher N.L. Brooke, *The Medieval View of Marriage*, Oxford, 1989, esp. pp. 173–210. On the negative aspect, see F. Brietzmann, *Die bose Frau inder deutschen Literatur des Mittelalters*, Berlin, 1912. One wonders about the position of a Cornish fragment concerned with marriage on a document which Jenner described in 1914

as 'the only process [in the fourteenth century] by which a married woman could dispose of her land': Henry Jenner, 'The Fourteenth-Century Charter Endorsement Brit. Mus. Add. Ch. 19491', *Journal of the Royal Institution Cornwall*, 20, 1915–21, pp. 41–48. The relative dates of the Cornish addition and the charter as such are not clear, however, and the juxtaposition may simply be fortuitous.

22. On which see, for example, D.H. Green, 'Orality and Reading: The State of Research in Medieval Studies', *Speculum*, 65, 1990. Green's essay is a useful introduction to the problem with further reading, although he has developed the issue with special reference to medieval German in more detail since. See also Proinsias Mac Cana, *The Learned Tales of Medieval Ireland*, Dublin, 1980, esp. pp. 1–32.

'LINGUISTICALLY SOUND PRINCIPLES': THE CASE AGAINST KERNEWEK KEMMYN

N.J.A. Williams

INTRODUCTION

In a recent book (*Cornish Today*, hereafter CT) I provided a critique of the forms of Neo-Cornish (revived Cornish) currently in use.[1] Among other things, I listed 25 ways in which I believe the sound-system and spelling of Kernewek Kemmyn ('Common' or 'phonemic' Cornish) to be mistaken. I further suggested that, in the interests of the Cornish revival, Kernewek Kemmyn should be replaced. This article sets out to re-articulate these arguments for the general reader, as well as making some brief comments about the future of the language revival.

Kernewek Kemmyn is the creation of Dr Ken George of the Institute of Marine Science at the University of Plymouth. His new pronunciation and orthography were first published in *The Pronunciation and Spelling of Revived Cornish* (PSRC) in 1986.[2] The Cornish Language Board accepted his proposals in July 1987 on the grounds that the new system was more 'authentic' than Unified Cornish. This assessment was premature, however, and even proponents of Kernewek Kemmyn have subsequently admitted that the system, as it was first proposed, contained a serious flaw. The error in question involved the spelling and pronunciation of words like *chy* 'house', *karensa* 'love', and *wosa* 'after'.

THE 'PHONEMES' *tj* AND *dj*

Cornish differs from Welsh and Breton in its treatment of inherited internal and final *d* and internal *nt*. The Welsh and Breton for 'father' is *tad* whereas the Cornish is *tas*. The Welsh for 'after' is *wedi* and the Breton is *goude*. In Middle Cornish 'after' is written *wose* or *woge*. The Breton for 'love' is *karantez* whereas the Middle Cornish is either *kerense* or *kerenge*. George interpreted this alternation of *s* and *g* in the Middle Cornish texts as reflecting a sound that was difficult to represent. He assumed that the underlying sound in *wose/woge* was similar to the combination *d* + *y* in the English phrase *could you*, for example. He argued that this collocation of sounds was difficult to represent properly and that therefore the scribes sometimes wrote *s* and sometimes *g*. Dr George's interpretation of *s:g* was not his own, since he was taking up a suggestion first made by Joseph Loth in 1897.[3] George recommended spelling the sound in question as *dj*. Similarly he recommended spelling the *s/g* of *kerense/kerenge* as *tj*. He also proposed spelling *chy* 'house' as *tji*.

In an article which was eventually published in 1990 I adduced a whole range of arguments, theoretical, orthographical and toponymic, to show that the 'phonemes' *dj* and *tj* had never existed and should not therefore be introduced into the revived language.[4] Dr George read my article in unpublished form and agreed with my arguments. As a result *dj* and *tj* were removed from Kernewek Kemmyn and were replaced by *s*, *j* or *ch*, exactly as I had proposed. The graphs *s*, *j* and *ch* were those used in Unified Cornish and by the Middle Cornish scribes themselves, though the texts used *g* rather than *j* in certain cases. Several things should be noticed about this episode. In the first place, Kernewek Kemmyn before 1989-90 might have contained sentences like *Nyndj edjov vy ow krydji yth edja Kerentja gantjo yn dji* 'I do not believe that Kerensa was with him in his house', where Unified would have written *Nyns esof vy ow cryjy yth esa Kerensa ganso yn y jy*. The spelling of Unified Cornish is very much closer to the spelling of the Middle Cornish texts than Kernewek Kemmyn is to them. The Unified forms *nyns*, *esof*, *Kerensa*, *ganso* are all attested in the Middle Cornish texts; *cryjy* and *jy* are more usually *crygy* and *gy* respectively. None of the Kemmyn forms is attested in Cornish at any period. Unified Cornish attempts to systematize the spelling of Middle Cornish while Kernewek Kemmyn rewrites it.

In the second place, the two graphs *dj* and *tj* were so bizarre that many Cornish-speakers could not bring themselves to use them. When it was demonstrated that they had never existed, some supporters of Kernewek Kemmyn were delighted. If *dj* and *tj* were abolished, then the major obstacle to the general acceptance of Kernewek Kemmyn would be removed. They were indeed replaced but the opportunity was not taken to look again at Kernewek Kemmyn in a more general sense. When one major feature of a system has been shown to be seriously mistaken, it is wise of to pause and take stock. After all, it had been claimed that *dj* and *tj* were an integral part of Cornish that had gone unnoticed hitherto. W. Brown put it as follows:

> Some of these genuine Cornish sounds have not before been recognized though they occur in other Celtic languages. Such a pair are the 'tj' and 'dj' of the new system where the j' acts like the glide vowels 'i' and 'e' of Gaelic in palatalizing the preceding sound.[5]

Brown's comparison of Gaelic here is baffling. The Gaelic languages have a fully-developed opposition between palatalised and velarized consonants. The Brythonic languages lack such a double series of consonants and the comparision is therefore invalid. The reason that *dj* and *tj* had not hitherto been recognized was because they never existed.

I explained the alternation of *s* and *g/j* as follows. Everywhere Old Cornish *d* became *dz* and this latter in final position simplified to [z], written *s*. In some cases, however, the consonant [dz] was palatalized to [dʒ] where [ʒ] is the sound of *s* in the English words *leisure, pleasure*. The whole complex [dʒ] was effectively the same as the English *j*-sounds in *jam* and *gentle* and was in consequence written *j* or g in Middle Cornish. The variation seen, for example, in *wose:woge* was to some extent one of dialect. Western Cornish tended to favour *j/g*, whereas more easterly dialects preferred *s*.

At first Ken George accepted this explanation, but later he changed his mind and suggested that Old Cornish *d* became some kind of *s* in the Middle Cornish period and that this idiosyncratic *s* became *j/g* in about 1675.[6] This raises some interesting questions. In the first place, George has yet to describe this special kind of *s* in precise terms. Secondly, George has arrived at his new opinion as a result of an analysis of place-names throughout Cornwall, although he has yet to cite the place-names that he has studied. Thirdly, George's view that a particular kind of *s* in Middle Cornish became *j/g* in Late Cornish (c.1675) conflicts with his earlier demonstration that *s* and *j/g* were contemporaneous in Middle Cornish.[7] At all events, George no longer claims that *dj* and *tj* were part of the sound-system of Middle Cornish, and as a result he has removed them from his own orthography. As I have hinted, this itself involves an important question of method and, in fact, Kernewek Kemmyn contains two further errors in its phonology which, though less obvious than *tj* and *dj*, are much more serious. I have space here to deal with them only very briefly.

VOCALIC ALTERNATION

The sound-systems of Welsh and Cornish differ from that of Breton in a significant way. In Welsh and Cornish certain vowels alternate with each other according to whether they occur in monosyllables on the one hand, or disyllables or polysyllables on the other. This vocalic alternation arose because, in the very earliest Welsh, Cornish and Breton, the accent in disyllables was on the final and not the penultimate syllable. In the case of Breton, however, the alternation has subsequently been lost. In Welsh the word for 'carry!' is *dwg*, where the vowel *w* is the approximate equivalent of English *oo* in *food*. 'I carry', on the other hand, is *dygaf*, where the *y* in the disyllable is pronounced rather like the vowel in the English words *worm*, *heard* or *firm*. In Cornish 'carry!' is *dog*, while 'I carry' is *degaf*. When in Welsh *y* occurs in monosyllables it is pronounced like a long *i* as in English *seen* or a long centralised *i*, the latter being a distinctively North Welsh pronunciation. In Welsh, therefore, the 2nd singular imperative *bydd* 'be!' (*dd* = the *th* of English *smooth*) is pronounced with a long *i* (of either kind), whereas the 2nd plural imperative *byddwch* 'be!' has the vowel of English *worm*, etc. The pronunciation of the two vowels is different in Welsh, although both are written *y*. The same alternation also occurs in Cornish where the alternation appears as *y:e*. Thus the singular imperative is *byth* 'be!' but the plural is *betheugh* 'be!' (*bedheugh* in Unified Cornish).

Kernewek Kemmyn is aware of the vocalic alternation *o:e* and *y:e* in Cornish, since it writes *dog* 'carry!' (singular) but *degav* 'I carry' and *bydh* 'be!' (singular) but *bedhewgh* 'be!' (plural).[8] Further examples of *o: e* alternation are not common in Middle Cornish and there are good reasons why this should be so. The alternation *y:e* is very frequent indeed in the Middle Cornish texts, however. Kernewek Kemmyn prefers to ignore it in the overwhelming majority of cases and to write and pronounce the historic *e* as *y*. Here are some examples of historic *e* written *y* in Kernewek Kemmyn. For the sake of comparison, I include the Unified Cornish spellings and at least one example from the traditional Cornish texts:

Kemmyn	Unified	Traditional
blydhen 'year'	bledhen	blethen BM 565
gwydhenn 'tree'	gwedhen	gvethen OM 186
hwyja 'vomit'	wheja	huedzha AB: 177b
hwytha 'blow'	whetha	wethugh!BM 4563
ynys 'island'	enys	enys OM 2592
Ynys 'Shrovetide'	Enes	Enez AB: 46b

It should be noticed, however, that Kernewek Kemmyn is inconsistent in its spelling of such words. We have already noted *bydh* but *bedhewgh*. Other items with *e* and not *y* include *eva* 'drink', *krena* 'tremble', *ledan* 'wide' and *tevi* 'grow'. It is perhaps significant that Dr George himself is perplexed by some of these words, for he believes the root vowel should be *y* and not *e*. He says of *tevi* 'N.B. This word is found only 7 times in trad. Cor., with the commonest spelling *tevy* (4 times); the cognates suggest that *tyvi* might be more correct'. Of *ledan* he says 'N.B. Regular development would give **lydan*, but the limited textual evidence favours<e>'.[9] *Ledan* is in fact the expected form.

The *y:e* alternation is particularly strking in the case of the diphthong *yw*. In Welsh *yw* is pronounced differently, for example, in the monosyllable *byw* 'alive' and the disyllable *bywyd* 'life'. In the monosyllable the vowel is *i* (or centralized *i*) + *w*, whereas in the disyllable the vowel is the neutral vowel + *w*. The equivalents in the earliest stratum of Middle Cornish are *byw* or *byu* 'alive' but *bewnans* or *beunans* 'life'. A variant **bywans* with *yw* in the stressed syllable is unknown in the Middle Cornish texts. *Bywnans*, however, is the form in Kernewek Kemmyn. The *y* in this word and others like it is entirely due to a false analogy with Welsh, George defending his re-spelling of the the play *Beunans Meriasek* (*The Life of St Meriasek*) as *Bywnans Meryadjek* by pointing to the Welsh usage *byw*.[10] He ignores the difference between the vowel of the Welsh monosyllable *byw* 'alive' and the Welsh disyllable *bywyd* 'life'. He apparently forgets that the Cornish equivalent of Welsh *yw* in dissyllables is *ew*. One might also note that Kernewek Kemmyn is not consistent in the matter of *yw/ew* for it writes *Kernewek* and not **Kernywek* (Welsh *Cernyweg*).

THE PROSODIC SHIFT

The absence of vocalic alternation is a serious enough fault in Kernewek Kemmyn. There is, however, a further error in the sound-system of Kernewek Kemmyn which is graver still, for it involves almost all the vowels and many of the consonants.

Breton and Welsh have three possible lengths of stressed vowel: short, half-long and long. Short vowels are pronounced with one duration of length, half-long vowels have two and fully long vowels have three. The technical name for a duration of length is *mora*, the Latin word for 'delay'. One can say, therefore, that in Breton and Welsh stressed vowels can have one, two or three morae. In Welsh the stressed vowel of *tad* 'father' has three morae, the stressed vowel of *tadue* 'fathers' has two morae, whereas the root vowel of *mam* 'mother' and *mamau* 'mothers' has one mora only. Native speakers of Welsh and

Breton consider long and half long to be varieties of the same thing, since in neither case is the vowel short. The unconscious opposition in the minds of speakers is between short and not-short. Indeed, in Breton grammars it is customary to treat long and half-long as long and to deal with short by itself.

There can be no doubt that at one stage Cornish shared the Welsh and Breton system of threefold length. There is no doubt either that before the period of our earliest Middle Cornish texts the threefold distinction had given way to a double distinction of short and long. I assume that the shift from long: half-long: short to long: short occurred in early Middle Cornish under the impact of English.

When we say that short, half-long and long became short and long, we are really saying the following: short remained, half-long became short and long became half-long. Vowels with one mora retained it, whereas vowels with two or three morae lost one. Schematically this can be represented as follows: 1>1, 2>1, 3>2. It is apparent that old half-long vowels and old short vowels after the shift are identical in length. This whole process I refer to as the Prosodic Shift. After the Prosodic Shift, the stressed vowel in *tas* 'father' had two morae, in *tasow* 'fathers' the stressed vowel had one mora while the stressed vowels in *mam* 'mother' and *mamow* 'mothers' each had one mora.

I mentioned that the Prosodic Shift occurred under the influence of English. English has a distinction of short and long only. Morover, stressed vowels in English are pronounced with relatively greater vigour than in Welsh or Breton. This feature was brought over into Middle Cornish. In Middle Cornish syllables lost in length but gained in intensity. Not only did long and half-long vowels shorten as a result of the Prosodic Shift, but unstressed vowels lost much of their intensity and were reduced to the neutral vowel or schwa (of which more in a moment).

The immediate cause of this Anglicization of the sound-system of Cornish was, I believe, the Norman Conquest of England. Before the conquest Cornwall had been in the West Saxon sphere of influence and the West Saxon kings were also kings of England. At the conquest English lost much of its status, Bretons settled in considerable numbers in Cornwall and links with Brittany were re-established. Many Cornish people who had become English-speaking under the West Saxons started to relearn Cornish. Within a generation or two many erstwhile English-speakers were now Celtophone, but they brought into their Cornish English features, particularly in the matter of the length and vigour of vowels.

My reasons for believing that the Prosodic Shift was already in place before our earliest Middle Cornish texts is this: the Middle

Cornish texts exhibit in their spelling a whole range of features that can be explained only by assuming that in the language of the Middle Cornish scribes, half-long had become short and long had become half-long. In CT I list 17 separate features that can be explained only by reference to the Prosodic Shift.[11]

No one disputes that the Prosodic Shift is a fact of Cornish phonology but Dr George dates it to around 1600.[12] However, the Prosodic Shift was a major event in the history of the language and would have had far-reaching effects on the entire sound-system. Were George's dating to be correct, we would expect to find huge differences in phonology between *Tregear Homilies* (TH) (*c.* 1555) on the one hand and *Creacion of the World* (CW) (1611) on the other. This is not the case. Indeed, in some ways the phonology of CW is more archaic than that of *Beunans Meriasek* (BM) (*c.* 1504).

There is a further argument against the later dating of the Prosodic Shift. We know from spellings like *pleau* 'parish' in Lhuyd (*c.* 1700) that in Late Cornish stressed monosyllables had actually lengthened. *Pleau* seems by the Late Cornish period to have acquired three morae. This lengthening was presumably well-established by Lhuyd's day. Yet, according to George's dating, syllables were shortening *c.* 1600. They can hardly have shortened *c.* 1600 only to lengthen again before 1700. We must assume, therefore, that the shortening had taken place much earlier. I date the Prosodic Shift to *c.* 1300 at the latest. Certainly, there are no fewer than 17 features of Middle Cornish phonology which indicate that the Prosodic Shift was already a *fait accompli* before our earliest Middle Cornish texts. However, Kernewek Kemmyn is unaware that the Prosodic Shift had already occurred in Middle Cornish. For example, it therefore spells both monosyllabic and disyllabic forms of *myres* ('to look'), *scryfa* ('to write') and *whylas* ('to seek') with *i*, that is to say with a 'half-long' closed *i*: *mires*, *skrifa*, *hwilas*, which are clearly mistaken.

THE DIPHTHONGIZATION OF FINAL LONG *i/y*

It is a commonplace of Cornish phonology that long final *i* or *y*, when it is not followed by a consonant, tends to diphthongize to *ei* or *oi* in the later language. It is for this reason that Lhuyd writes *ky* 'dog' as *kei* and *ny* 'we' as *nei*.[13] George believes that the shift of long *i* to a diphthong *ei*, *oi* occurred in the period *c.* 1525–*c.* 1625 and was a result of the Great Vowel Shift. The Great Vowel Shift was a major reshaping of the vocalic system of English that began in the latter part of the fifteenth century. As a consequence of the Shift the long *i* of Middle

English 'ride' (with approximately the vowel of Modern English 'read' or 'reed') became a diphthong *oi* or *ai* as it is in Modern English.

There are problems with ascribing a phonetic change in one language to a similar change in another. Cornish was, it is true, heavily influenced by English and lived and died under the shadow of English. It was, nonetheless, a different language. If one vowel in Cornish underwent the English shift, we should expect other vowels to do so. If Cornish *ky* became *kei* because of the Great Vowel Shift, then we would expect Cornish *gun* 'down' to become **gown*, just as Middle English *hous* (pronounced *hoose*) became Modern English *house*. If the shift long *i/y>ei* were based on English, one would expect it to operate in the same kind of environment as the English change. The shift of English long *i* to a diphthong occurs everywhere. The change long *i/y* in Cornish, on the other hand, is confined to absolute final position.

This Cornish diphthongization has nothing whatever to do with the English Great Vowel Shift. It is much earlier and is entirely to do with the Cornish Prosodic Shift. We know that the diphthongization of Cornish *i/y* is early in Cornish because it is already present in the rhymes of *Pascon agan Arluth* (PA). Since PA was composed c. 1400 the diphthongization is probably earlier still. PA rhymes *otry* 'outrage' (which is stressed on the second syllable) and *dry* 'to bring' with *pray* 'prey' and *joy* 'joy'. Similar rhymes occur throughout the *Ordinalia* and the rest of the Middle Cornish texts. The reason for this diphthongisation is as follows. In final position when unprotected by any consonant, final long *y/i* in Cornish before the Prosodic Shift had three morae. It could therefore be represented as [iii], for example in [driii] 'bring' or [kiii] 'dog'. Since the final segment is at the end of an unprotected syllable, it would tend to become semi-vocalic. I therefore analyse the sequence [iii] in final position as [ii] followed by [j], where [j] is approximately equivalent to *y* in English *yes*. I therefore write [iij] rather than [iii]. After the operation of the Shift [iij] was reduced to [ij]. In this reduced vowel, however, the first element is now short. In consequence the short first element decreased in tension *i* to give [Ij], where [I] is the *i* in English *sit*. The two elements of the vowel continue to differentiate themselves and the end result is [əj] where [ə] is the neutal vowel. It is this new diphthong in *dry* and *otry* that rhymes with *prey* [prej] and joy [dʒoj] in PA.

OPEN AND CLOSED LONG *o* IN MIDDLE CORNISH

Cornish before the Prosodic Shift had two distinct long *o*-vowels. Open long *o* was the result of lengthening before single consonants and occurred in such words as *bos* 'to be', *mos* 'to go', *ros* 'gave'. This vowel was probably similar to a lengthened variety of the vowel in English *dog* or *knot*. In phonetic script this long open *o* is usually written [ɔ:]. The second variety of long *o* derived from Old Cornish *ui*. *Ui* in Old Cornish appears first to have become a monophthong, i.e. long *u*, and later to have lowered to become a long closed *o*. This latter long *o* occurred in words like *mos* 'table', *los* 'grey' and *ros* 'net'. It was similar to the vowel of English *pause, cause*. Phonetically it is usually written [o:].

As a result of the Prosodic Shift, it seems that in standard literary Cornish [ɔ:] and [o:] fell together as [ɔ:]. This loss of distinction can be seen from the way in which the two vowels rhyme with each other. In BM, for example we find the following rhymes (in each case I cite the form with [o:] first): *woys* 'blood'–*mois* 'go' 130–31, *goth* 'behoves' –*voth* 'wish' 584–85, *goys* 'blood'–*boys* 'to be' 1599–1603, 1642–43, *loys* 'grey–boys* 'to be' 2168–71, *boys* 'food'–*moys* 'to go' 3926–29, *poys* 'heavy'–*moys* 'to go' 4092–94, *loys* 'grey'–*voys* 'to be' 4415–18, *loys* 'grey'–*toys* 'to come' 4476–77. The loss of distinction between [o:] and [ɔ:] is exactly what we would expect. As a result of the Prosodic Shift open *i* (or closed *e*) fell together with open *e*. This is why *dyth* 'day' is usually *deth*, *cryf* 'strong' is usually *cref* and in some texts *byth* 'will be' is almost invariably *beth*. The principle of symmetry would lead us to expect something similar in the *o*-vowels, i.e. that [o:] should have become [ɔ:].

In the case of [o:], however, there is a further complication. In the later language Middle Cornish [o:] sometimes appears as long *u* [u:], in forms like *luz* 'grey' and *kuz* 'wood' (Middle Cornish *cos, coys*). It is possible that in such words [o:] had not fallen together with [ɔ:] but remained separate and became long *u* in Late Cornish. This is the view of Ken George, who claims that 'the long vowel became closer: [o:]> [u:] *c.* 1625'.[14] There are difficulties with this explanation. In the first place, we should remember that in Late Cornish *luz* 'grey' and *kuz* 'wood', the vowel is in origin Old Cornish [ui]. If, for example, *luz* 'grey' had really been [lo:s] in Middle Cornish, we would have to assume that the word went through the following steps between the twelfth and seventeenth centuries: [luit luis lu:s lo:s lu:z]. This implies that [u:] was lowered to [o:] and then was raised again to [u:] soon afterwards. Moreover, there are place-names which show [u:] for [o:] on the one hand but also contain distinctively Middle Cornish features on the other. *Carrick Luz* in St Keverne, for example, contains [u:] in *luz* 'grey' but the name also contains *carrick* 'rock'<Middle Cornish *carrek* and not the expected *carrack* of Late Cornish. If *Carrick Luz* were later than *c.* 1625, it ought really be **Carrack Luz*.

I assume that there were two reflexes of Old Cornish *ui* in Middle Cornish. In the dialect of central Cornwall, which formed the basis of the literary standard, Old Cornish *ui* monophthongised to [u:] and after the Prosodic Shift fell together with [ɔ:] from other sources. This is the reason that words like *goys* 'blood' rhyme with words like *bos* 'to be' in BM. In western Cornish, however, I assume that *ui* monophthongised to [u:] and remained [u:] until the death of the language in the eighteenth century. This [u:] is what is written <û> in the Late Cornish sources.

I suggested elsewhere that the plays *Passio Domini Nostri Jhesu Christ* (PC) and *Resurrexio Domini Nostri Jhesu Christi* (RD) were more westerly in language than OM.[15] It is significant that in PC and RD the reflex of Old Cornish *ui* is on occasion written *ou* as though it were pronounced [u:] and not [o:]. Note, for example, *scouth* 'shoulder' PC 658, 2623, *duscouth* 'shoulders' RD 2500 (rhyming with *ruth* 'red'), *gouth* 'falls' PC 2626, *glous* 'pang' PC 1147, *lous* 'grey' PC 19, *trous* 'foot' PC 860, 1223 and *bous* 'food' RD 541 (rhyming with *cafus* 'to get'). The word *oys, os* 'age' is spelt *yvs* at PC 786 and rhymes with *tus* 'people'.

It is apparent from the above discussion that the attempt by Kernewek Kemmyn to distinguish the Middle Cornish phonemes /o:/ and /ɔ:/ is unjustified. As a result of the Prosodic Shift, standard Middle Cornish had /ɔ:/ only. The more westerly dialects had /ɔ:/ and /u:/. There was no separate phoneme /o:/ distinct from /ɔ:/ in Middle Cornish. Such forms as *koes* 'wood', *loes* 'grey', *goes* 'blood' in Kernewek Kemmyn are without warrant. Items like these should be spelt either with *o* (standard) or with *u* (western), i.e. as they occur in the sources. To spell these words with *oe* for [o:], as Kernewek Kemmyn does, is not only at variance with the practice of the Middle Cornish scribes, it is phonetically unjustified as well.

CONSONANT DOUBLING IN KERNEWEK KEMMYN

The Prosodic Shift, then, is an integral part of Middle Cornish phonology. Middle Cornish has no half-long vowels, only long and short. Kernewek Kemmyn on the other hand insists on three lengths. Since Kernewek Kemmyn wants its spelling to represent the pronunciation as clearly as possible, the system attempts to distinguish short vowels from 'half-long' ones by doubling the following consonant. The vowels in *cam* 'bent' and *bron* 'hill' are both short and since Kernewek Kemmyn mistakenly believes that Cornish also had half-long vowels, *cam* must be spelt as *kamm* and *bron* as *bronn*. Thus the placename *Camborne*, which is everywhere spelt in Middle Cornish as

Cambron, in Kernewek Kemmyn becomes *Kammbronn*. Such a spelling would have some justification if Cornish had three vocalic lengths. Because Cornish has only two, *Kammbronn* is without justification. The initial *k* is another problem, and this I discuss briefly below.

Before I leave the question of vocalic length I should like to make some apology for my previous negligence in this matter. When I wrote my article against *dj* and *tj* in Kernewek Kemmyn, I posited such forms as [wo.ze] 'after' and [e.ze] 'was' with half length in accordance with Dr George's assumptions.[16] Subsequent investigation has convinced me that such forms were fictions. My praise for George's new orthograph in the first section of the article was also unwise. It was prompted by a desire to encourage Cornish revivalists but was based on an inadequate examination of Kernewek Kemmyn. Quite apart from *dj* and *tj*, I already had reservations about the new system and indeed had communicated some of them to Dr George himself.

EW > OW

We have seen above that Kernewek Kemmyn insists on spelling disyllables with *yw* when the vowel ought to be *ew*. This is not all, however. As a result of the Prosodic Shift the whole system of Cornish diphthongs was reshaped. Diphthongs before the shift could have either a half-long or a short first element. Thereafter, the first element of all diphthongs was short. This had far-reaching effects. Among other things, *yw* in monosyllables became *ew* and *ew* in disyllables became *ow*. Thus, for example, earlier *clyw!* 'hear' but *clewes* 'to hear' became *clew!* 'hear' but *clowes* 'to hear'. Disyllabic forms of the verbs *kewsel* 'to speak', *tewlel* 'to throw' and *clewes* 'to hear' almost always have *ow* in their root syllable in BM, TH and CW. Here are some examples of the verb 'to hear' from these three texts: *ny clowys* BM 191, *re glowes* BM 527, 802, *pan glowe* BM 1030, *del glowas* BM 1160, *clowugh* BM 1890, *clowys* BM 2224, *ny glowys* BM 2238, *a glowes* BM 2394, *a glowas* TH 4a, 30, *clowas* TH 4a, 5, 41, *the glowes* TH 38a, *clowes* TH 41a, *a glowas* CW 140, *tha glowas* CW 637, *a glowses* CW 770, *pan glowa* CW 1136, 1205, *a glowaf* CW 1166; cf. *Klouaz, dho glouaz* 'to hear' in Lhuyd: 44a. It will be readily seen, therefore, that *klyw, klywes*, etc. of Kernewek Kemmyn are all the more at variance with the traditional texts.

UNSTRESSED VOWELS

Nowhere are the effects of the Prosodic Shift more clearly seen than in the unstressed vowels. When stressed syllables were shortened but reinforced as a result of the Prosodic Shift, unstressed syllables were correspondingly weakened. This meant that the quality of unstressed vowels was very largely lost and that most unstressed vowels fell together as the neutral vowel schwa. This is the *uh*-like vowel heard in the unstressed syllable of such English words as *mother, gammon, Christmas* or like an unstressed variety of the first vowel in Welsh *bywyd* to which reference has already been made.

The reduction of unstressed vowels can be clearly seen in the Middle Cornish texts by the way in which such vowels are indifferently spelt. The word for 'one', for example, is variously spelt *onan, onen, onon* or *onyn*. Similarly 'to wait' is *gortes, gortos, gurtas* or *gortays*, while 'people' is either *pobal, pobel* or *pobyl*. In these words and in others like them Kernewek Kemmyn seeks to maintain the quality of the unstressed vowel. In the word for 'one' the unstressed vowel is *a* in Kernewek Kemmyn and this is, in theory at least, to be pronounced *a*. Such an unjustifiable spelling and pronunciation has presented editors with a problem. In the introduction to his Kernewek Kemmyn edition of PA Ray Edwards discusses the spelling of the words *onan* 'one' and *honan* 'self' and says:

> This is the G.M. [i.e. *Gerlyver Kernewek Kemmyn* (GKK)] spelling though in only one case in our Poem do we find honan rhyming with a word ending in *-an*. Ken George has come to the conclusion that these ·words were written with ·*yn, -an* or *-on* endings depending of the words with which they were set to rhyme. In almost every case the rhyming words in the Poem end in *-on* so that *onon/honon* do likewise in the MS. implying, I would think, that these final rhyming syllables are just neutral vowels. Out of the three, the ending *-an* was chosen [i.e. by Kernewek Kemmyn] in imitation of Welsh and Breton forms with the unfortunate result for this Poem that these syllables will appear not to rhyme and the reader will have to treat them as neutral vowels for them to do so.[17]

Edwards here, with his customary acuity, has come upon a major flaw in Kernewek Kemmyn. It is not, therefore, astonishing that Edwards, though a user of Kernewek Kemmyn, has consistently expressed doubts about aspects of it. Indeed, Edwards' observation concerning the nature of unstressed vowels in PA leads inevitably to a further conclusion. Kernewek Kemmyn has been made to conform to Welsh and Breton in the matter of unstressed vowels. Yet it is quite clear from the rhymes in the PA that Cornish by the late fourteenth century was already radically different from the other two languages in having reduced unstressed vowels to schwa. This cannot be an isolated phenomenon. If unstressed vowels are reduced in Cornish it must be that stressed vowels are correspondingly more vigorous. It is *a priori* likely, therefore, from Edwards' conclusion, that the Prosodic Shift was a fact by the time of PA. His pertinent observation implies firstly, that the phonology of Cornish was radically different from Welsh and Breton in a variety of ways and secondly, therefore, that Kernewek Kemmyn is mistaken.

THE ORIGINS OF THE ERRORS IN KERNEWEK KEMMYN
If we understand how Kernewek Kemmyn came to be so mistaken, we can ensure that never again need revived Cornish be disfigured by similar errors. The first and most immediate reason for the defects of Kernewek Kemmyn is that the handbooks of Celtic linguistics which deal with Cornish are themselves inadequate. The best book ever written about Cornish is Henry Jenner's *Handbook of the Cornish Language* (HCL) of 1904. The work was written by a revivalist for the incipient revival and yet it contains much of interest to the academic Celticist. It does not explicitly deal with the question of vocalic alternation. As far as vocalic length is concerned, it assumes that Cornish has short and long only. The two other readily available works that deal with Cornish are Holger Pedersen's and Henry Lewis' *A Concise Comparative Celtic Grammar* (CCCG) of 1937 (reprinted with a supplement in 1961), and Henry Lewis's *Llawlyfr Cernyweg Canol* (LlCC), published in 1923 and revised in 1946.[18] Henry Lewis was a Welshman and a Celtic scholar. His knowledge of Cornish was not particularly profound and he had, of course, no interest in speaking the language. In his section on morphology in LlCC Lewis does not even trouble to write his own paradigms. Rather, he appears to have based his verbs and prepositional pronouns on Norris.[19] Although Norris was editing the *Ordinalia*, he appended to his work a very useful 'Sketch of Cornish Grammar' which forms the basis of Lewis' descriptions. Lewis' work on Cornish appears to have been used extensively by George for GKK and presumably elsewhere.

Lewis's section on Cornish phonology in LlCC is as unsatisfactory as it is brief. Nowhere, for example, does he explicitly discuss the question of vocalic alternation, and generally his remarks are inaccurate and misleading. Moreover, at no point does Lewis discuss the question of vocalic length in Middle Cornish and the way in which the inherited system has given way to an English-based one. If, then, the treatment of Cornish phonology in the academic handbooks is mistaken and confused in places and wanting in others, the treatment of both topics in Kernewek Kemmyn becomes intelligible.

There are more basic reasons for the errors of Kernewek Kemmyn.

It is almost always true that if an academic enterprise is unsuccessful, it is so because the underlying theory is defective. Kernewek Kemmyn is constructed on such an inadequate theoretical basis. We know that Dr George had read Loth's article of 1897, for it was from there that he derived his ideas about *tj* and *dj*. In the same article Loth makes the following observations (translated here from the French to English):

> Our regrets at the death of Cornish are to some degree alleviated by the fact that the two living Brythonic languages are very close to it, Breton in particular forming with Cornish such a close linguistic group that we can consider them as two related dialects of the same language. Middle Cornish was without doubt closer to Breton as a whole than the modern Breton dialect of Quiberon is to that of St-Pol-de-Leon.[20]

This statement of Loth's is untrue. The unique treatment of *d* and *nt* in Cornish is sufficient evidence that Cornish was in significant ways quite unlike Breton. Cornish was a language in its own right with its own history and its own individual phonology. To claim otherwise is to misread the evidence. It is quite clear, however, that Loth's view has been an important influence on George's thinking, and therefore on Kernewek Kemmyn.

If Cornish and Breton were dialects of the same language (as George, following Loth, appears to believe) then the phonology of Cornish can be deduced from comparison with Breton. There is no need to read the Middle Cornish texts closely to see what the speakers of the language actually wrote. Worse still, if the comparison with Breton gives one result and a reading of the texts gives another, then it must be the Middle Cornish texts that are mistaken.

Caradar (A.S.O. Smith) liked to spell as far as possible as the texts did, and consequently on occasion found himself in disagreement with Nance. Compare Caradar's remarks about *annowy* 'kindle': 'Tregear a scryf "annowy". Mes chanjya annowy dhe "enawy" a wra Mordon. Prag? Awos bos "enaoui" yn Bretonek! Mes annowy a yl yn ta bos nes dhe'n Keltek Cotha ha Kernewek yu' ['Tregear writes "annowy". But Nance changes annowy to 'enawy'. Why? Because "enaoui" is the Breton form! Bur annowy may well be closer to the earliest Celtic and it is Cornish'].[21]George, perhaps following Nance's example, says of Caradar's desire to imitate the spelling of the Middle Cornish texts: 'This is a weak principle, because it again takes no account of the pronunciation'.[22] George implies that the Middle Cornish scribes could not write their own language properly. If what they wrote does not agree with the phonology of Middle Cornish as understood by a comparison with Breton, then the scribes are wrong. This is indeed a curious approach to the study of Middle Cornish.

But although on occasion he allowed himself to be swayed by Breton, Nance based Unified Cornish on the texts. Unified Cornish is mistaken, I believe, in a few relatively trivial ways, but because it adheres closely to the sources, it is recognizably Cornish. The same cannot be said for Kernewek Kemmyn. Agan Tavas, the society for the promotion of Unified Cornish, recently declared:

> Sadly, students of revived Cornish must now choose between several differing forms of the language. Agan Tavas recognises the validity of any form based on the language as used by Cornish people at any time, but favours the continued use . . . of Unified Cornish, the form settled by Nance over sixty years ago and used by everyone until recently. Agan Tavas opposes the use of invented forms of the language which lack any historical authenticity.[23]

Similarly, as the late P.A.S. Pool tellingly observed:

> Kemyn is something quite different, an entirely artificial creation whih does not resemble Cornish as used by Cornish people at any time in history. To those accustomed to Unified . . . Kemyn has an alien and somewhat sinister appearance, as if the language had somehow been taken over by robots and reduced to the status of a code.[24]

A 'PHONEMIC' ORTHOGRAPHY

Kernewek Kemmyn is sometimes known as 'Phonemic Cornish' because its orthography claims to adhere closely to phonemic principles. Put simply, 'phonemic' means that any sound in the language will always be represented in writing by the same letter or combination of letters. Moreover, any letter or combination of letters will have only one phonetic value. As an attempt at a phonemic orthography, Kernewek Kemmyn can be criticized on four grounds. In the first place, it uses the same combination of letters to represent different sounds. In the second place, it uses different letters to represent the same sound. In the third place, since the phonology of Kernewek Kemmyn is mistaken, the spelling makes false distinctions. In the fourth place, by squeezing a fifteenth-century language into the strait-jacket of an arbitrary twentieth-century spelling, Kernewek Kemmyn violates the orthographical traditions of Cornish.

The spelling of Kernewek Kemmyn has been recast according to a faulty phonology. Because the phonology is mistaken, the spelling is also inadmissible. But even if the phonology had been largely correct, the spelling of the texts should not have been arbitrarily altered. Traditional Cornish is extinct. The language revival is attempting to resuscitate a dead language. It cannot legitimately recast that language and simultaneously claim that it is reviving a traditional form of speech.

We have possibly two parallels for the case of Cornish. Hebrew has been successfully revived, although it had ceased to be a vernacular for almost two millennia. Yet Israeli Hebrew, although it has lost much of its Semitic character, uses the traditional orthography of the biblical and rabbinical language. A parallel closer to home is that of Manx. Manx died as a traditional language in the early 1970s. The revived language uses the traditional orthography of Manx, even though it is notoriously difficult for learners. The Cornish revival should do the same. It should use the traditional orthography for the language rather than a 1980s orthography that is itself based on a whole series of misconceptions—and which is inconsistent as well.

Before leaving the question of the spelling of Kernewek Kemmyn, a final observation ought to be made. Kernewek Kemmyn has deliberately recast the traditional orthography of Cornish in order to make it correspond with the phonology of the language. Since the devisers of Kernewek Kemmyn have, in my view, failed to understand the phonology of Middle Cornish adequately, we cannot expect Kernewek Kemmyn to reflect the sounds of traditional Cornish very closely. Yet the spelling of Kernewek Kemmyn is not even successful on its own terms. It was the intention of the devisers of the system that the pronunciation of each word would be immediately apparent from the spelling. In which case it is odd that GKK should give the phonetic representation of so many headwords alongside their Kernewek Kemmyn spelling. If the orthography were truly phonetic, these phonetic representations would be redundant, since the pronunciation of each word would be obvious.

DEFENDING THE STATUS QUO
In July 1987 the Cornish Language Board accepted Kernewek Kemmyn in its entirety because, as they announced themselves,

> The Cornish Language Board feels that the work that has been done by Dr Ken George in his book 'The Pronunciation and Spelling of Revived Cornish' is a great improvement for the language. Therefore for the sake of the authenticity of the language and for the sake of those who come after us, the Language Board accepts the proposals.[25]

It is apparent, then, that the advocates of Kernewek Kemmyn proposed and promoted their system because they thought it to be more 'authentic' than any other form of revived Cornish. If it can be shown that Kernewek Kemmyn is less authentic than other varieties of Cornish, Kernewek Kemmyn loses whatever *raison d'etre* it may have had.

It is unlikely that those who support Kernewek Kemmyn will be prepared to abandon their system immediately, in spite of all its manifest faults. At least five different, and in some cases mutually exclusive, reasons are being put forward in favour of the status quo. Let us look at them briefly:

1. To replace Kernewek Kemmyn with a revised variety of Unified Cornish would be to add to the varieties of Neo-Cornish. There are already enough forms of revived Cornish without increasing their number.

Until 1987 there was only one variety of Neo-Cornish, namely Unified Cornish. The proponents of Kernewek Kemmyn introduced their system (and in so doing split the language movement) on the grounds that Kernewek Kemmyn was authentic in a way that Unified was not. To the proponents of Kernewek Kemmyn, then, authenticity is the sole criterion of legitimacy. The most authentic form of Neo-Cornish is the only one to which revivalists can give their loyalty. If Kernewek Kemmyn is the most authentic form of Neo-Cornish, then Kernewek Kemmyn is the system to follow. If Kernewek Kemmyn is not authentic, as I am now suggesting, then Kernewek Kemmyn has no legitimacy. The number of varieties of Neo-Cornish is irrelevant.

2. There is no need to replace Kernewek Kemmyn because it is only a spelling. Unified Cornish and Kernewek Kemmyn are the same thing.

This view is widely held even by those who do not support Kernewek Kemmyn. In a recent review of a Celtic phrasebook, for example, the reviewer says of the Cornish in it: 'Strictly Unified and Common [Cornish] differ only in spelling'.[26] This view is without foundation. It is apparent from PSRC that the deviser of Kernewek Kemmyn intended that his new system should be pronounced very differently from Unified Cornish. If Unified and Kernewek Kemmyn differ only in spelling, then the introduction of Kernewek Kemmyn was unnecessary. If Kernewek Kemmyn is the same thing as Unified but in a different garb, then the introduction of Kemmyn and the ensuing split were frivolous. If Kemmyn and Unified really do not differ significantly, the proponents of Kernewek Kemmyn can hardly justify the continuing use of their system, particularly since Unified Cornish is the more authentic of the two.

3. Kernewek Kemmyn spells phonetically and is therefore easier to learn than any other form of Cornish.

This was the view expressed by the reviewer of CT in *An Gannas*, who wrote,

> Skila veur dhe as a KU war agan lergh o bos res dhe lytherennans arnowydh sywya an sonyow, a-ban vydh ogas pub dallether sowsneger dre nas, nyns o hemma an kas yn Oesow Kres pan wodhya an dus leverel an geryow yn ewn ha ny vern yn tien fatell vedhens skrifys!

> [An important reason for leaving Unified Cornish behind was that there was a need for a modern orthography to follow the sounds, since almost every beginner is a native speaker of English; this was not the case in the Middle Ages when people knew how to pronounce the words properly and it did not matter completely how they were spelt].[27]

Notice first of all the non sequitur in the first part of this passage. Kernewek Kemmyn had to be introduced because the overwhelming majority of Cornish learners were native-speakers of English and the orthography of Unified Cornish was apparently less than ideal for them. It is indeed a novel principle in linguistic planning that a minority language must adapt its spelling to suit the native language of its learners. Could one imagine Welsh, Irish or even Manx doing so? The real point to notice in the passage is this: the reviewer claims that the orthography of Kernewek Kemmyn is close to the phonology of Cornish. His claim, however, is far from being true. The orthography of Unified, though not aspiring to be either 'modern' or 'phonemic', is far closer to the pronunciation of Middle Cornish than Kernewek Kemmyn is. If the spelling of Kernewek Kemmyn were really accurate, if it did in fact reflected the pronunciation of Middle Cornish, there might possibly be some justification for it.

It should also be observed that the reviewer does not claim the spelling of Kernewek Kemmyn reflects a different phonology but merely that it is more closely related to the sounds than is Unified Cornish. Nowhere does he suggest that the underlying sound system is different. If the sound system of Unified and of Kernewek Kemmyn are effectively the same, why was Kernewek Kemmyn ever introduced?

4. Any form of Cornish is as good as any other.

A correspondent of mine, who is a firm supporter of Kernewek Kemmyn, wrote to me recently to defend the continued use of the system. He suggested that any orthography for Cornish was as good as any other since all forms of the language were varieties of Cornish. He asserted, moreover, that the spoken, and not the written language was the crucial thing. In addition, he confessed that he liked talking to speakers of Unified Cornish because he found them easy to understand.

If the proponents of Kemmyn really do believe that one system is as good as any other, it is difficult to understand why they insisted on replacing Unified Cornish. And if the written form is much less important than the spoken form, then the proponents of Kernewek Kemmyn have split the movement and hindered the revival and all for a mere orthography.

5. it is too late to replace Kernewek Kemmyn with another system. Kernewek Kemmyn is too well established to be emended or replaced.

The argument from expediency is perhaps the most frequent reason put forward by speakers of Kernewek Kemmyn in favour of the status quo. It is also the weakest. Unrevised Unified Cornish was a perfectly serviceable system, but the Cornish Language Board replaced it with Kernewek Kemmyn on the grounds that Kemmyn was more authentic. Unified Cornish was in place from 1928 to 1987 but the supporters of Kernewek Kemmyn substituted their own system after a minimum of consultation.

KERNEWEK KEMMYN

None of the arguments in favour of maintaining Kernewek Kemmyn carries any real weight. Many people have understood for the last eight years that Kernewek Kemmyn is mistaken both in conception and in execution, a view that has been elaborated in depth and at length in CT. Far from being the new dawn the Language Board believed it to be, Kernewek Kemmyn has proved to be something of a blind alley—'an unjustifiably wrong turn' as Professor Charles Thomas so famously put it.[28] For the good of the revival and for the sake of unity, the Cornish Language Board should now replace Kernewek Kemmyn with a more authentic Cornish, based on the 'linguistically sound principles' which Dr George himself advocates.[29]

We are not dealing here with a matter of convenience, of not 'rocking the boat', of administrative difficulties. The question is a moral one. Kernewek Kemmyn bears little resemblance in sounds or spelling to the traditional language of Cornwall at any period in its history. It is, therefore, fair neither to the present generation nor to future generations to persist with Kernewek Kemmyn. Since Kernewek Kemmyn is flawed and since it cannot be satisfactorily revised, it should be abandoned.

THE WAY FORWARD

In CT I suggested ways in which Unified Cornish might be improved. My recommendations included reforms to the sound-system that would render Unified more authentic and modifications to the accidence and syntax that would simplify the grammar in line with the later texts. Before I say a little about my recommendations, I should like to make a few general observations about the Cornish revival and the methods by which we arrive at our Neo-Cornish systems.

Let us start from first principles. We wish to revive Cornish but are uncertain which form of the language to use. It is clear, however, that the Middle Cornish of the texts and the Late Cornish of the seventeenth and eighteenth centuries are phonetically one and the same language. As far as inflexion and syntax are concerned, Middle and Late Cornish are very close indeed. As Jenner wrote:

> As for grammatical forms, it will be seen that the writer is of [the] opinion that the difference between Middle and Modern Cornish was more apparent than real, and that except in the very latest period of all, when the language survived only in the mouths of the least educated persons, the so-called 'corruptions' were to a great extent due to differences of spelling, to a want of appreciation of almost inaudible final consonants, and to an intensification of phonetic tendencies existing in germ at a much earlier period.[30]

It is, I believe, imprudent to base revived Cornish on the late language for two main reasons. In the first place, Late Cornish is relatively limited in scope when compared with the medieval and Tudor texts. In the second place, Late Cornish uses a spelling based on English. This orthography did not arise through choice but was forced upon the later writers because they knew no other. Someone who can read Late Cornish only will find reading any other form of the language virtually impossible. If we wish to revive the traditional language of Cornwall, then we should revive it with its traditional orthography.

Unified Cornish was based on the mediaeval language and in particular upon the *Ordinalia* and PA. I am not convinced that this was completely sensible. It would surely have been more prudent to base the revived language on the latest possible period at which the language was still a full vernacular and still written in the traditional orthography.

We have five extensive Middle Cornish texts, PA, the *Ordinalia*, BM, CW and TH. The last three form a unity as far as date is concerned. BM was written *c.* 1504. Tregear wrote his *Homilies c.* 1550. Although William Jordan wrote CW in August 1611, the original text was almost certainly composed before the Reformation, i.e. *c.* 1530–40. Together, these texts form a linguistic unity. Their spelling is traditional yet they exhibit grammatical features that become common in the later language.

In *Cornish Today* I recommend using BM, TH and CW, the 'Tudor texts', as the basis for a revised version of Unified Cornish. This revision I call Unified Cornish Revised or UCR. Since Late Cornish is identical with Tudor Cornish from the phonetic point of view, we can legitimately base the phonology of UCR on Lhuyd's description. This is an important point, because Lhuyd's description of Cornish, though imperfect, is the only phonetic description of the language that we have. As a result of a detailed analysis of Lhuyd and of the Cornish texts themselves, I recommend revising the phonology of Unified Cornish slightly in five ways:

1. Unified Cornish does not distinguish the long *y* (pronounced *ee*) of *mys* 'month' from the vowel of *gwyth* 'trees' or *byth* 'will be'. These latter should probably be pronounced *gwedh* and *bedh* respectively. There is much uncertainty here, however, since it is clear that *bys* 'world' and *ys* 'corn' were pronounced with a long *i* (*ee*) in some varieties of Late Cornish, rather than with the long *e* that one would posit by comparison with other words. UCR writes *gwedh* 'trees', *bedh* 'will be' and allows both *bes* and *bys* 'world'. (The hesitation between *y* and *e* in some etyma may have something to do with the analogy of *y:e* in *scryf* but *screfa*).
2. Unified Cornish does not properly distinguish between the œ-vowel of *dues* 'come' and the ü-vowel of *y dus* 'his people'. That the two sounds were distinct in Middle Cornish is guaranteed by the way in which one unrounds to *e* in Late Cornish and the other to *i/y* (*ee*). Even so, the failure of Unified Cornish to distinguish the two vowels is not entirely unjustified, since we know, for example, that on occasion *ues* 'is' becomes *ees* in Late Cornish rather than *ês*.
3. Unified Cornish spells 'to hear' as *clewes* and 'Cornish' as *Kernewek*. It is quite clear, however, that from the period of PA onwards, original *ew* in disyllables and polysyllables is becoming *ow*. UCR, therefore, writes *clowes* 'to hear', *cowsel* 'to speak', *towlel* 'to throw', *Kernowek* 'Cornish' and is thus faithful to the practice of the Tudor scribes.
4. Unified Cornish is uncertain about the value of *g/k* in words like

wheg 'sweet', *medhek* 'doctor'. After an exhaustive analysis of the evidence, I conclude that final consonants were heavily affected by the Prosodic Shift. Stressed syllables have *g* whereas unstressed syllables have *k*: *wheg* 'sweet' but *anwhek* 'bitter', *rag* 'for' but *marrek* 'knight'. The same alternation is also operative in UCR for *b/p*: *mab* 'son', *neb* 'who but *morrep* 'seashore', *modryp* 'aunt'. Similarly, after a stressed vowel, *f* is pronounced *v* in words like *nef* 'heaven', *of* 'I am', etc. Final *th/dh* is a problem and I conclude that *dh* is the norm everywhere. I write *ladh* 'kill!', *bedh* 'be!' and also *menedh* 'mountain', *gwragedh* 'wives'. This was also Jenner's practice.

5. Unified Cornish writes *gh* both finally and medially. The commoner practice of the Cornish scribes, however, is to write *myrgh* 'daughter' but *myrhes* 'daughters', *yagh* 'healthy' but *yehes* 'health'. I follow the scribes here and alternate medial *h* (pronounced *h*) with final *gh* (pronounced as *ch* in Scottish *loch*). This alternation was also observed by Jenner who says: 'Note that when a syllable is added to a word ending in *gh*, the *g* is omitted'.[31]

In CT I also make detailed recommendations for the simplification of the inflexion and syntax of Neo-Cornish. A full discussion of my recommendations would be out of place here but it is worth mentioning three points. Firstly, I recommend using *fatel, tel, del* to introduce indirect statement. This means that UCR will say *Yth esof vy ow crejy tel wrug ow mab y whul solabrys* ['I believe my son has already done it'] where Unified would use the more cumbersome *My a grys ow map dh'y wul solabrys* or *My a grys y'n gwruk ow map solabrys*. This UCR syntax is well established in Middle Cornish. Secondly, I recommend using *mynnes* 'to wish' as an auxiliary to express the future, for example *Me a vyn screfa lyther avorow* ['I shall write a letter tomorrow']. This syntax is to be found in all the Middle Cornish texts with personal subjects. It is also attested on occasion with impersonal subjects, for example *mar myn ov descans servya* ['if my learning will be adequate' BM 524]. George's opinion that *mynnes* expressing the future occurs in Late Cornish only, is groundless. Thirdly, it should be noticed that many of the reforms of syntax and inflexion are already in use by some speakers of Unified Cornish.[32]

CONCLUSION

Cornish Today has generally met with a warm welcome from revivalists. Most of those who have read the book appear to believe that there is now a strong case against Kernewek Kemmyn. Ray Edwards is typical when he writes: 'Dr Williams' book . . . should be studied by all serious students of the language and in particular members of the Cornish Language Board. Our ultimate aim should be to make our revived Cornish as authentic as possible even if further changes are seen to be necessary.'[33] The proposals for UCR are now being studied in depth by Agan Tavas to determine how far the society should adopt them. The Cornish revival cannot afford conflicting systems. More than anything, the revival needs unity of purpose and action, but unity is unlikely to be achieved until Cornish-speakers agree upon one generally acceptable variety of Cornish. Such agreement cannot be reached, however, until spurious forms of the language are rejected.

NOTES AND REFERENCES

1. N.J.A. Williams, *Cornish Today: An Examination of the Revived Language*, Sutton Coldfield, 1995.
2. Ken George, *Pronunciation and Spelling of Revived Cornish*, Torpoint, 1986A.
3. *Revue Celtique*, 18, 1897.
4. N.J.A. Williams, 'A Problem in Cornish Phonology', in M.J. Ball, J. Fife, E. Poppe and J. Rowland, *Celtic Linguistics: Ieithyddiaeth Geltaidd*, Amsterdam and Philadelphia, 1990.
5. *Carn*, 66, 1989.
6. Ken George, 'An Delinyans Pellder-termyn: Toul rag Studhya an Yeth Kernewek', in G. Le Man and Y-L. Le Moing, *Bretagne et Pays Celtiques: Melanges Offerts a la Memoire de Leon Fleuriot*, Rennes and Saint-Brieuc, 1986B.
7. Ken George, 'The Use of a Mainframe Computer to Analyse Cornish Orthography', in G.W. MacLennan (ed.), *Proceedings of the First North American Congress of Celtic Studies*, Ottawa, 1986C.
8. Wella Brown, *A Grammar of Modern Cornish*, Saltash, 1993, pp. 138–139, 130.
9. Ken George, *Gerlyver Kernewek Kemmyn*, Saltash, 1993, pp. 309, 197.
10. Personal communication, George to Williams, September 1987.
11. Williams, 1995, section 12.1.
12. George, 1986A, p. 68; Ken George, 'Which Base for Revived Cornish?', in Philip Payton (ed.), *Cornish Studies: Three*, Exeter, 1995.
13. Edward Lhuyd, *Archaeologia Britannica*, London, 1707, repub. Shannon, 1971, pp. 46a, 100a.
14. George, 1986A, p. 129.
15. Williams, 1990, p. 267.
16. Williams, 1990.
17. Ray Edwards, *Pascon Agan Arluth: Passhyon Agan Arloedh*, Sutton Coldfield, 1993, p. 20.
18. Henry Jenner, *Handbook of the Cornish Language*, London, 1904, repub. New York n.d.; Henry Lewis and Holger Pedersen, *A Concise Comparative*

Celtic Grammar, Gottingen, 1937 repub. 1961; Henry Lewis, *Llawlyfr Cernyweg Canol*, Cardiff, 2nd. ed., 1946.

19. E. Norris, *The Ancient Cornish Drama*, London, 1859, repub. New York, 1968, pp. i–ii.
20. *Revue Celtique*, 18, 1897.
21. E.G.R. Hooper, *Kemsyk Kernewek: A Cornish Miscellany*, Camborne, 1963, p. 43.
22. George, 1986A, p. 27.
23. W. Morris, *Cornish Dictionary Supplement, No. 3: Geryow Dyvers*, Redruth, 1995.
24. P.A.S. Pool, *The Second Death of Cornish*, Redruth, 1995, p. 6.
25. Ray Edwards, *Kernewek dre Lyther: Kynsa Gradh*, Sutton Coldfield, 1994, p. 111.
26. *Carn*, 91, 1994, citing M. Gunn, *Da Mihi Manum*, Dublin, 1994.
27. *An Gannas*, 226, October 1995.
28. *Associates' Newsletter: Institute of Cornish Studies*, Spring 1990.
29. George, 1986A, p. 41.
30. Jenner, 1904, pp. x–xi.
31. Jenner, 1904, p. 86fn.
32. Rod Lyon, *Everyday Cornish*, Redruth, 1984.
33. Ray Edwards in *Kernewek dre Lyther Annual*, July 1995.

ABBREVIATIONS

AB   Edward Lhuyd, *Archaeologia Britannica*, London, 1707, repub. Shannon, 1971.

BM   Whitley Stokes, *Beunans Meriasek: The Life of St Meriasek*, London, 1872.

CCCG   Henry Lewis and Holger Pedersen, *A Concise Comparative Celtic Grammar*, Gottingen, 1937 repub. 1961.

CW   Whitley Stokes, 'The Creation of the World', *Transactions of the Philological Society*, Part iv, 1864 (the title page is dated 1863).

GKK   Ken George, *Gerlyver Kernewek Kemmyn*, Saltash, 1993.

HCL   Henry Jenner, *Handbook of the Cornish Language*, London, 1904, repub. New York n.d.

LICC   Henry Lewis, *Llawlyfr Cernyweg Canol*, Cardiff, 2nd ed., 1946.

OM   'Origio Mundi' in E. Norris, *The Ancient Cornish Drama*, London, 1859, repub. New York, 1968.

PA   Whitley Stokes, 'Pascon agan Arluth: The Passion of our Lord', *Transactions of the Philiological Society*, 1860–61, Appendix 1–100.

PC   'Passio Domini Nostri Jhesu Christi', in Norris, 1859.

RD   'Resurrexio Domini Nostri Jhesu Christi', in Norris 1859.

TH   John Tregear, *Homelyes xiii in Cornysche*, British Library Additional MS 46,397; quoted from a cyclostyled text published by Christopher Bice in 1969.

LANGUAGE REVIVAL AND LANGUAGE DEBATE: MODERNITY AND POSTMODERNITY

Bernard Deacon

INTRODUCTION

The world of the Cornish language revivalist has been in turmoil since the breakdown of the 'Nancean synthesis' in the mid-1980s.[1] Every so often the tremors caused by this event break through into more public domains, as supporters of various spelling systems clash in the columns of the local press.[2] These public skirmishes are, however, only the more superficial manifestations of a deeper debate, one felt at its most intense within the relatively closed sub-culture of the language revival itself.To those uninvolved in the Cornish language movement this debate, largely conducted within the singular terminology of linguistics, may be seen as on a par with that well known medieval predilection for assessing the number of angels who could stand on a pin-head. Yet, as I shall argue below, if we raise our focus from the details of morphology, phonology, orthography and syntax we can perceive interesting links to broader social changes. What I intend to suggest in this contribution is that social theory, the theories used by social scientists to explain the social world, can help us better understand the current Cornish language dilemma and, perhaps, also help us move beyond it.

THE COLLAPSE OF THE NANCEAN SYNTHESIS

The story of the emergence and progress of the current debate within the Cornish language movement need not detain us long as most of the details have already appeared in print.[3] Ken George produced a detailed critique of the phonological base (the sound system) of Unified Cornish during the early 1980s. This led to the adoption by the Cornish

Language Board of George's new spelling system in 1987. It was claimed that the new orthography, by bringing the graphemes (the written representations of sounds) closer to the phonemes (the sounds) of the revised language, would both make Cornish easier to learn and would align the pronunciation of the revived language with that of the historic Cornish language of around 1500.[4] However, others who were equally dissatisfied with the Nancean synthesis, but perhaps for somewhat different reasons, were simultaneously moving in another direction. They attempted to base their pronunciation of the language on the historic Cornish of a later period, around the 1690s. This group was impatient with the 'elfish jargon, written in ornamental blackletter and enunciated only at the Gorseth and in the annual Cornish evensong. They wanted a language that could be used, speech that smacked of the quayside, the pub and the street.'[5]

Nevertheless, their streets were soon deserted by the majority of speakers and learners who, swayed by the legitimation provided by the Cornish Language Board, changed over to George's phonemic Cornish, later given the name Common Cornish or Kernewek Kemmyn. But not all did. A third group of revivalists refused to make the shift from Unified Cornish to Kernewek Kemmyn and decided to stick with Nance's spelling system. By 1990 the revival had fragmented into a majority group advocating the new Kernewek Kemmyn system, which had succeeded in holding on to the institutions of the revivalist movement, and to smaller groups of Unified Cornish and Late Cornish users, the latter preferring to call their version 'Modern Cornish'. Each of these evolved new institutions, in Agan Tavas and the Cornish Language Council, to further their versions of Cornish.

Fragmentation did not end there. The debate over what was the best base for the revived language re-surfaced in 1995 with the publication of Nicholas Williams' book *Cornish Today*, together with his article 'Linguistically Sound Principles' in this volume. Williams, like George, based his work on a close analysis of the texts of historic Cornish, but reached very different conclusions. He claimed to identify a 'prosodic shift' in Cornish, occurring at some time 'before the earliest Middle Cornish texts' and caused by Cornwall's linguistic history, as English speakers were re-acculturated into Cornish during an expansive phase of the Cornish language.[6] For Williams this meant that George, who dated the sound changes involved in Williams' 'prosodic shift' to a period 350 years later, had been 'rather wide of the mark'.[7] Kernewek Kemmyn was therefore 'faulty from the phonetic point of view and its orthography leaves much to be desired'.[8] Williams was even more scathing about the attempt to base the spelling of revived Cornish upon Late Cornish, as proposed by Richard Gendall. This, for him, was 'probably the most unwise' of a series of 'imprudent choices' that had 'littered' the history of the Cornish Revival.[9] Instead, he proposed yet another spelling system, Unified Cornish Revised, based on a later period than Kernewek Kemmyn, and with its focus on Tregear's *Homilies* of 1555.

THE RIGHT TO SPEAK: SOCIAL THEORY AND LANGUAGE

Before reviewing the way in which social theorists have approached the Cornish langauge debate so far we need to establish the right of social theorists to intervene in a debate about language. This should not take long. Language is intrinsically social. It is both the product of complex histories and social processes and a part of the reproduction of those histories and processes. The production and reception of language happens within social relationships and social interactions where some speakers have more authority than others. It is not just that without language there can be no society and without society no language. Language is itself bound up with social relations of power, with relations between people. Because of this way in which language is part of the social world it must be fair game for sociologists and other social theorists.[10] We can go further. Because words are always uttered or written by people in situations where communication is taking place, their use and their meanings are always socially constructed. It is only through language that we construct our reality and express our values. It is therefore impossible and futile to try to detach the structure of language from the process of language, the words people use from the values they have.[11] The two are inextricably bound together.

However, the linguistic approach, as adopted by George and Williams, does exactly this. It tries to 'freeze' language, focusing on language as a structure and seeking the rules that govern this structure.[12] From the perspective of social theory, this approach to language is itself part of a process of staking out disciplinary boundaries, within which the status of linguistics and its right to pronounce authoritatively on language is vigorously defended. What is created is a particular discourse, a 'unified and structured domain of language-use that constrains what can be said or thought'.[13] This discourse of linguistics both establishes the authority of some to pronounce on language and denies that right to others unless they first learn the rules of the discourse. But those rules, as we shall see, are bound up with other discourses that constrain the debate about language and language planning within excessively narrow limits.

THE LANGUAGE DEBATE AS A CLASH OF IDEOLOGIES

When discussing the Cornish language revival, social theorists have up to now focused on the concept of ideology, meaning 'a set of related beliefs, attitudes and opinions'.[14] The twentieth-century revival is argued to be part of a broader medievalist, nostalgic ideological project that reacted against the problems of de-industrializing Cornwall by seeking refuge in a distant, safely pre-industrial past.[15] The Kernewek Kemmyn revision is then interpreted as an attempt to 'secure revived Cornish even more firmly on its medieval base, thus reinforcing the ideological focus of the early revivalists'.[16] This explanation makes much of George's rationale for choosing the date 1500 as the base for the phonology of revived Cornish; 'an ideological rationale for this date, should one be required, is that it just precedes the Protestant Reformation, the death-blow for traditional Cornish'.[17] In contrast to the medieval ideological project of Unified Cornish and Kernewek Kemmyn, the attempts to base revived Cornish on Late Cornish is, in this view, seen as an 'ideology of modernity', an attempt to link the language to 'Methodist–industrial Cornwall (and make it) a natural element of Cornish modernity'.[18] On this reading, Williams' proposed Unified Cornish Revised, by moving the basis of Cornish from the medieval to the Tudor period, is presumably a Tudor ideological project.

While an attractive way of making sense of the language debate in that it links the arcane debate over the details of phonology, morphology and syntax to broader world views, this reliance on ideology is problematic. Using 'ideology' helps us to generalize about the Cornish responses to the problems posed by de-industrialization and the associated political and cultural 'great paralysis' but a classification based on it becomes a little too neat and simple when applied to the more particular case of the Cornish Revival. The concept of ideology is being used in a descriptive way rather than as a tool for analysing how the world-views of the language revivalist are constructed and reproduced over time. The content of a medievalist, as opposed to a modernist, revivalist ideology, or how it hangs together, or how the ideology relates to social practice has not been spelt out in detail. In the last resort the existence of such ideologies is asserted rather than demonstrated. Unified Cornish or Kernewek Kemmyn are based on Middle Cornish; therefore, those revivalists who use these reconstructions are adopting or are at least influenced by a medievalist ideology. Is it this clear cut, though? For instance, while Henry Jenner looked explicitly back to a medieval age, other revivalists who learnt, even spoke, Unified Cornish, especially after the 1939–45 War, saw it as a part of building a 'New' Cornwall, post-industrial rather than pre-industrial.[19] The pages of *An Gannas*, the Kernewek Kemmyn newsletter, are not noticeably more 'medieval' than the pages of *An Garrack*, the Modern Cornish newsletter, while the latter is not discernibly more 'modernist'.

This suggests a deeper problem with using the concept of ideology in this manner. The agents themselves, the actual revivalists, do not understand it this way. Indeed, Kernewek Kemmyn activists will vehemently deny the thesis as applied to them.[20] It has been pointed out (by a defender of the ideology concept) that 'there is the danger of arrogance, complacency or worse in the use of terms like "ideology" . . . terms that may connote an offensively us-and-them attitude, a presumption of superior (undeluded) wisdom on the part of the enlightened . . . intellectuals'.[21] What this suggests is that, if we are going to impute a medievalist ideological consciousness to the majority part of the revivalist movement, then we had better be very sure of the grounds for this. Otherwise social theory is at best in danger of being viewed as arrogant presumption and at worst as being merely a tool of a particular platform in the language debate.

In view of these problems, adopting ideology as the central organizing concept is perhaps not the best way to help us understand the current Cornish language dilemma. In the rest of this article I intend, therefore, to turn to broader theories of modernity and postmodernity in order to reflect on the contemporary language revival, set it into its wider social context and provide some preliminary conclusions about the language debate.

MODERNITY AND POSTMODERNITY

Recently, a neighbour said to me: 'nothing is the same anymore is it'. Another neighbour involved in the same conversation heartily agreed. Now, although we might respond to this by citing many examples of continuity, such comments are indicative of a popular perception of overwhelming change. The Cornish language dilemma may be the local variant of something much wider and more global. There is a sense, at least in the wealthier parts of the world, that we are living through a complex transformation, that society is changing more rapidly and in different directions than before. This has given rise to the idea of a shift from modernity to postmodernity. Modernity, the period ushered in by the Enlightenment, has, by this argument, reached its limits. It has been, or is being, replaced by something qualitatively different, that which comes after modernity, or postmodernity. Even analysts who play down the idea of a temporal rupture will still often use terms such as late modernity or high modernity to indicate that something is, nevertheless, changing.[22] While postmodernist theories themselves come in a variety of shapes and sizes and range from the thought-provoking to the bizarre, it is possible to detect a broad consensus among social theorists about what is involved in this shift to 'post-modernity'. From this we might isolate three aspects.

First, as already suggested, postmodernity is marked by growing apprehension. 'Doubts, uncertainties and anxieties . . . seem increasingly to be a corollary of modernity'; a 'feeling of anxiety, out-of-placeness, loss of direction . . . constitutes the true referent of the concept of "postmodernity"'.[23] This generalized anxiety appears to raise questions about the modernist belief in a progressive improvement in the human condition, a belief shared by both defenders of consumer capitalism and its socialist and Marxist critics. Several writers go on to suggest that more uncertainty is accompanied by greater self-reflexivity as individuals reflect on what they are doing and why.[24]

The second feature is the so-called 'crisis of representation' that began to make itself felt in the 1970s. The work of philosophers, literary theorists and social scientists began to emphasize the difficulties of representing the 'real'. Words seemed to be drifting apart from the things they described. Indeed, the signs and symbols of things in the late twentieth century themselves become the 'real'. Such distinctions, as between advertisements, drama and 'real life', are obscured. It is no longer an easy or unproblematic matter to access 'reality'.[25] With this breakdown of representation, culture in turn becomes the focus of attention rather than economics, to the point where the divisions between the economic and the cultural are no longer meaningful; commodities become cultural, culture itself is commodified.[26]

Anxiety and the crisis of representation combine with a third aspect of postmodernity, a generalised suspicion of meta-narratives, of grand explanations for the human condition like 'progress', 'reason', Marxism or the major religions which purport to offer a unified or 'total' view of the world.[27] The result is a growing perception of fragmentation, particularity, difference and contingency in the place of the former grand and ordered narratives.[28] Examples of this fragmentation are not hard to spot. With the end of the Cold War the binary struggle of two monolithic powers has given way to a confusing mosaic of inter- and intra-state struggles. In domestic politics the old political parties suffer attrition at their margins; the Tories are challenged by the UK Independence Party and Goldmith's Referendum Party, Liberal Democrats by the Liberals, Labour by Socialist Labour and Militant Labour, all three by the Greens and by sub-state nationalist parties, electoral politics in general by an undergrowth of direct action orientated social movements. The tired ritual of traditional party politics is increasingly only held together by an outdated electoral system. At the same time, old social classes dissolve and 'dealign', globalization inserts post-colonial peoples into the heart of their former empires and individuals both seek and are presented with new identities. Culturally, broadcast media implode into a multiplicity of offerings, even as all tend towards offering the same thing.

Fragmentation, difference and doubt 'signify that the limits of the modern have been reached, that the pursuit of unshakeable foundations for analytic truth constitutes a fruitless project'.[29] Old certainties are seen as losing their credibility. Among these old certainties is the belief that science has a particularly privileged role in the 'project' of civilization and modernity. Giddens points out that 'high modernity is characterized by widespread skepticism about providential reason, coupled with the recognition that science and technology are double-edged, creating new parameters of risk and danger . . .'[30]. Newtonian science's dominance has been questioned since the 1960s, both externally and, perhaps more crucially, from within the scientific community, as prediction is scrutinized and found wanting, precision is deemed impossible and simplicity replaced by complexity and 'chaos'.[31] Science is now more likely to be seen as that project that has given us the dubious benefits of nuclear weapons, chemical pesticides, animal feeds that produce BSE, or regional planning that rides roughshod over the the wishes of local communities, than as the answer to all our problems. Instead of a belief in an ordered progression to a better world we are therefore left with finding 'a way of relating to the limits and limitations of modernity, a way of living with the realization that the promise of modernity to deliver order, certainty and security will remain unfulfilled'.[32]

THE CORNISH LANGUAGE REVIVAL, SCIENCE AND MODERNITY

How do we insert the language revival into this modernity/ postmodernity categorization? The striking aspect of the twentieth-century revival, particularly in its post-war manifestation, was not its medievalism but its modernism. It may not be just coincidence that Toynbee placed the beginnings of modernity in the last quarter of fifteenth-century Europe, the precise period on which Kernewek Kemmyn attempts to ground its version of Cornish and the earliest of the periods currently being canvassed as alternative bases for the revived language.[33] There are, however, stronger reasons than this accident of chronology for suggesting that the Cornish language debate in general, while itself a symptom of postmodernist doubts, uncertainties and scepticism, is largely conducted within the discourses and structures of modernity. In particular, the appeals to science and to authenticity made by various contributors to the language debate are classically modernist appeals. But it is my argument here that this dominant discourse of modernity is no longer appropriate for the conditions of postmodernity. In order to unravel the Cornish language dilemma, it will be necessary to open up and transcend this discourse.

Modernist science is concerned to seek patterns and unities, laws and regularities. To do this it categorizes, classifies and hypothesises in order to build theories about the world. These theories are then tested against reality and subjected to a continuous process of modification and sophistication. If careful interpretation of the data suggests a theory is consistently found wanting then that theory is ultimately abandoned. It follows that, in modern science, only one of two contradictory theories can be 'correct'. 'Modern science still holds that if an erroneous theory is mistakenly accepted, it would eventually be uncovered and corrected through replication and further research.'[34] This is exactly what Williams is now saying about Kernewek Kemmyn, a theory that he regards as 'faulty', 'mistaken', 'flawed', 'spurious' and prone to 'errors'.[35] As a result, he believes that Kernewek Kemmyn 'will ultimately be abandoned' as befits an 'erroneous theory'.[36]

But the real world does not appear to be that simple. Since the 1960s, as suggested above, the assumptions of modernist science have been under challenge. Two aspects of this challenge are particularly relevant to the language debate. First, the possibility of scientists being detached, value-free and objective is now questioned rather than being taken for granted. The theories and concepts scientists use to make sense of the world themselves construct the world.[37] On this reading, the scientist is not so much dispassioned theory-tester as participant-observer. His or her theories cannot be detached from the 'reality' being studied; they become part of that reality. Reconstructions of the Cornish language do not just reveal the historic language; they create it. In a similar way, modernist science has been driven by the search for order and regularity. Therefore, it is order and regularity it finds. But in following this quest for order we may lose sight of the complexity and contingency of the world.

Those embracing postmodernist theory will argue that the world is, indeed, complex and contingent rather than ordered and that our sense of order is a product of the dominant form of knowledge, scientific knowledge. While it might be suggested that order and complexity might co-exist and are not so mutually incompatible as is often implied

by postmodernist writings, these doubts do raise a second question
mark over modernist science. The latter adopts a language of certainty
and precision. But this language conceals the complexity of the world.
As certainty and precision, disinterested and value-free inquiry are
actually impossible then a gap emerges between the rhetoric of science
and its practice. This critique is particularly relevant when levelled at
those studying the social, which includes language.

The work of the main contributors to the Cornish language debate
illustrates these problems of the scientific approach. Both Williams and
George appeal to science, to the interpretation of data which 'proves'
or 'disproves' their respective theories. However, this appeal is hardly
as clear cut as they presume. By taking Ken George's work as an
example, and focusing on his 1995 article 'Which Base for Revived
Cornish?', we can see how the practice of rationalist science does not,
indeed cannot, match up to the rhetoric. It fails to match up in that it
is partial, it uses evidence as part of a rhetorical game, and it appeals
to non-scientific discourses.[38]

Its partiality is nicely illustrated, for example, by the way George
deconstructs the use of the term 'Modern' by those who prefer to base
their version of revived Cornish on the Late period. There is no
equivalent deconstruction of the word Kemmyn (common) adopted by
users of Kernewek Kemmyn for equally ideological purposes.[39] Such
silences and the partial use of evidence keep reappearing among the
erudite reconstructions of verbal paradigms. Thus, to illustrate his point
that 'there has been upsurge of interest in poetry in Kernewek
Kemmyn', we are informed that 'a new group, Berdh Arnowydh
Kernewek, has been giving public recitals of their works, in Cornish
with English translation or vice versa. Saunders and Snell are writing
poetry in Cornish using specifically Celtic verse-forms'.[40] What the
reader is not told is that only one of the three poets in Berdh Arnowydh
Kernewek writes in Cornish, the other two being neither Cornish
speakers nor writers, while Saunders' poetry is written in his own
orthography and not in Kernewek Kemmyn. Such partial use of
evidence is actually included to bolster a particular case, something
that it is difficult to see how science, whatever its rhetoric of 'objectivity', can possibly avoid, given the complexity of evidence in the
world. Indeed, the very adoption of the scientific discourse itself is
partial as it closes off other possibilities and makes conclusions based
on methods outside this discourse automatically unreasonable and
therefore plain wrong. George writes that 'it is surprising that, when
choosing an orthography for Kernuak, Gendall did not use as a basis
Lhuyd's system, which is far more scientific than that of the writers in
the Newlyn School'.[42] This is, of course, only 'surprising' when the only

knowledge deemed admissible is that acceptable to the rules of modern science. The discourse that George uses thus closes off the possibility that other forms of knowledge have their own value.

Second, the response of George to criticism of his reconstruction of revived Cornish is perhaps better seen as part of a rhetorical game than as scientific method. Replying to Williams in *Kernow*, the magazine which adopts a robust defence of Kernewek Kemmyn not unlike that of the Spanish Inquisition to heretics, Williams' 'prosodic shift' seems to have developed upper case initial letters and an extra word. It has expanded into the 'Great Prosodic Shift'.[43] This small enough textual addition is then picked up by the accompanying poem, written in the style of balladeer of the early nineteenth century, perhaps the high point of modernity in Cornwall.[44] George's text thus legitimates the lampooning poem, which helps to undermine Williams' arguments through ridicule. In a similarly uncompromising fashion, George sees Williams' work as providing a 'devastating' critique of 'Carnoack', not a spelling that either Williams or Modern Cornish users themselves use, but by which George means the Modern Cornish version of the revived language.[45] And yet, while Williams is most definitely critical of the Modern Cornish version as advocated by Gendall, he is also suggesting that most of the pronunciation and indeed syntax associated with Modern Cornish was being used much earlier and that there is no real difference between Middle and Late Cornish.[46] So Williams' 'Tudor Cornish' is to be spoken like Modern Cornish, the difference lying in the spelling system. Middle Cornish, we discover on this reading, is actually a disguised Modern Cornish. Or perhaps Modern Cornish is a disguised Middle Cornish. Whichever way we look at it Williams' conclusion, that revived Cornish should be spoken like Modern Cornish, seems strangely at odds with George's premature obituary for the latter.

Third, modern science finds it impossible in practice not to resort to non-scientific appeals. George appears to accept without question the notion that there are 'true' languages, which he argues that Late Cornish, being 'geographically and socially restricted', certainly was not. In support of this statement we are invited to 'look at Brittany today to see the truth of this statement'.[47] What exactly we are supposed to be looking for is not made plain. Underlying such assertions of what are and are not 'true' languages are surely highly questionable assumptions. As Payton has pointed out, notions of 'corruption' and 'confinement' that are usually directed at Late Cornish are best seen as ideological projects boosting the legitimacy of one form of Cornish over another, rather than scientific 'truth statements'.[48] Indeed, Williams has followed Jenner in suggesting that many of the so-called 'corruptions' of Late Cornish were 'to a great extent due to differences of spelling'.[49]

What we are thus presented with is a mixture of appeals to scientific reason interlaced with rhetorical claims and unstated assumptions that are designed to further a particular revivalist project. When this is realized we can perhaps make sense of the astonishing non sequitur that concludes George's 1995 paper: 'The superiority of Kernewek Kemmyn is demonstrated by the fact that it is the form of Cornish used by the majority of Cornish speakers and writers'.[50]

George's work also illustrates the way modern science obscures doubt in the interest of uniformity and generalization. Replying to his critics, he claims that the pronunciation and spelling of Kernewek Kemmyn 'are closely wedded' and that 'the orthography of Kernewek Kemmyn is an improvement on that of Nance'.[51] There is not much room for doubt here. But the evidence for the accuracy of this statement depends on the reader accepting George's own reconstruction of Cornish phonemes. In contrast, Williams claims that George has got it wrong and comes up with a different phonemic system, despite using the same texts.[52] It seems that this area is thus open to a lot more doubt than the confident language implies. Indeed, as analysis of the texts of written Cornish proceeds, what we seem to be presented with is not increasing consensus and certainty but growing doubts and complexity. The language of certainty and truth adopted by writers like George and Williams is misleading but is typical of the language of science and modernity. There is a disjunction between the available data, which is partial, contradictory, complex and open to a variety of interpretations, and the scientific discourse which closes off possibilities and asserts that there can be only one truth. Ken George at times seems to be aware of this; 'it is impossible *sensu stricto* to recover historical Cornish [of any phase]',[53] but refuses to accept what this growing complexity implies both for modernist, scientific methodology in general and for his analysis in particular, the foundations of which are sandier than he might like to think.

THE HOLY GRAIL OF AUTHENTICITY

The quest for the authentic, the true, original, genuine, has transfixed all sides of the Cornish language debate since the mid-1980s. In the preface to his *The Pronunciation and Spelling of Revived Cornish*, which brought his findings to a wider audience in 1986, George states that 'if Cornish is to be seen as authentic, then it is essential that they [criticisms from outsider academics] be examined and answered'.[54] When the Cornish Language Board decided to adopt George's new spelling in 1987 it was 'for the sake of the authenticity of the language'.[55] At the same time, those who prefer to stick with Unified Cornish have turned this argument against the supporters of Kernewek Kemmyn. Rather than adopt the new spelling, they respond that 'Agan Tavas [the organization set up to promote Unified Cornish] opposes the use of invented forms of the language which lack any historical authenticity'.[56] Authenticity is also at the heart of the Modern Cornish project;

> given the modern character of Modern Cornish, the comparative simplicity of its grammar, its everyday language, its unique access to an authentic, historical system of pronunciation and intonation, this latest and most developed form of the language seems not only ideally but also logically suited as the basis for a revived Cornish.[57]

Some Modern Cornish supporters even go so far as to posit the 'basic premise: that authenticity is the most desirable quality of a revived language'.[58] Finally, the most recent reconstruction of revived Cornish, Williams' Unified Cornish Revised, also stakes its case for further reform 'in the interests of authenticity' and asks the reader to 'judge for himself (sic) which of the two (sic) modern orthographies looks the more authentic'.[59]

Saunders has rightly condemned this wholesale use of 'authenticity', along with notions of 'purity'. These, he argues, 'are categories from the realms of ethics and aesthetics,and to import them into a scientific discourse is to impose value-judgements where dispassionate and cool analysis are essential'.[60] However, while Saunders, writing from within a scientific and modernist discourse, is correct in pointing to the logical contradictions of combining authenticity and science, he nevertheless misses a broader point here. Authenticity, like science, is a product of modernity. And the problem of authenticity is a peculiarly modern problem.[61] It was the nineteenth century, the century of industrialization and urbanization, that also saw the emergence of antiquarian societies devoted to collecting and saving old customs, folk songs, dialect stories and even dead or dying languages, all of which were seen as threatened by the forces of change and burgeoning modernity.[62] There is, therefore, a paradox here. Modernity changes and destroys places, landscapes and communities and adds constantly to 'inauthenticity' as the 'true origins' and 'roots' of things are overlain by the modern. But it also creates the quest for authenticity, as people deliberately seek to root themselves, their families and their places in the past. Perhaps 'the final victory of modernity . . . is not the disappearance of the non-modern world, but its artificial preservation and reconstruction'.[63]

At one level then, the whole history of the Cornish Revival can be seen as a product of modernity, involving a quest for authenticity. But of course, while being a part of it, it also resists a simple modernist logic. The existence of the Revival suggests an alternative construction of a place—Cornwall—an alternative, that is, to the dominant modernist logic that has produced a de-industrialized periphery, a place of holidays and retirement, passion and romanticism for the jaded urbanite.

However, the condition of postmodernity undermines the certainties of modernity. Just as mass tourism gives way to niche markets, green tourism, weekend breaks and the like, so alternative constructions of Cornwall fragment and dissolve, to re-cohere in different and changing forms. The general fragmentation and speeded-up social change associated with postmodernity has two consequences. First, the authenticity searches become ever more frantic. As the possibility of achieving authenticity recedes further, so the value given to authenticity strengthens. This leads to what Baudrillard has termed the 'hyperreal', manufactured images that seem more real than the 'real'.[64] When the images come up against 'reality' it is often reality that is then denied. This phenomenon might be observed in those tourists or migrants to Cornwall who become disappointed that the place does not live up to their own 'reality', a reality constructed through avid consumption of romantic novels, tourist brochures and media images of Cornwall. Similarly, it is not unknown for returning exiles, steeped in a 'reality' of heroic Celtic nationalism, to encounter serious problems in matching this to other 'realities' on the ground, which must then be denied or ignored.[65]

Along with ever more frantic authenticity searches, postmodernity —or late or high modernity—is making it increasingly impossible to reach a consensually agreed authenticity. A plurality of authenticities is created. All believe their's to be the only authentic voice. Of course, this makes the notion of authenticity itself, meaningless. Academic defenders of the term are then forced to adopt relativist positions on it; authenticity is 'at best a relative term' and 'authenticity may be a desirable goal, but absolute authenticity is quite unattainable'.[66] Again, George seems more aware of the problems of authenticity than most, admitting that 'our knowledge of historical Cornish has a degree of uncertainty ('experimental error') associated with it'.[67] Nevertheless, he is reluctant to admit that this opens the door to a number of coexisting 'authenticities' and continues to argue for relative authenticity as a principle for the revived language.[68]

Authenticity is one of the two 'fundamental questions' considered by George in his 1995 article. If authenticity now seems difficult to achieve, we are invited to turn from it to George's 'language planning'. Unfortunately, no clear criteria are offered for judging the suitability of different versions of the revived language for 'language planning'. As a result, George actually slips back in this article to discuss the accuracy of the phonological base and the historical reconstruction. This is safer, more 'objective' and more 'scientific' ground. But it inevitably brings the discussion back to the issue of authenticity. The difficulty here is that potential criteria for language planning, for example the ease of learning the language or the ability to express ideas in it, are not easily measurable within a scientific discourse. Indeed, all sides can, and do, frequently make these claims for their own version of the revived language. While George claims that Kernewek Kemmyn is a 'vibrant, living, modern, everyday language, capable of expressing ideas in more than one register', Gendall makes similar claims for Modern Cornish; it 'is a rich, interesting and surprisingly easily-learnt idiom'.[69] Such claims cannot be easily proven. All that we can observe at this stage is that people succeed in learning Cornish of all kinds and that there are relatively fluent and relatively indifferent speakers of Cornish of all varieties.

MOVING BEYOND MODERNITY

What I have been suggesting is that the debate about the language has been, hitherto, conducted largely within a scientific discourse that is a part of classic modernity. However, the new context of postmodernity has resulted in increasing challenges to the pretensions of modernist science. We seem to live in a world of growing uncertainty, where difference and disorder is as likely as uniformity and order. The breakdown of the 'Nancean synthesis' is perhaps our local manifestation of this. In such conditions the quest for 'authenticity', a modernist problem, becomes more frantic but, at the same time, more meaningless. What is produced is a plurality of authenticities that argue past each other, largely within a discredited scientific discourse that cannot any longer achieve a consensual legitimacy.

If this interpretation has any validity then it would clearly be presumptuous of me to offer a 'solution'. The postmodern dilemma seems to be that there are no longer simple solutions. Nonetheless, some reflections are worth making. First, it seems fruitless and a waste of intellectual effort to pursue the chimera of absolute 'authenticity' with such passion. Here Ken George's criterion, 'keeping true to the spirit of historical Cornish' seems to be eminently sensible.[70] But this implies also that there is a number of possibilities, all of which may be relatively 'authentic', according to their own lights. The second observation flows from this abandonment of absolute authenticity. Somehow, those involved in the language revival will have to recognize and accept the plurality that has emerged within the language movement. No one form of revived Cornish is likely to re-establish the 'Nancean synthesis', so there has to be a toleration of other forms. The rather triumphalist and intemperate language of some enthusiasts, for example 'Kernewek Kemmyn is certainly an immense success, so much so that all other systems are marginalized, with consequent annoyance and frustration of their few supporters'[71] is not the best way of achieving this. Such language obscures the crucial role of maintaining institutional legitimacy through commanding the Cornish Language Board. Numerical advantage is the result of this rather than of any inherent superiority of the orthographic or phonological system itself.[72] In similar fashion, attacks on Kernewek Kemmyn as 'merely an Englishman's idea of how Cornish might have sounded 500 years' should be roundly condemned.[73] Such a language of exclusion is counter-productive. Each variety of revived Cornish has a right to exist, even though we might have serious reservations about some of them. Meanwhile, these reservations must be debated so that there can be reflection on each reconstruction.

My third suggestion is that, in moving towards this reflexivity, those individuals involved in the language movement need also to become much more sceptical about the local 'grand narratives' of the Cornish Revival. If postmodernity is about 'scepticism towards meta-narratives', then heaping slavish praise on the works of one's chosen guru seems behaviour overly reminiscent of modernity. Increasing scepticism directed at Nance's 'grand narrative' played a productive part in breaking the log-jam that had prevented open discussion of the spelling and pronunciation of Cornish before the 1980s. But to replace one major guru with a series of more minor ones is to leave the process uncompleted.

Fourth, the language debate must move beyond the scientific discourse and open up the debate to such things as speculation, reflection, intuition and feelings. Such knowledge should be admitted as equal and no longer, as assumed by modernism, inferior to the knowledge produced by scientific method. After all, it may well be possible that different versions of revived Cornish can appeal to different fragments of society, usually on grounds that have little to do with scientific reason.

The problem with this recognition that, in conditions of post-modernity, we have to live with fragmentation and diversity, is that it might lead to an 'anything goes' approach that institutionalizes divergence. To some extent this danger can be alleviated by avoiding the language of exclusiveness and triumphalism. But it would clearly be naive to expect this to happen overnight, given the frequently bitter and personal attacks that have been hurled across the linguistic barricades over the past decade or so. What is required, therefore, is a recognition of plurality, but within some over-arching unity.[74] This leads to my fifth and final reflection. Institutional reforms are required that might help move the Cornish language movement beyond the structures of modernity that it seems to be sealed into. Some form of over-arching 'umbrella' institution that has a publicity role, co-ordinates grant applications, encourages cooperative ventures and interactive events, while respecting the different versions of revived Cornish, will be essential if the language movement is to overcome its current dilemma.[75]

CONCLUSION

As we approach the end of the century, the future of the Cornish language revival, itself the product of modernity, seems to lie in the ability of those involved in it to reflect on its history and on ways of transcending it. New forms of relating, both internally and to the mainstream of Cornish society, are needed to steer the movement safely through the shoals of postmodernity. For the conditions of postmodernity offer new opportunities too. In the rediscovered emphasis on the 'local', the 'particular' and the 'unique', a space may be being created for the Cornish language that did not exist in conditions of modernity. But to take advantage of that space those active in the language revival will have to realize that the Cornish language is not just a question of phonemes and graphemes; it is part of a wider society, a society that is changing rapidly. It is because of this that the future of Cornish is far too important to be left entirely to the linguists.

NOTES AND REFERENCES

1. The term 'Nancean synthesis' was coined by Tim Saunders, 'Cornish —Symbol and Substance', in Cathal O'Lain, *For A Celtic Future*, Dublin, 1983, pp. 253–58.
2. See, for example, *Cornish Times*, October 1995–January 1996.
3. Philip Payton and Bernard Deacon, 'The Ideology of Language Revival', in Philip Payton (ed.), *Cornwall Since the War: The Contemporary History of a European Region*, Redruth, 1993, and Philip Payton, 'The Ideology of Language Revival in Modern Cornwall', in Ronald Black, William Gillies and Roibeard O'Maolalaigh (eds), *Celtic Connections*, Tuckwell,

Edinburgh, forthcoming 1997. Some key texts of the language debate are Ken George, *The Pronunciation and Spelling of Revived Cornish*, Torpoint, 1986; P.A.S. Pool, 'A Plea for Unified Cornish', *Old Cornwall*, 10.9, 1989; Wella Brown, 'The Reform of Revived Cornish', *Old Cornwall*, 10.9, 1989; Richard Gendall, 'The Language of the Cornish People', *Old Cornwall*, 10.11, 1990.

4. George, 1986, p. 60.
5. N.J.A. Williams, *Cornish Today: An Examination of the Revived Language*, Sutton Coldfield, 1995, p. 159.
6. Williams, 1995, pp. 95–99.
7. Williams, 1995, pp. 111
8. Williams, 1995, p. 168.
9. Williams, 1995, p. 153.
10. L.D.Wacquant, 'Towards a Reflexive Sociology: A Workshop with Pierre Bourdieu', *Sociological Theory*, 7, 1989.
11. Richard Jenkins, *Pierre Bourdieu*, London, 1992, p. 155. This dialectic between the structure and process of language is why Williams' assertion that 'from the ideological point of view languages are completely neutral. People can have value systems, the languages they speak cannot' (Williams, 1995, p. 12) is fundamentally mistaken.
12. cf Jenkins, 1992, pp. 153–154.
13. Nicholas Abercrombie, Stephen Hill, Bryan S.Turner, *Dictionary of Sociology*, London, 1988, pp. 71 and 119.
14. Abercrombie et.al., 1988, pp. 118–119.
15. Payton and Deacon, 1993, p. 273; this is set out at more length in Payton, forthcoming 1997.
16. Payton and Deacon, p. 285.
17. George, 1986, p. 60.
18. Payton, forthcoming 1997.
19. See issues of the magazine *New Cornwall* for the early 1950s.
20. For instance, see the critical review of Payton and Deacon, 1993, in *An Gannas*, 209, 1994.
21. Christopher Norris, *The Truth about Postmodernism*, Oxford, 1993, p. 14.
22. For example, Frederic Jameson, 'Postmodernism of the Cultural Logic of Late Capitalism', *New Left Review*, 146, 1984; Anthony Giddens, *Modernity and Self-Identity: Self and Society in the Late Modern Age*, Cambridge, 1991, p. 10.
23. Barry Smart, *Postmodernity*, London, 1993, p. 12; Zygmunt Bauman, 'Is there a Postmodern Sociology?', *Theory, Culture and Society*, 5, 1988.
24. Steven Connor, *Postmodernist Culture: An Introduction to Theories of the Contemporary*, Oxford, 1989, p. 5.
25. Jameson, 1984, p. 71.
26. See Scott Lash and John Urry, *Economies of Signs and Spaces*, London, 1994.
27. Jean Francois Lyotard, 'Interview', *Theory, Culture and Society*, 5, 1988.

28. Judith Squires, 'Introduction' to Judith Squires (ed.), *Principled Positions: Postmodernism and the Rediscovery of Value*, London, 1993, p. 2.

29. Barry Smart, 'Modernity, Postmodernity and the Present', in Bryan S.Turner, *Theories of Modernity and Postmodernity*, London, 1990, p. 24.

30. Giddens, 1991, pp. 27–28.

31. Immanuel Wallerstein, 'The Challenge of Maturity: Whither Social Science?', *Review*, 15, 1992.

32. Smart, 1993, p. 27.

33. Arnold Toynbee, *A Study of History*, Vol. 8, London, 1954, p. 144.

34. Kenneth Hoover, cited in Pauline Rosenau, 'Modern and Post-modern Science: Some Contrasts', *Review*, 15, 1992.

35. Williams, 1995, p. 168, and N.J.A. Williams, ' "Linguistically Sound Principles": The Case Against Kernewek Kemmyn', in Philip Payton (ed.), *Cornish Studies: Four*, Exeter, 1996.

36. Williams, 1995, p. 168.

37. John Shotter, *Cultural Politics of Everyday Life: Social Constructionism, Rhetoric and Knowing of the Third Kind*, Buckingham, 1993, pp. 26–27.

38. Ken George, 'Which Base for Revived Cornish?', in Philip Payton (ed.), *Cornish Studies: Three*, Exeter, 1995. Selecting Ken George's work as an example of the scientific paradigm should not be taken to imply that it is only his work that suffers from the shortcomings identified here. Similar silences, non-scientific appeals and rhetorical games can be identified in other purportedly scientific texts such as Williams, 1995, or Richard Gendall, *A Student's Grammar of Modern Cornish*, Menheniot, 1991. However, as George is arguably the most prominent of the contemporary writers of the Cornish Revival, his work can be taken as an exemplar.

39. George, 1995, p. 105.

40. George, 1995, p. 117.

41. Tim Saunders and Alan Kent, *Awen*, unpublished ms.

42. George, 1995, p. 111.

43. Ken George, '*Cornish Today*—A Provisional Response', *Kernow*, 34, 1996.

44. Anon (Lowena Sillifant), 'The Great Prosodic Shift', *Kernow*, 34, 1996.

45. George, 1996.

46. Williams, 1995, pp. 96 and 159.

47. George, 1995, p. 117.

48. Payton, forthcoming 1997.

49. Williams, 1995, pp. 13 and 66–67.

50. George, 1995, p. 122.

51. George, 1995, p. 113.

52. Williams, 1995, pp. 111–116.

53. George, 1995, p. 118.

54. George, 1986, p. 4.

55. Cornish Language Board, cited in Ray Edwards, *Kernewek dre Lyther: Kynsa Gradh*, Sutton Coldfield, 1994, p. iii.

56. W. Morris, *Cornish Dictionary Supplement 3: Geryow Divers*, Redruth, 1995, p. 52.

57. Richard Gendall, *1000 Years of Cornish*, Menheniot, 1993, p. 12.
58. Charles Penglase, 'Authenticity in the Revival of Cornish', in Philip Payton (ed.), *Cornish Studies: Two*, Exeter, 1994, p. 96.
59. Williams, 1995, pp. 121 and 134.
60. Tim Saunders, 'Authenticity, Purity and Ideology', *Kernow*, 30, 1995.
61. David Harvey, 'From Space to Place and Back Again: Reflections on the Condition of Postmodernity', in Jon Bird, Barry Curtis, Tim Putnam, George Robertson, Lisa Tickner (eds), *Mapping the Futures: Local Cultures, Global Changes*, London, 1993, p. 12.
62. Charles Dellheim, *The Face of the Past: The Preservation of the Medieval Inheritance in Victorian England*, Cambridge, 1982.
63. Harvey, 1993, p. 12.
64. Jean Baudrillard, *Simulations*, London, 1983, originally published as *Simulacres et Simulation*, Paris, 1981. Thus Baudrillard has made the ironic claim that, in the USA, only Disney is properly authentic, as there are no real worlds left, only images (Baudrillard, *America*, 1989).
65. The disappointment found on discovering that images and 'reality' do not apparently match is also a strong underlying theme in Malcolm Chapman, *The Celts: The Construction of a Myth*, London, 1992; see Tim Saunder's review of Chapman, 'The Celts: The Deconstruction of an Anthropologist', *Kernow*, 34, 1996.
66. Williams, 1995, p. 161 and George, 1995, p. 104.
67. George, 1995, p. 106.
68. George, 1995, p. 118.
69. George, 1995, p. 118; Richard Gendall, *An Curnoack Hethow*, Menheniot, 1992, p. i.
70. George, 1995, p. 118.
71. George, 1996.
72. Payton, forthcoming 1997.
73. J. McGrath, letter to *Cornish Times*, 6 October 1995.
74. Harvey, 1993, p. 16 makes this point about coping with postmodernity in general.
75. The joint publication by Wella Brown, Denise Chubb, Neil Kennedy and Jane Ninnis, *The Cornish Language*, 1991, and the establishment in 1995 of a Cornish sub-committee of the UK committee of the European Bureau for Lesser Used Languages, perhaps point the way forward.

'REFORMING THIRTIES' AND 'HUNGRY FORTIES'—THE GENESIS OF CORNWALL'S EMIGRATION TRADE

Philip Payton

INTRODUCTION

The concept of 'emigration trade' has been developed successfully by Brashay,[1] the term referring not only to the movement of population from one place to another but embracing too the myriad patterns of socio-economic activity that arose in response to this movement. Government officials, shipping agents, local provisioners, newspapers, publicans, coaching operators, clergymen, solicitors and a host of other public and business interests became directly involved in the mechanics of the emigration trade as it emerged in early nineteenth-century Britain. Those areas that experienced emigration on the grand scale found their economies influenced profoundly by this trade. Cornwall was one such area, its burgeoning emigration trade soon matched by a parallel and inter-relating 'emigration culture' which came to dominate Cornish life. By the end of the century the welfare of large sections of the Cornish population—particularly in the mining areas— was dependent upon the labours of their émigrés in distant parts, while the sheer complexity of the emigration process had led to the creation of a briefly significant Cornish international identity.[2]

The existence of an extensive Cornish emigration is generally recognized but the full characteristics of Cornwall's emigration trade are often obscured by two popular half-truths that have come to colour our perceptions of the phenomenon. First of all, there is the insinuation that the emigration was a brief paroxysm of mass departure after the copper crash of 1866, a belief encouraged by Hamilton Jenkin's emphasis upon the 'Exodus of the 'Seventies' and his insistence that

'During this period, the short space of a few years witnessed the breaking-up of a tradition of centuries' as a wave of emigrant Cornish folk, 'answering the call of necessity, was seeking new fields of action overseas'.[3] Secondly, there is the associated view that the Cornish emigration was overwhelmingly and essentially that of copper and tin miners.

The fact is, however, that while changes in the international copper market in the 1860s did precipitate a new era of mass movement, emigration from Cornwall had been noticeable by the 1820s and was already a significant phenomenon by the 1830s and 1840s. Equally, whilst many Cornish emigrants were indeed miners or connected with mining, numerous others were drawn from other occupational categories—particularly from those working on the land.[4] Significantly, much of the early movement—first stirring in the 1820s, and growing apace in subsequent decades—was from the non-mining districts of Cornwall, especially in the north and far north-east where even in the hey-day of Cornish mining the extent of extractive activity was negligible.

FIRST STIRRINGS
The dark days after 1815 triggered this early emigration. In 1822 a 'County meeting' of Cornish landowners at Bodmin called for general reductions in taxes, tithes and rents, the poor harvest of 1829 forcing many from the land, with the *West Briton* noting in April 1832 that 'The rage for emigration that now prevails in the north of this county is wholly unprecedented in Cornwall; in different parishes from 200 to 300 persons each, have either departed or are preparing to leave'.[5] A decade later in February 1843 the *West Briton* noted that rents and taxes were still the principal determinants of emigration from North Cornwall: 'The spirit of emigration continues active in the neighbourhood of Stratton. High rents, heavy rates, and obnoxious and impoverishing taxes are driving some of the best of our agriculturalists to climes where these demons of robbery and ruin are unknown'.[6]

Economic considerations were clearly of significance here but inextricably entwined were political issues and ideological principles, the critical tone of the *West Briton's* reporting reflecting a growing radicalism in Cornwall which was impatient for reform after the period of post-Napoleonic repression. The already profound impact of Nonconformity (given further impetus by the foundation of the radical Bible Christian sect in North Cornwall in 1815) was marshalled to this radicalism as it found itself questioning institutions of Church and State and expressing a desire for religious freedom, social and economic mobility, and civil liberty. For some, there seemed little hope of fulfilling such aspirations at home, with emigration to apparently more progressive societies such as those of the United States or South Australia offering the only way forward. In 1839 one Thomas Sleep from Falmouth wrote home from South Australia to explain that 'none of us desire to return to the bondage which holds our fellow country-men',[7] while in 1840 John Holman wrote from the same colony to his father at South Petherwin in North Cornwall: 'I am freer than when I was in England . . . we would not be back to South Petherwin for £500.'[8] Another Cornishman in South Australia, John Oats, wrote to doubting relatives in Cornwall in exasperated tones: 'if you mind to bind yourself in the chains of slavery all the days of your life, you had better stay where you are.'[9] More than a hint of this link between radical sentiment and emigration was expressed in the poem 'The Cornish Emigrant's Song', written during this period by the Revd. R.S. Hawker—Vicar of Morwenstow in North Cornwall:

Oh! the eastern winds are blowing;
The breezes seem to say.
'We are going, we are going,
To North Americay.

'There the merry bees are humming
Around the poor man's hive;
Parson Kingdon is not coming
To take away the tithe.

'There the yellow corn is growing
Free as the king's highway;
So, we're going, we're going
To North Americay.[10]

Rather more prosaically, Samuel James—a yeoman farmer on the Lizard peninsula in the west of Cornwall—rationalized and articulated his reasons for emigration. Foremost amongst his considerations was the need 'To escape the heavy charges of supporting certain useless institutions'.[11] To this was added the desire 'To escape from supporting a State religion . . . [and] To live under free and useful institutions'.[12] Taking stock of these concerns, James sailed in the *Orient* from Falmouth for New York in April 1842, together with 188 other Cornish folk from the environs of Redruth, Camborne and Helston.

Agricultural depression and political discontent may have been motives for emigration during the 1830s and 1840s, but the fortunes of Cornish mining had relativley little effect at that time. As Deacon has shown,[13] the relative decline of the west Cornish copper mines during those decades was more than matched by the discovery of new deposits on Caradon Hill and in the Tamar Valley, with many miners (often with their families) making the move from West to East Cornwall. However, if the economic state of Cornish mining as yet failed to feature amongst the significant 'push' factors, conditions in the mining areas were certainly of importance, especially during 1845–47 when the failure of the potato crop caused widespread hardship in Cornwall. As William Allen (the emigration agent at Penzance) explained, 'there is great excitement in this county and neighbourhood. Many persons in the Penzance district are preparing to emigrate to South Australia, and amongst them a fair proportion of first rate miners'; a view echoed in the colonial press which reported that 'Mr Allen says business was dull in Cornwall, and as the potato crop in his neighbourhood participated in the general failure, much distress was felt and anticipated.'[14]

POTATO BLIGHT AND MINERS' RIOTS
Curiously, while much energy has been devoted recently to marking the potato famines in Ireland and the Highlands and Islands of Scotland (not least through the scholarly writings of T.M. Devine, Christine Kinealy and others),[15] Cornwall generally has not sought to commemorate its own disaster of 1845–46. Indeed, not only have the potato blight and its effects in Cornwall been ignored in the main by the local media, Cornish schools and other potentially engaged organizations, but there seems also to have been little scholarly interest in the subject amongst academic commentators. Almost universally, recent historians appear to have overlooked the Cornish blight. Todd Gray, for example, has opined that 'the last period of severe food shortages in Cornwall (and Devon) was probably during the 1590s, even then the consequences were not as serious as those caused by the great Irish famine of 1846–51'.[16] Although Cornwall was able to avoid the worst excesses of starvation, emigration was a major safety-valve as it was in Ireland and the Highlands and Islands. The population of Stratton Hundred in north-east Cornwall declined by some ten per cent during the 1840s, and the contemporary observer J.R. Leifchild estimated that in 1849 nearly five per cent of the Penzance Poor Law Union district had emigrated to Australia and New Zealand. As he put it, 'Emigration has tended to keep down the Cornish population'.[17]

The particular impact in the Penzance area, noted by both Allen and Leifchild, reflected the fact that it was the Penwith peninsula that had developed a particular dependency upon the potato crop. As early as 1801, potatoes had become established as a major element in the diet of the mining communities of Marazion, St Just and St Ives,[18] local farmers learning (ironically, from the Irish experience) that potatoes were a useful preparatory crop for barley on heath or bog land. In 1758 Borlase had written that the potato was 'a more useful root'[19] than turnips but Henwood, observing Cornish life a century later, could note with nostalgic regret that 'Until within the last ten years, Cornwall was celebrated for the excellence of its potatoes; these were also abundant and cheap.'[20] In other words, the 'Hungry Forties' had witnessed the fall from grace of the Cornish potato, reducing it (almost) from important staple to fond memory. The *West Briton* had chronicled this demise, noting in July 1846 that

> A correspondent from Lelant informs us that the blight among the potatoe [sic] crops, which occasioned such a sensation last year, has again made its appearance in that neighbourhood; and, according to various reports, he fears it has become extensive . . . thus cutting off from the farmer and poor labourer their hopes of the next year's potatoe crop.[21]

And it was not only in Penwith that the effect of blight was felt. Despite the repeal of the Corn Laws, bad harvests had doubled the price of grain, excacerbating the shortage and distress occasioned by the failure of the potato crop. After the hard winter of 1846–47, bands of angry miners set seige to Cornish towns such as Callington, Launceston, Wadebridge, St Austell, Redruth, Helston, and Penzance to prevent the export of corn and to force 'fair prices'. For example, at Wadebridge in May 1847

> the owners of the corn in the cellars proceeded to ship it on board a vessel . . . when information was received that a large body of men from the Delabole quarries was approaching . . . and soon afer about four hundred men entered the town, and proceeded at once to the Quay . . . [as] a great proportion of the men were really in want of food, the magistrates and others purchased all the bread procurable in the town, and distributed it amongst them, each receiving a part of a loaf on his passing over the bridge on his way home. Most of them had crossed the bridge when a rumour was spread that the party of the preceding day were again at hand. This rumour was soon realised, and between three and four hundred men entered the town, each armed with a bludgeon, and marched on the Quay, cheering as they proceeded. The quarrymen, or most of them, then returned, and mixed with the others (streamers, china clay men, and tinners from Roche, Luxulyan, St Austell, &c.), and when assembled together they presented a most formidable appearance, and created great consternation.[22]

Similarly, A.K. Hamilton Jenkin recorded the reminiscences of an 'old miner' who had been a boy during the Hungry Forties:

> One Saturday I went with my mother to Helston market, and it was pay-day for the miners. I shall never forget what I saw on that Saturday afternoon. Coinage Hall Street was thronged with miners from the bottom to the Market House on the top of the street, all armed with shovel handles and and pick handles. I saw the soldiers march with difficulty up the street; they were about sixty or seventy in number, very young men. They were so pressed by the miners that they could scarcely move along. I saw a gentleman on the Market House steps reading; my mother told me it was the Riot Act. I could not hear what was said because of the tumult. I was told that the commanding officer ordered his men to fire a volley in the air, but they refused, and no wonder. I should think the miners were twenty to one soldier. If they had fired, every man of them would have been killed or disarmed. I saw a great quantity of bread distributed among the hungry crowd.[23]

Another old miner recorded what life was like in Cornwall during the 1840s:

> Everything was very dear and the working people were half starved . . . For our breakfast we had barley gruel, which consisted of about three quarts of water and a halfpenny-worth of skimmed milk thickened with barley flour . . . We lived about half a mile from the mine, and I had to go home to dinner. I . . . was sometimes so feeble that I could scarcely crawl along. For dinner we had sometimes a barley pasty with a bit or two of fat pork . . . and for supper a barley cake or stewed potatoes or turnips with a barley cover.[24]

NEW WORLDS

Although it was conditions in the mining towns rather the fortunes of minng *per se* that constituted the 'push' influences, amongst the 'pull' factors mining featured strongly, with Cornish miners already attracted to Mexico by the 1820s and with the Wisconsin lead mines being opened-up by 1830. Initially, Wisconsin drew many from the neighbourhood of Camborne, Redruth and Illogan, and by 1850 there were as many as 9,000 Cornish at Mineral Point in that State. As early as February 1836 the imminent departure of the *Royal Adelaide* from Falmouth for New York had prompted the comment that this was 'an excellent opportunity for persons wishing to settle at or near Mineral Point'.[25] Soon after, the 'Copper Rush' of 1843 and 1844 drew many from Cornwall and Wisconsin to the Keweenaw district of Michigan, and five years later the discovery of gold in California led to all manner of wild and enthusiastic stories in the Cornish press. Cuba, too, drew its Cornish emigrants (William Whitburn, from Gwennap, lectured on the Cuban copper mines on his return to Redruth in 1839), while the 1830s also saw the arrival of Cornish miners in India.[26] Other places as disparate as South America and New Zealand had by this time also emerged as destinations for emigrant Cornish folk.[27] More particularly, following the foundation of South Australia in 1836 and an initial wave of Cornish emigration to that colony, the discovery of rich copper deposits at Kapunda (1844) and Burra Burra (1845) attracted many Cornish 'Cousin Jacks'. Indeed, the *South Australian Gazette* was by September 1845 suggesting already that the embryonic copper industry of South Australia might come to challenge that of Cornwall:

> The greatest excitement has been produced in Cornwall by the attempt to get rid of the import duty on copper . . . The copper of Chili and Cuba is at present the great bugbear of Cornwall, but these foreign mines, will, by this time, have given partial ground to the rival who has so suddenly started up in an unexpected quarter, ready to supply Britain with copper in unlimited abundance. South Australia, a British Province, with mines worked by Cornish hands, and supported by English capital, has at this moment upon its known surface, and within one hundred miles of port of shipment, copper ore in quantity sufficient to supply one year's consumption of Great Britain.[28]

Significantly, the *Gazette* added that, 'We look forward, indeed, with serious anxiety, not only to the men but to the masters and capitalists of Cornwall transferring their energies to the more rich and generous mines of South Australia.'[29]

'OFFICIAL' EMIGRATION

Amongst other 'pull' factors were the conditions of religious, civil and economic liberty that had supposedly been established in the United States (the 'American Dream') and South Australia (a 'Paradise of Dissent').[30] But purely economic considerations were of course also of importance, not least the prospects of cheap land and free or assisted passages to British colonies such as Upper Canada and (after 1836) South Australia. Indeed, the existence for much of the nineteenth century of a vigorous colonial settlement policy led to the emergence of what might be termed the 'formal' or 'official' government-sponsored emigration trade, its development and progress charted in great detail in the so-called Parliamentary 'Blue Books'.[31] In addition to the General Reports of the Colonial Lands and Emigration Commissioners, these Blue Books contained colonial government reports and miscellaneous colonial correspondence. They reveal, for example, the extent of 'official' emigration from Cornwall to Canada, with details of regular departures from Cornish ports such as Padstow, St Ives, Penzance, Falmouth, Truro, and Fowey, together with data for Plymouth and Bideford from which sailed many East and North Cornwall emigrants.

James-Korany has estimated that at least 42,000 emigrants left Cornwall for Canada between 1831 and 1860, with a peak in 1832 and a further surge during the potato famine of the 1840s.[32] However, this figure must be treated with some caution, for there is evidence that many Cornish emigrants took advantage of Canadian settlement schemes to slip across the border to the United States when once in North America.[33] A fair proportion of the 42,000, therefore, should be counted American rather than Canadian immigrants. Similarly, departure from Cornish ports did not necessarily imply Cornish origins, local harbours often acting as 'staging posts' for emigrants from other parts of Britain. Be that as it may, it is humbling to note that from the port of Padstow alone some 6,200 emigrants sailed to Canada between 1831 and 1860. Indeed, in 1841 Padstow was the third most important departure point for Canada, surpassed only by Liverpool and London.[34] Not surprisingly, Padstow—with its strategic geographical situation half way along the north coast—was a major point of departure for North Cornwall emigrants, particularly between 1829 and 1857. A distinctly Padstonian variant of the emigration trade developed during these years, with emigrant ships sailing for Quebec and returning two or three months later laden with Canadian timber.[35] Ships such as the *Clio*, the *Economist* and the *Springflower* were familiar sights in Padstow harbour at that time, the last-named vessel earning an enduring place in Padstow lore as a result of its extraordinary experience in 1842. Carrying 40 emigrants bound for Canada, the *Springflower* ran into heavy gales some 1400 miles out into the Atlantic and sustained considerable damage. Although so close to her destination, she turned her back to the prevailing wind and, partially dismasted, limped home to Padstow where she was met 'with sympathy and respect'.[36]

As well as drawing attention to the extensive emigration from Cornwall to Canada, the Blue Books also confirm that South Australia was a major destination for Cornish folk in this early period. They indicate, for example, that in the period 1846–50 Cornwall was of all British counties far and away the most important source of South Australian settlers. Some 4775 persons left Cornwall for the colony during those years, the next most significant county being Middlesex with a mere 1412 emigrants. Indeed, 25 per cent of all emigrants from the United Kingdom to South Australia in this period were from Cornwall,[37] establishing a significant and enduring link between the two areas. In later years the statistics were to be equally extraordinary and impressive, as in 1857 when 28.6 per cent of the 3,920 South Australian immigrants were Cornish, or in 1865 when 42.5 per cent of the colony's 4,665 'new chums' were from Cornwall.[38]

The Poor Law Amendment Act of 1834 added potentially a new dimension to the 'official' emigration trade, although curiously Cornwall was slow to make use of the new opportunities for parish-assisted emigration. Cornish parishes might have begun to exploit the system as early as 1836 or 1837, but in fact pauper emigration was hardly measurable until 1841–42 when ten parishes in Cornwall used the scheme to aid some 69 emigrants. After 1843 the system was rarely employed, and in the entire period 1836–47 only 260 pauper emigrants were sent from Cornwall: 123 to Canada, 70 to Australia, and 67 to New Zealand.[39] James-Korany has suggested that the lack of a large landowner/philanthropist class, coupled to the existence of a fiercely independent 'self-help' Nonconformist ideology, might account for this reluctance or inability to resort to pauper emigration. But it should also be recalled that in this period pauperism was itself much less a problem in Cornwall than it was elsewhere in southern Britain. The situation in both Devon and Somerset was far worse than in Cornwall, while Dorset and Wiltshire had amongst the highest levels of pauperism in Great Britain.[40]

The 'official' emigration trade documented in the Blue Books was to a considerable extent facilitated by the appointment of local agents who actively promoted government-sponsored schemes. These agents, in turn, used the local press to communicate with potential emigrants in their various constituencies, furnishing details of ships' sailings and explaining the intricacies of free passage arangements. In the *West Briton* in March 1839, for example, a notice entitled 'Emigration to Sydney, New South Wales' informed readers that a Mr T.H. Edwards of Helston would provide details of free passage to that colony, with the next ship for the Antipodes due to leave Plymouth on 8 April.[41] Similarly, the *West Briton* announced in April 1839 that 'A line of First Class Packet-ships sail punctually every month . . . from London and Plymouth, for Sydney. These ships are from 500 to 800 tons each, with poops, and very superior accommodation for the conveyance of Cabin, Intermediate, Steerage Passengers.'[42] Mr Edwards of Helston was again named as agent, with other emigration agents including William Broad of Falmouth, Charles S. Edsall of Truro, John Oliver of St Teath,

George Jennings of Liskeard, and James Lynn of St Austell. The geographic spread here is interesting, with agents appointed strategically in each of the different parts of Cornwall.

In March 1839 it was reported that Isaac Latimer of Rosewin Row, Truro, a *West Briton* journalist and public figure of some repute, had been appointed agent by the Colonization Commissioners for South Australia.[43] Latimer was immediately a highly visible and energetic propagandist for the colonial cause, contributing effectively to the effort that secured from Cornwall 10 per cent of all applications for free passage to South Australia between 1836 and 1840.[44] In many respects he exemplified the spirit of 'progress' and 'self-improvement' that reflected the vigour of early nineteenth-century Cornwall, particularly the Methodist ethos that had permeated so many aspects of Cornish society and supported emigration as an 'improving' cause and thus helped precipitate the early emergence of Cornwall's emigration culture. In December 1839, for example, Latimer delivered lectures on the art of printing to the 'St Austell Useful Knowledge Society' and the 'Truro Institution', an incidental but telling insight into his commitment to 'improvement'.[45] Together with his colleagues—A.B. Duckham at Falmouth, John Geake at Launceston, and J.B. Wilcocks across the border at Plymouth—Latimer preached tirelessly to the lower classes of Cornish society, seeking 'Every kind of laborer and artizan [who] may, if married, of good character, and within the age prescribed by the Commissioners, obtain a free passage to this flourishing colony.'[46]

MARKETING EMIGRATION

In addition to the newspaper advertisements, Latimer and the other agents also made great use of public meetings as a device to reach their prospective clients, lecturing to large audiences up and down Cornwall in places such as St Austell, Bodmin and Chacewater. In August 1839, for example, it was said of Latimer's meeting at the Market House, St Austell, that 'The place was extremely crowded, by persons from a great distance.'[47] As well as explaining the 'improving' benefits of emigration and detailing the particulars of free passage (even to the extent of carefully elucidating Wakefield's principle of 'systematic colonization'), such meetings were also an opportunity to read impressive testimonials from those who had already gone forth from Cornwall to the colonies. Thus, at the Market House, 'Many letters of the most pleasing nature were read, which had been received from Cornish emigrants, who all spoke in most flattering terms of the province, and invited their friends to come over and join them'[48] in

South Australia. But audiences on occasions took some convincing, and in late 1839 a particular cause of concern for many would-be emigrants was the charge for children made to adults who had otherwise secured free passage to South Australia. As Latimer himself admitted,

> there are hundreds of families, said an intelligent labouring man to me on Monday last at St Austell, across the water (alluding to the parishes of Fowey, Tywardreath, Lanteglos and their neighbourhood) who would be glad to emigrate, who would do anything to pay for their children, but who could not remove from their parish if it cost them a shilling.[49]

To his credit, Latimer took up the issue with the Commissioners, and by the December could place 'South Australia: Important Notice' in the *West Briton*, informing readers that henceforth the children of emigrants would receive free passage so long as 'they are under one, or full seven years of age'[50] at time of embarkation.

As intimated above, letters written home to Cornwall from emigrants in the colonies were powerful propaganda tools in the cause of the 'official' emigration trade. Typically, these letters were used in one or more of four distinct ways. They might be read aloud at the public meetings, or they might find their ways into the correspondence columns of local newspapers (especially the radical, 'improving' *West Briton*, with Latimer on its staff). Additionally, letters would be quoted at length in public posters displayed in towns and villages across Cornwall, and on occasions they could even appear in journals such as the *South Australian News* and the *South Australian Record*, which were published by the Commissioners in Britain to promote emigration to the colonies. One such letter was published in a poster by A.B. Duckham at Falmouth on 24 June 1839, a missive that was realistic but reassuring in its assessment of South Australia, addressing itself frankly to common fears about the climate, the obligations of free emigrants in the colony, and the disposition of the Aborigines. It was also careful to hint at the potential mineral wealth of the province:

> Work, I expect, will be very brisk near winter; the ground then, is soft: plenty of heavy rains fall in the winter, and their [sic] is neither frost or snow; it is is now very warm in the day, but the nights are cold: the summers are very hot, they say; when the wind sets in from the northward, it blows very warm and sultry: it is a fine climate and very healthy . . . an Emigrant is free the moment he lands, he is allowed a home to live in for six months, with 14 days rations; his luggage is brought from the ship to Adelaide, free of expense, to his very door . . . I was out the other day with three

others, unarmed, and met two natives, one called Capt. Jack and
the other Peter, I walked up to them and shook hands, they were
pleased as you like . . . I tell you this to show you how friendly
they are with us: . . . I saw a piece of silver ore about 28lbs weight,
last week, that was picked up by a young man of the name of
James Nichols, who was a shipmate of mine; on the mountains he
traced the load [sic] for a mile, and picked up about thirty pieces
as big as hens egg, all of which he showed me.[51]

Similarly, other letters employed to facilitate the 'official' emigration trade dwelt upon such issues as wages and prices in the colonies,
conditions on-board the emigrant ships, colonial social life, availability
and suitability of land, and—inevitably—the prospects for agriculture
and mining. For example, in November 1839 Mrs E.J. Willoughby from
Newlyn wrote home from Adelaide to her father at St Clement, near
Truro, explaining that in the year she had been in the colony she had
set-up a shop with a turnover of £150 a week. She employed a shop
assistant on £50 per annum, together with a personal maidservant at
£18 a year: 'She is a Cornish girl, from near Launceston.'[52] With her
advice to relatives to join her in the colony, for 'if you are steady and
careful, you could soon make your fortune',[53] it was not surprising that
Mrs Willoughby's letter found its way swiftly into the pages of the *West
Briton*. In the same way, in 1838 a letter from William, Joseph and
James Pedler to their brother Thomas at Perranarworthal was soon
republished in the *South Australian Record:*

> It is with much pleasure that I am able to inform you that, after a
> very pleasant passage of sixteen weeks, we arrived safely here;
> with the appearance of the country and my future prospects I have
> no reason to be dissatisfied. The price of provisions is as follows
> fresh meat, 1s per lb, salt meat 8 1/2d; butter and cheese, from 2s
> to 3s per lb; tea, 4s per lb; coffee, 2s per lb. Taking things as they
> are, I can maintain my wife and four children very comfortably
> for 1 10s per week. Wages for labourers are from 6s to 7s per day;
> contractors for work, 8s to 12s per day; masons and carpenters,
> 10s to 12s per day; sawyers, 15s to 20s per day. I am engaged to
> shoemaking at 2 14s per week. The climate is excellent, especially
> for those of an asthmatic affection; therefore, the only thing that
> makes us uncomfortable is the absence of our families.[54]

Thomas Scown, a builder from Launceston, had emigrated to
South Australia in 1838 in the *Katherine Stewart Forbes*, a ship that in
the years ahead was to appear regularly on the Australian run. Scown
wrote approvingly to his brother that 'This vessel is a most noble ship

for strength, accommodation, and fast sailing . . . we gave our captain, doctor, and mates, and ship's crew, three cheers each when we were asked by the Emigration Agent what causes of complaint we had during our voyage. To you this must be cheering.'[55] Scown also emphasized that the demand for labour in the colony was high, with Cornishmen being especially sought after: 'We have not only given general satisfaction, but other mechanics are surprised at these Cornish operatives. Londoners, in South Australia, are already put by by Cornish men.'[56] Samuel Bray, from Falmouth, commented on the importance of the Methodist church as a vehicle for social relationships in the colony, writing in 1838 that 'We have a chapel as large as Budock Chapel, and about one hundred in society. They held their quarterly meeting on 27th March; we were invited to take tea with them; we went, and enjoyed ourselves very much.'[57] In the following year John Holman wrote home to South Petherwin, enthusing over 'the promised land . . . Hundreds and thousands of acres, uninhabited, looking green as a wheat-field in May, with some clumps of trees, and the ranging hills covered with timber.'[58]

A decade later the prospects, apparently, had not changed, William Rendell of Linkinhorne (near Liskeard) receiving an excited letter from his father in the colony who claimed that 'We have gold, silver, copper and iron mines in abundance . . . [but] Do not think I want you to come out to go mining, for I can put you in a farm, that for the remainder of your life you may live in more ease and comfort.'[59] Other Cornish settlers had also done well, for 'William Tonkin has had this year about 400 bushels of wheat, and will have more next year. The rain is coming down beautifully as I write this.'[60] Thomas Davey, another Cornishman, wrote to a friend at home, explaining that 'I am working at the Burra Burra mine, and my wages is from £3 to £4 a week, and I hope I shall have the pleasure of seeing you out at South Australia, and your sister Mary.'[61] Peter Medland, from Biscovey (near St Blazey), penned his letter with some passion: 'Brother and sister, and neighbours, we wish to let you know what a rich and splendid province this is. There are mines in the province that are worth all Cornwall . . . we should like to see all the miners in Biscovey and Turnpike-gate out here, to have £3 or £4 per week, in such a flourishing country.'[62]

THE LAND OF PROMISE
The cumulative effect of all this correspondence, skilfully woven together and exploited by the emigration agents and other propagandists, was to create in Cornwall not only an enthusiasm for

emigration but also a sense of anticipation and expectation, the community always eager for news of success from its fast-growing body of émigrés overseas. Perhaps for this reason, more negative reports from abroad (the Canadian 'mutinies' in 1837–38, the South Australian recession in the early 1840s) were played down in the press and elsewhere, although on occasions critical letters did appear in the newspapers. For example, James Sawle—from Truro—wrote home with news of what it was like to arrive in Adelaide at the height of the South Australian depression. 'It is necessary that the public should know what to expect on the voyage,' he wrote, for 'hundreds have found a watery grave through the unkindness of those under whose care they have been placed.'[63] One arrived in Adelaide 'exhausted with hunger and fatigue, your dear children crying with hunger and cold' to find that 'We are subject to diseases, painful and distressing; I could name many who left Cornwall who have found a grave in Australia.'[64] As to reports of an abundant demand for labour, 'this is not true . . . it is truly distressing to be out of employ in this place . . . trade is at at a standstill. Do not let any of my neighbours be deceived by false representations.'[65]

Perhaps inevitably, the most harrowing accounts of the emigration experience were left unpublished, their grim reality contrasting too strongly with the plausibility and breathless enthusiasm of the emigration agents. In 1839 the *West Briton* carried a fulsome advertisement for the emigrant ship *Java*, bound for South Australia. She was a 'fine first-class teak-built ship . . . burthen 1,200 tons. This splendid ship's accommodations are unusually spacious and lofty, and are so arranged as to ensure the comfort of the Cabin and Intermediate Passengers . . . She will carry an experienced Surgeon and Assistant.'[66] However, the unpublished account of the *Java's* subsequent voyage (compiled by a Cornish emigrant, George Richards) reveals a different tale: 'no nourishing food on board for the sick . . . the intermediate cabins are insufferably hot . . . great complaints about the provisions'.[67] Crossing the Equator was a barbaric ritual:

> Neptune came on board 7pm . . . The shaving commenced, no respect to persons was paid, those that resisted were treated very bad, had the razor with teeth like a saw applied and bedaubed with tar all over, blind folded, made to take pills of sheeps dung, and bitter Draughts, bled, and thrown into a Cistern of water . . . A French gent was served so bad that he ran into the Cabin and struck the Captain which put an end to such a foolish custom.[68]

A number of children succumbed to disease during the voyage, including Richards' own daughter:

> Dear little Caroline died this morning about 5 am committed to the deep 12 o'clock about 4000 miles West of Australia, for 12 days she made use of nothing but cold water. 3 days before her death when she could eat something we had nothing to give her but Red Herring or Salt Pork which was poison for her complaint.[69]

Emigration agents at home must have been aware of nightmare journeys such as that of the *Java* but in their determination to promote the emigration trade they were prepared to overlook inconvenient difficulties. For example, Isaac Latimer also acted as emigration agent for Van Diemen's Land, but when acting for South Australia this did not prevent him from asserting that 'the vice and demoralization of Australia, has reference only to the penal settlements of New South Wales, Van Diemen's Land, and Norfolk Island . . . the morality of South Australia is secured in every way that can be thought of'![70]

'INFORMAL' EMIGRATION

Alongside the 'official' or 'formal' emigration trade detailed above was a parallel 'unofficial', 'informal' or 'entrepreneurial' trade in which business interests managed their own emigration schemes, usually in support of their particular commercial activities overseas and often to destinations that were not British possessions. An early example of such activity in Cornwall was that of the British mining magnate John Taylor[71] who in the early 1820s contracted with John Rule of Camborne, a Captain at United Mines in Gwennap parish, for Rule to undertake a technical inspection of Mexican silver-lead mines.[72] Rule reported favourably (later becoming a director of the Real del Monte Mining Company) and part of his brief was to recruit like-minded Cornishmen to join him in Mexico. Inevitably, he sought after those whom he had known personally or by reputation (a 'networking' mechanism that was an essential part of many 'informal' emigration schemes), recruiting Cousin Jacks to work as miners, carpenters, sumpmen, engineers, wheelwrights, foundry-men and mill-men. Among them were the Captains James Morcam, John Dalley, and Garby, together with three miners of the names Glasson, Penberthy and Allen.[73] The advance party sailed from Liverpool on 24 March 1824 in the transatlantic packet *Corinthian*; on arrival at New York they chartered a brig to take them to Tampico, and then travelled overland by horse and mule to arrive at Real del Monte on 11 June. Meanwhile, a main party of men and machinery (including Cornish beam engines) had been carefully assembled, the *Western Luminary* noting that 'Great numbers of miners have been engaged'[74] to sail from Falmouth for Mexico, with mine Captains enticed by salaries from £700 to £1000 per annum. As before, Rule's network of contacts was important, the recruits including Henry Tregonning (formerly of United Mines, but then working at Perran Great St George) and John Painter and Thomas Simmons (both from Poldice).

There was a similar 'informal' emigration to the United States and to Central America during this period. In February 1835, for example, the *West Briton* advertised on behalf of the Union Gold Mines in Virginia for an engineer 'competent to erect some steam engines',[75] along with three engine-men, one foreman blacksmith, one foreman mason, one pit-man, and nine sumpmen. Once again, the local network of knowledge and contacts was important, prospective applicants for the posts being invited to get in touch with William Petherick of Redmoor Mine, Callington, or William West at Fowey Consols.[76] In the same way, in 1846 the Boston and Lake Superior Mining Association recruited from Cornwall, employing the offices of the Falmouth merchants, G.C. & R.W. Fox & Company. Included in the team of miners that subsequently sailed from Falmouth was the well-known Captain Henry Clemo.[77] Similarly, John Vivian of St Agnes acted as agent for the Eastern Coast of Central America Commercial and Agricultural Company which was anxious to attract emigrants to work land that it had been granted by the government of the Federal States of Central America.[78] Later, during the Californian gold-rush of 1849, amongst the many prospecting syndicates formed was the Cornwall Association for Streaming of Gold in California. Set-up under the Cornish cost-book system with Joseph Wood of St Austell as its secretary, the Association sought Cornish participants, for 'If ever there was a call for the skilled labour of Cornwall . . . this gold district demands it.'[79]

Cornish shipping interests were also directly involved in this 'informal' trade, it being advertised in March 1837 that the vessel *Caroline* of Gweek (a small harbour on a creek of the Helford River) was due to sail shortly for Philadelphia. Described as an A1, copper-fastened fast sailing ship of 400 tons burthen, the *Caroline* was commanded by John Broad (from his name, probably a Cornishman), with intending emigrants requested to contact the Gweek offices of the Penzance solicitors, Messrs Cornish & Borlase, for details.[80] Elsewhere in Cornwall—such as at Penzance or Boscastle, or Restronguet and Malpas on the Truro River—small harbours and quays were also the scenes of similar 'informal' activity.[81] Often ships were locally-owned and locally-manned and, despite their generally small size, sailed not only for Falmouth or Plymouth (where emigrants might disembark to join larger vessels) but also across the Atlantic to America.

In practice, the distinctions between the 'official' and 'informal' emigration trades were often blurred, especially in Cornwall where the emigration agents enjoyed a complex series of relationships with shipping, mining and land-settlement interests at home and abroad. For example, in 1846 the 'official' emigration agent J.B. Wilcocks recruited 120 emigrants from Cornwall and Devon who sailed from Plymouth in the *David Malcolm* under the auspices of the South Australian Mining Company,[82] the company having specifically sought the services of Wilcocks to assist their endeavours. Other South Australian entre-preneurs also resorted to 'informal' activity, as in 1846 when Captain Richard Rodda (from Penrice, near St Austell) was engaged by a newly-formed mining company to exploit mineral deposits on proper-ties in the Barossa Valley owned by the Scottish capitalist George Fife Angas. Rodda and his team of 80 miners sailed in the *Britannia* and the *Hooghly*, armed with a letter of introduction from Angas to the authorities at Port Adelaide: 'I embrace the present opportunity of introducing to your attention Capt. Richard Rodda who has gone to South Australia with some miners to work the copper lodes in my lands at the Valleys in the Barossa Range, which I have let to the 'Barossa Range Mining Company' on a lease of 21 years.'[83]

Again in South Australia, one interesting instance of this coale-scence between the 'official' and 'informal' emigration trades was the activities of the Cornwall and Devon Society that had emerged by the early 1850s. In contrast to the many overseas Cornish associations that grew up towards the end of the century, the Cornwall and Devon Society was not so much a social-cultural body dedicated to the celebration of Cornwall and Cornishness but rather a pressure group designed to win specific advantages for the Cornish (and Devon) community. Formed by those who had settled in the colony in the late 1830s and 1840s and had assumed positions of importance in its commercial and public life, the Society was led by its secretary John Bentham Neales—the enigmatic Plymothian who had created a con-siderable stir in Cornwall by boasting that from his initial investment of £250 in the Burra Burra mine he had received a dividend of £1000 in the first year. There were two treasurers (one a Cornishman, the other a Devonian!) and the Society's committee included a sprinkling of Adelaide businessmen and a solid body of Cornish mine managers —men such as Captain Henry Roach of Burra Burra, Captain Gundry from North Kapunda, Captain Lean at Wheal Prosper, Captain Rowe at Wheal Barton, Captain Trestrail at the Phoenix Mine, and Captain Trewartha, the Government Mineral Surveyor.[84]

The Society's aims were to 'encourage Emigration direct from the Counties (Cornwall and Devon), devise the best means by which that desirable end can be accomplished, to watch over the interests of Devon and Cornish colonists, and generally to promote harmony and good feeling among them'.[85] In encouraging emigration, the Society used the well-tried device of manipulating its 'informal' network of contacts at home, writing directly to selected mine captains in Cornwall to publicise 'the highly remunerative employment that awaited the skill and enterprise of Cornish miners'.[86] But it also lobbied at 'official' levels, in 1851 petitioning the Governer of the colony for more miners to be brought out from Cornwall. It argued that the creation of homogeneous Cornish mining communities was in the colony's interests for Cornish folk stuck together and understood one another in a way that was not possible with 'foreigners': 'early association and knowledge of each other's habits and character are calculated to preserve the best moral restraint on the conduct of all'.[87] The Society also requested that more emigrant ships be sent directly from Cornish ports.

CONCLUSION

The Governer replied by pointing out that between June 1850 and May 1851, one-seventh of all colonists despatched from the United Kingdom to South Australia were Cornish miners. Indeed, the very existence of the Cornwall and Devon Society was a measure of both the extent of emigration from Cornwall in the preceding decades and the level of sophistication that the Cornish emigration trade had by now achieved. Its international networking complemented the 'official' and 'informal' activities in Cornwall itself, activities that spanned the work of emigration agents, shipping operators, improvement societies, local newspapers, and a whole range of other practitioners and participants. Moreover, this early period had laid the institutional and psychological foundations for the further development of Cornwall's emigration culture in response to the unfolding crisis of the Cornish economy in the second half of the nineteenth century. When, in the mid and late 1860s, the crash of Cornish copper created widespread unemployment in the mining communities, Cornish society was well placed to turn to the cause of emigration as a means of relieving distress at home.[88]

NOTES AND REFERENCES
1. Mark Brayshay, 'The Emigration Trade in Nineteenth-Century Devon', in Michael Duffy, Stephen Fisher, Basil Greenhill, David Starkey, Joyce

Youings (eds.), *The New Maritime History of Devon; Vol. 2: From the Late Eighteenth Century to the Present Day*, London, 1994.

2. Philip Payton, *The Making of Modern Cornwall: Historical Experience and the Persistence of 'Difference'*, Redruth, 1992, see especially chapter 5.

3. A.K. Hamilton Jenkin, *The Cornish Miner*, 1927, new edn. Newton Abbot, 1972, p. 321.

4. For example, see Philip Payton, *The Cornish Farmer in Australia*, Redruth, 1987.

5. *West Briton*, 6 April 1832.

6. *West Briton*, 17 February 1843.

7. *South Australian Record*, 11 September 1839.

8. *South Australian Record*, 30 May 1840.

9. *South Australian News*, September 1847.

10. R.S.Hawker, 'The Cornish Emigrant's Song', in A.L. Rowse (ed.), *A Cornish Anthology*, 1968, new edn. Penzance, 1982, p. 6. Ironically, Hawker was himself a High Church Anglo-Catholic.

11. A.C.Todd with David James, *Ever Westward the Land*, Exeter, 1986, p. 9.

12. Todd and James, 1986, p. 9.

13. Bernard Deacon, *Migration and the Mining Industry in East Cornwall in the Mid-Nineteenth Century*, Exeter, 1985.

14. *South Australian Register*, 20 March 1847.

15. T.M. Devine, *The Great Famine*, Edinburgh, 1988; T.M. Devine, *Clanship to Crofters' War: The Social Transformation of the Scottish Highlands*, Manchester, 1994; Christine Kinealy, *This Great Calamity: The Irish Famine 1845–52*, London, 1994.

16. Todd Gray, *Harvest Failure in Cornwall and Devon: The Book of Orders and the Corn Surveys of 1623 and 1630–31*, Redruth, 1992, p. xi.

17. J.R. Leifchild, *Cornwall: Its Mines and Miners*, 1857, repub. Newcastle-upon-Tyne, 1968, p. 270.

18. Mark Overton, 'The 1801 Crop Returns for Cornwall', in Michael Havinden (ed.), *Husbandry and Marketing in the South West 1500–1800*, Exeter, 1973, p. 56.

19. John Rowe, *Cornwall in the Age of the Industrial Revolution*, Liverpool, 1953, repub. St Austell, 1993, p. 231.

20. Roger Burt (ed.), *Cornwall's Mines and Miners*, Truro, 1972, p. 72.

21. *West Briton*, 17 July 1846.

22. *West Briton*, 21 May 1847.

24. Hamilton Jenkin, 1927 and 1972, p. 287.

24. T. Oliver, *Autobiography of a Cornish Miner*, nd, cited in Hamilton Jenkin, 1927 and 1972, p. 251.

25. *West Briton*, 12 February 1836.

26. *West Briton*, 29 November 1839, 6 December 1839.

27. *West Briton*, 28 February 1840, 6 March 1840.

28. *South Australian Gazette & Colonial Register*, 20 September 1845.

29. *South Australian Gazette & Colonial Register*, 20 September 1845.

30. Payton, 1992, p. 109.

31. See Margaret James-Korany, "Blue Books" as Sources for Cornish Emigration History', in Philip Payton (ed.), *Cornish Studies: One*, Exeter, 1993.
32. James-Korany, 1993.
33. John Rowe, *The Hard-rock Men: Cornish Immigrants and the North American Mining Frontier*, Liverpool, 1974, p. 50.
34. James-Korany, 1993.
35. Donald R.Rawe and Jack Ingrey, *Padstow and District*, Padstow, 1984, p. 30; cf Ann Giffard, *Towards Quebec*, London, 1981.
36. Rawe and Ingrey, 1984.
37. James-Korany, 1993.
38. Payton, 1987, pp. 114–115.
39. Korany-Jones, 1993.
40. John Langton and R. J. Morris, *Atlas of Industrializing Britain 1780–1914*, London, 1986, p. 161.
41. *West Briton*, 1 March 1839.
42. *West Briton*, 12 April 1839.
43. *West Briton*, 4 March 1839.
44. Payton, 1987, p. 114.
45. *West Briton*, 6 December 1839.
46. *West Briton*, 13 September 1839.
47. *West Briton*, 30 August 1839.
48. *West Briton*, 30 August 1839.
39. *West Briton*, 13 September 1839.
50. *West Briton*, 27 December 1839.
51. State Archives of South Australia (SAA), PRG 174 *George Fife Angas Papers*, SA Colonial Commission 666, Letter from Marmaduke Laurimer to his mother in Falmouth.
52. *West Briton*, 29 April 1840.
53. *West Briton*, 29 April 1840.
54. *South Australian Record*, 11 July 1838.
55. *South Australian Record*, 12 September 1838, 10 October 1838.
56. *South Australian Record*, 10 October 1838.
57. *South Australian Record*, 2 December 1839.
58. *South Australian Record*, 20 October 1839.
59. *South Australian News*, April 1847.
60. *South Australian News*, April 1847.
61. *South Australian News*, December 1847.
62. *South Australian News*, January 1848.
63. SAA PRG 174, Letter from James Sawle to his Brother.
64. SAA PRG 174, Letter from James Sawle to his Brother.
65. SAA PRG 174, Letter from James Sawle to his Brother.
66. *West Briton*, 20 September 1839.
67. SAA D4718L *Journal of a Voyage to South Australia* by George Richards.
68. SAA D4718L
69. SAA D4718L

70. *West Briton*, 13 September 1839.
71. see Roger Burt, *John Taylor: Mining Entrepreneur and Engineer 1779–1863*, Buxton, 1977.
72. A.C. Todd, *The Search for Silver: Cornish Miners in Mexico 1824–1947*, Padstow, 1977, pp. 33–34.
73. Todd, 1977, p. 34.
74. *Western Luminary*, 22 February 1925.
75. *West Briton*, 13 February 1835.
76. *West Briton*, 13 February 1835.
77. Rowe, 1974, p. 71.
78. *West Briton*, 6 March 1840.
79. *West Briton*, 1 January 1849.
80. *West Briton*, 10 March 1837.
81. D.B. Barton, *A History of Tin Mining and Smelting in Cornwall*, Truro, 1967, repub. Exeter, 1989, p. 85.
82. SAA 313 *Passenger Lists*, Letter from J. B. Wilcocks, 1846.
83. SAA 94 *Letters, Chiefly Commercial, from James and Robert Frew*, 7 May 1846, G. F. Angas to R. Frew.
84. *South Australian Register*, 1 January 1851.
85. *South Australian Register*, 1 January 1851.
86. *South Australian Register*, 8 January 1851.
87. La Trobe Library, *Despatch: Cornwall and Devon Society to Young, Memorial as to Emigration of Cornish Miners*, Despatch No 19, 31 January 1851.
88. Philip Payton, 'Cornish Emigration in Response to Changes in the International Copper Market in the 1860s', in Philip Payton (ed.), *Cornish Studies: Three*, Exeter, 1995.

A CENTURY OF CENTRALIZATION: CORNISH HEALTH AND HEALTHCARE

Rod Sheaff

INTRODUCTION

Analyses of health and healthcare from a Cornish Studies perspective must surely start by asking: What are the peculiar characteristics of the Cornish health system and how did they originate?; how (if at all) are they linked to Cornwall's 'peripheral' status?; and what implications do they have for health policy analysts and Cornish Studies alike? One way to address these questions is by reviewing the history of health and healthcare in Cornwall.

TRADITIONAL HEALTHCARE

Only meagre and fragmentary knowledge remains of 'traditional' pre-scientific healthcare in Cornwall, and once one steps beyond these fragments it becomes very hazardous to try to reconstruct the corresponding belief-systems about aetiologies, diagnostic categories and treatments. Certain aspects of traditional Cornish medicine have parallels recorded surprisingly far afield, indeed well-nigh universally. Among these are the medicinal use of herbs (in Cornwall, including seaweed) and prognosis by astrology.[1] Medicinal uses of what Fraser called 'contagious magic' and 'sympathetic magic' have been documented in many societies.[2] A Cornish treatment for warts was to bury the ninth pea from a pod, or a piece of meat. The reason for this treatment is known and clearly uses 'contagious magic': as the pea or meat decayed, so would the wart.[3] Perhaps this reasoning that disease could be transferred by physical contact from the patient to some other body was involved in attempts to cure warts by touching them with the hand of a dead child. A presumably equally ancient belief was in the sacrifice of live animals to cure an illness, one surviving well into this century and reflected in such practices as cutting a live pigeon in two and placing the halves against the soles of the patient's feet; or of a man trying to treat his lumbago by killing a cat and wearing the skin on his back; and even the sacrifice of live animals by fire.[4] Hamilton Jenkin recorded the beliefs that a person could not easily die when lying 'athwart the planshun', and that opening windows and doors would ease his passing; possibly a form of belief in sympathetic magic.[5]

Hardly surprisingly, many elements of traditional Cornish medicine have close parallels in other Celtic cultures. Two pan-Celtic beliefs about health and ill-health concerned the curative powers of holy wells and of certain stones. Some Cornish holy wells were held to have specific powers: those of Chapel Farm (St Breward), Castle Horneck (Madron) and Joan's Pitcher (Lewannick) were believed efficacious for sore eyes; Alsia well (St Buryan) and St Piran's well (Perranzabuloe) for rickets; Cubert and Madron wells for children's diseases. More generic curative powers were attributed to Constantine's well at St Merryn, Dupath, Lady Wells (Mevagissey) and Nance (Colan).[6] St Nun's well at Altarnun and a now-lost well at Camborne were thought to cure insanity. In 1602 Carew described 'bowsenning' of the insane:

> The water running from St Nunn's well fell into a square and close walled plot, which might well be filled at what depth they listed. Upon this wall was the frantic person set to stand, his back towards the pool, and from thence with a sudden blow in the breast tumbled headlong into the pond, where a strong fellow, provided for the nonce, took him and tossed him up and down, alongst and athwart the water. Then he was conveyed to the church, and certain masses sung over him . . . if there appeared small amendment he was bowssened again and again, while there remained in him any hope of life for recovery.[7]

Similar treatments were still used in eighteenth-century France and Brittany, to dissolve the extravagant ideas of the insane by the combined effects of shock and purification. The Bretons also attributed curative powers to certain dolmens and menhirs but the Penwith custom of passing through the hole in the central stone at Men-an-Tol to cure rickets is the only, albeit well known, Cornish parallel.[8]

An apparently more distinctively Cornish belief was that an 'ill-wisher' could cause illness (amongst other misfortunes). A remedy was for the patient or his relative to draw the ill-wisher's blood but to do this one had first to discover who the ill-wisher was. Here 'conjurers' and 'pellars' (Cornish: *peller*) could assist, besides being supposedly able to prognosticate the outcome of the sickness. John Stevens, a Polperro shoemaker, has been recorded as someone claiming such powers and some pellars, for instance one Anne Jeffries, claimed they could enlist the aid of pyskies in curing distempers, sickness, sores, agues, falling-sickness and broken bones.[9] In the nineteenth century we find more baffling reports such as the belief that wearing the colour yellow would exacerbate rheumatism or lumbago. To cure a range of sicknesses that included bleeding, ringworm, thrush, deafness, warts, sore eyes, shingles, epilepsy and scrofula various charms were in use, varying from the macabre (e.g. keeping a piece of used hangman's noose in a bag around one's neck) to the bizarre (e.g. swallowing a rolled ball of spiders' webs to cure asthma). No less interesting is the fact that such beliefs appear to have been widely held until well into the last century. Indeed, traditional healers continued functioning into early this century.[10]

Besides shedding a somewhat faint light on pre-scientific beliefs about the body, health and illness these traditions also give clues to the symptoms, of ill-health which were apparently common enough in pre-industrial Cornwall for people to devise standard methods of treatment: rheumatism was evidently common as were skin diseases, as well as those conditions noted above. Carew recorded the existence of lazar-houses, implying that leprosy was also rife in medieval Cornwall. Plague seems to have been rare in Cornwall but devastating when it did occur. One can only conjecture that the pressure on agricultural land immediately before the Black Death may have caused food shortages and hence an even lower level of resistance to that disease than would have been normal in medieval times. A later plague killed about half the population of St Ives in 1647. Whatever results the Tudor Poor Laws may have achieved in stimulating parochial provision of a few forms of rudimentary health and social care in England, their effect in Cornwall appears to have been minimal. Perhaps this is not surprising in light of the difficulties English governments had in governing Cornwall during the sixteenth century. Indeed, the English state, as opposed to individual Cornish gentlemen, played almost no part in Cornish healthcare until the onset of industrialization.[11]

INDUSTRIALIZATION
More scientific and organized approaches to health and healthcare followed industrialization. Hard-rock tin-mining produced characteristic forms of occupational ill-health. Silicosis and phthisis were evidently prevalent among mid eighteenth-century tin-miners and

perhaps even more so among copper-miners (because they used dry stamping of ore as opposed to wet stamping for tin); so too were cardiac and pulmonary diseases which would have been exacerbated by the punishing ladder-climbs to and from workface and the by high temperatures at the bottom of Cornish mines—often 30 degrees Celsius or more. Traumas were common. Premature explosions were prone to result in eye injuries, and occasinally loss of limbs. By the middle of the nineteenth century things were little better. In 1857 the average age of underground miners at Balleswidden was 29 years and 4 months, at Levant 28 years 10 months, at Ding Dong 26 years 1 month. Contemporary reports give the mean age of miners' deaths as 47 (St Just 1837–56) or as 43 years 5 months (St Agnes). Cases of typhoid were also attributed to the quality of water in the mines.[12]

Miners were the extreme case when it came to occupational ill-health but life-expectancy was apparently little better for Cornish farm-workers. In St Agnes in 1859–61 their mean age of death was 55 years and 5 months, only a year longer than miners there. Separate data on the health status of farmers and fishermen seem to be rare however, usually being simply subsumed in general figures (where even these exist) for whole populations. Such figures reflected diseases of poverty, resulting from insanitary housing and diets of a sparsity almost unimaginable today. At the worst times (e.g. the 1840s) the poorest families would eat little or nothing for several days at a time. Poor housing appears to have contributed to accidental injuries (through scaldings, building collapse etc.) as did the recreations hurling and wrestling. Measles, smallpox, diphtheria, typhoid, maternal mortality, whooping cough, influenza and typhus appear to have been common causes of death. Poverty was an incentive to send children to work at young ages, with a corresponding reduction in life expectancy. Mean age at death was recorded in 1848 as ranging from 42 years and 11 months in Liskeard and the St Germans district, down to 28 years 4 months in the mining area of Redruth. One, but not the only, reason for such low figures was the high level of infant and child mortality. Couch estimated that in 1857 64.07% of males and 45.73% of females died before the age of five. At St Cleer the proportion of burials of males under the age of five rose from 6/31 in 1813–9 to 130/259 in 1850–9; of females under 5, from 2/37 in 1813–9 to 103/214 in 1850–9. Corresponding figures for St Just-in-Penwith during 1840–9 were 261/600 for males and 220/477 for females.[13]

Cholera was a chronic public health problem in Cornwall until the late nineteenth century. Outbreaks occurred in places as dispersed as Newlyn in October 1832, Falmouth in 1833, Mevagissey and Calstock in the summer of 1849; and throughout Cornwall during 1838.[14]

Unfortunately for fisherman, fish were widely believed to be a source of the disease and there was one (rather unsuccessful) attempt to close Falmouth fish market as a result. By 1833 the former Stannary prison at Lostwithiel had been refitted as a cholera hospital. Typhus broke out in Penzance in 1822 and typhoid in Liskeard seventy years later. No less common—and perhaps connected—were complaints that Cornish local authorities were neglecting such health risks as the scattered bones in Crantock graveyard and the haphazard disposal of sewage and of organic waste from slaughterhouses. In the mid-nineteenth century there were still complaints of poor sanitation in Camborne and Padstow, and similar complaints about St Neot, Callington and East Looe in 1890.[15]

Mains drainage was partly introduced in Truro during 1853 but a strong stomach is still needed when reading about the lack of hygiene at one Falmouth ice-cream maker's ('hokey factory') over forty years later. The quality of water supplies was equally haphazard. Two centuries earlier Carew had complained that in Bodmin 'their conduit water runneth through the churchyard, the ordinary place of burial for town and parish. It breedeth little cause of marvel, that every general infection is here first admitted and last excluded.' In the 1830s a leat providing drinking water in Truro made its way near or through kennels, stables and dyers. Marazion received a piped water supply in 1878, whilst that in Redruth was upgraded nine years later. An underground supply was laid-in within Dolcoath mine itself but Charlestown still had none even in 1893.[16]

By far the most effective healthcare in such conditions is to address the underlying causes of ill-health—poverty at home and poor working conditions; a matter for policy-makers and preventive measures rather than the individual doctor or nurse treating the casualties at the bedside. Regular public health reports for Cornwall began in 1912 but what is probably Cornwall's biggest contribution to public health appears at first sight almost trivial: Andrew Pears of Mevagissey invented a new soap which became one of the most widely-used brands in nineteenth-century Britain. Theoretically, vaccination for smallpox became compulsory in 1853 but in Bodmin at least it was suspected that the Public Vaccinator had charged for hundreds of vaccinations he never performed. Lax vaccinators may not have been entirely to blame though; Andrews records that Cornish people then were rather sceptical about the benefits of vaccination. Outbreaks of smallpox occurred near Gwennap the following year and around Redruth in 1858.[17]

As for occupational health shareholders and employers objected that preventive health and safety measures were impossibly burdensome and would bankrupt (in this case) the Cornish mines. Nevertheless, the installation of man-engines did prove feasible and where used were probably the most important occupational health improvement in Cornish mines until after 1918. Some mines had friendly societies for miners' widows, orphans and sometimes for sick or injured miners. In the eastern mining districts (around Caradon) a Miners' Mutual Benefit Association provided pensions for 'worn-out' miners and those blinded by mining accidents, in return for payment of weekly subscriptions over five or more years. Elsewhere, many miners paid a small weekly sum to receive, at need, the bal-surgeon's attentions. Some general charities also provided financial relief during times of sickness.[18]

Primary healthcare at this time consisted largely of self-care on the traditional lines noted above or dosing oneself with patent medicines. Among the more colourfully-marketed drugs in nineteenth-century Cornwall were 'Solomon's drops' for various skin diseases; cephalic snuff, Ching's worm lozenges and Rozeate Powder for Superfluous Hair; Lane's Haemacathartic Tincture for scrofula, cancer, leprosy and scurvy; and Dr Boerehaave's Infallible Red Pill. More dismally, the Poor Laws required mothers of illegitimate children to declare the the name of the father who had then to indemnify the parish for the cost of rearing the child, on pain of imprisonment if he refused. For this reason, and in the more repressive moral climate of that time, illegitimate births were often concealed. Women sometimes gave birth unattended, even in fields, and infanticide remained a major form of birth control in Cornwall as in England.[19]

What are nowadays more conventional cures, or rather treatments, were provided by the familiar figures of the apothecary, barber-surgeon and doctor, although even at best doctoring was apparently a far-from-lucrative occupation. Therapies ranged from leeches through home surgery to the new 'electrical treatment'. Some doctors and surgeons would see poor patients free of charge but Mr Dove of St Austell was not unusual in requiring a referral letter from 'some respectable person' confirming that the patient was both 'a proper object and in indigent circumstances'. Itinerant doctors also plied such trades as the analysis of urine although some were evidently regarded as quacks by their more settled contemporaries. Similarly for dentistry; the nineteenth-century Cornishman could either treat himself through such methods as the self-application of 'plastic' artificial enamel or resort to itinerant tooth-pullers at fairs and markets, or even have artificial or human teeth transplanted onto his own 'stumps'.[20]

Many British hospitals originated as the hospital wings of work-houses, turning after 1929 into local authority hospitals and taking over the former workhouse buildings. Cornish Poor Houses also functioned as local hospitals for long-stay patients (often mentally ill or elderly) who had no other resort. Possibly because of Cornwall's relative economic diversity then, with many working people able to move between work in mining, fishing and agriculture, the economic hardships of the early 19th century, although still severe, did not produce the riots and violent demonstrations directed against workhouses that occurred in many English industrial regions (e.g. around Manchester) during the 1830s and 1840s. Rowe points out that the riots in Stratton and the use of troops to protect Poor Law Commissioner Gilbert during his visit in 1837 occurred in what was then the most purely agricultural part of Cornwall. Yet violent demonstrations against the ending of outdoor relief also occurred in St Ives.[21] Cornwall also had voluntary hospitals. Although the Cornwall (later Royal Cornwall) Infirmary reported 100 per cent occupancy as early as May 1812, this was on a tiny scale. A hospital in Falmouth for disabled merchant seamen and their widows had 70 occupants by 1825. Its annual report for 1820–1 stated that the Penzance Dispensary had treated 639 patients, of whom 347 were cured, 172 'relieved', 13 had been 'discharged irregular', 18 had died and 90 were still 'on the books'; Penzance Dispensary, incidentally, seems to have anticipated Florence Nightingale's 'cured/relieved/dead' categorization of healthcare outcomes by some thirty years.[22]

Considering the risks of transporting a seriously ill or injured person in nineteenth-century Cornwall (the *West Briton* of 29 January 1819 reports how John Jewel died whilst attempting to walk home from Camborne to Wendron after breaking his arm in a mining accident), together with the workhouse regime and the mainly ineffective therapies available then, it is perhaps less surprising than first appears that many Cornish people of the time were unsympathetic to proposals to establish hospitals. Many Redruth miners, for example, were indifferent or even hostile to proposals in the 1840s to set up a hospital in the district. Older people's reluctance to report any contact with TB or to present for screening were still being reported in the late 1950s.[23] Suspicion of former workhouses and asylums was especially deep-rooted, as the author can attest from some of his own elderly relatives' remarks about Bodmin and Barncoose. From the early nineteenth century there survive reports of the chaining of mental patients in Cornish workhouses, although such regimes were becoming obsolete some twenty years earlier.[24] Proposals to establish a Cornwall lunatic asylum at Bodmin for pauper patients were first voiced in 1810. St Lawrence's appears to have been well managed by the standards of its day, and down to the present seems to have avoided the worst excesses of staff neglect, even abuse, of mental patients found in the worst parts of the English system. (Sedgwick describes a case in which Cornish hospitals accepted as an involuntary patient a man convicted of manslaughter, against whose admission staff in a Bristol mental hospital had threatened to strike, even though that would have resulted in the man's imprisonment). Nevertheless, until the 1950s little could be done for such patients other than contain their more extravagant behaviours. A combined effect of the stigma of asylum confinement and the cost of travel from elsewhere in Cornwall was that many patients, some of whom would stay there for decades, were seldom visited by relatives or friends.[25]

CORNWALL AND THE ENGLISH NATIONAL HEALTH SYSTEM

The creation of the National Health Service (NHS) has gradually accelerated the centralization of the UK health system as a whole. 'Accelerated', not 'initiated'. In Cornwall this centralizing process can be traced back to the nineteenth-century Poor Laws which introduced a system for the provision of (amongst other things) some forms of healthcare which was standard for the rest of the UK. Subsequent legislation (the 1858 Medical Act; the 1848 and 1875 Public Health Acts; the 1845 and 1890 Lunacy Acts) reinforced the standardizing tendency, as did the introduction of National Health Insurance for the provision of GP services for workers in 1911. State involvement in healthcare extended piecemeal from legislation to licensing practitioners and to stipulating how certain long-stay hospital services were to be funded, then to actually funding general practice and, finally, with the NHS, to actually providing and managing nearly all health services. Implementing the wartime Emergency Medical Service in 1939 was a critical step because it led to Cornish health services first being planned, and after 1947 managed too, as one element of a regional structure encompassing the south-western one-fourteenth of the English NHS. Since 1974 repeated NHS reorganizations have established ever more complex and stringent mechanisms for financing, managing, regulating and reforming the Cornish health system as a peripheral element in an ever more centralized English health system. In 1996 Cornwall became part of an amalgamated South West and Wessex Region nearly twice the size of the former South Western RHA and now a branch of the English NHS Executive, not a nominally independent Regional Health Authority. This burgeoning of the state's role was of course actuated by UK rather than Cornish policy interests. Throughout, 'the state' meant 'the state at UK rather than Cornish level'. In contemporary

Europe, the UK health system is unusual because local government plays so small a role; since the creation of the NHS in 1947 there has been slight—and diminishing—scope for Cornish local authorities autonomously to differentiate their health services and health policy to meet local healthcare needs. Since 1947 this centralizing process has been manifest in the area of hospital development, political control of the health system, and the successive structural reorganizations of the NHS.

Traces of the dispersed, small-scale pre-NHS pattern of Cornish hospital services are still evident. They reflect the distinctive Cornish pattern of settlement with only a third of the population living in towns of over 10,000 residents, only one conurbation bigger than 40,000 and a comparatively even distribution of villages and hamlets.[26] The NHS has converted some of these local hospitals to provide rehabilitative or long-term social care. Others have continued as GP hospitals, a role closer to that for which they were originally conceived. Twenty-six small (i.e. below 125 beds) old hospitals, or former hospitals, one NHS-built centre, and two private acute hospitals (also small) were functioning in 1996. From 1962 NHS policy favoured centralizing hospital services in District General Hospitals (DGHs). NHS opinion as to what size of DGH was necessary to support a comprehensive range of specialities at local level, and how big a catchment population was necessary for such a hospital to operate economically, fluctuated over the years. Initially DGHs for a population of 100,000 to 150,000 were favoured, a figure later increased to 200,000–300,000. By the 1980s it was assumed that the optimum catchment was one Health District, with a population usually in the range 200,000 to 500,000. By this reckoning the Cornish population of 486,000 (1995) warranted only one DGH. After considerable debate within the NHS as to whether it should be sited at Truro (as Cornwall's administrative centre) or Redruth (as the main industrial centre) Treliske in Truro was developed as a standard DGH. The latest of its five phases of construction continues during 1996, having resulted so far in 598 beds covering most acute specialties. Opening this extra in-patient capacity appears, however, to pose questions about the future of West Cornwall Hospital (Penzance), as the original project did about the future of maternity services at Redruth and acute hospital services in Falmouth, at the old Royal Cornwall Infirmary (Truro) and elsewhere.[27]

This gradual centralization of hospital services and the summer congestion of Cornish roads make helicopter ambulances seem, at first sight, especially apt for Cornish conditions. As one of the first in the UK, the Cornish air ambulance aroused some discussion in the UK health press, and much local publicity. Surprisingly, an initial study suggested that speed of delivery of patient to hospital was much the same as by road and that subsequent improvements were not great enough to make much clinical difference to the patient's prospects. Strangely, the air ambulance appears during its first year to have taken longer to reach patients than a land ambulance would but has got the patient to hospital more quickly. However, air ambulance supporters point out its flexibility and acceptability to patients.[28]

Cornish geography also resists the DGH model in another way. Long before the NHS there were cross-boundary flows of east Cornish patients to hospitals in Plymouth and beyond. For a period this 'Overlap Area' became officially part of Plymouth AHA and is still referred to in local NHS working practice. One effect of GP fund-holding has been to intensify this long-standing competition between the Cornish and Plymouth NHS trusts for patients from that overlap area. Nowadays approximately a third of Cornish residents use Devon health services: especially North Devon Healthcare Trust (Barnstaple), Plymouth Community Services NHS Trust, Exeter and Devon Community Health Services Trust (for child, family and forensic psychiatry), and, above all, Plymouth Hospitals NHS Trust (mainly Derriford, the DGH for Plymouth, and Freedom Fields). In some specialities—e.g. plastic surgery, neurosurgery—Derriford takes all Cornish caseload. This tendency is likely to increase since some tertiary referrals to London, e.g. those for certain specialist cardiac treatments, will revert to Plymouth when new facilities open in Derriford. Adding up all kinds of units of activity for 1995 gives a total of 145,267 contacts for Cornish patients in Derriford. Numbers of contacts do not, however, equal numbers of patients; one patient may make several contacts. For instance, the 3130 obstetrics units of activity cover only 1400 inpatients. Another bizarre, if nominal, transfer of Cornish patients to Devon services came when NHS non-General Practitioner (GP) assets on the Isles of Scilly were transferred to the Plymouth NHS trust for community services during 1995–6.

At first sight, the policy of replacing institutionalized care of people with learning difficulties and long-term physical and mental illness with community care might seem a counter-example to this centralizing tendency. After all, similar policies have been pursued on technical, therapeutic grounds in many European countries and it is a policy to which the small, dispersed health facilities which historically developed in Cornwall are well adapted. Even community care, however, has been in large measure implemented in response to the increasingly central-ized line-command relationship between Health Authorities and (since 1991) NHS trusts (locally) and the NHS Executive and Department of Health (in London and Leeds). Cornish NHS bodies have functioned as peripheral implementers of central NHS Executive policy, much as their non-Cornish equivalents have. In this respect community care differs little from the implementation of general management, from establishing NHS Trusts (starting with Cornwall Mental Health and Eldercare in the 1992 'first wave'), from the policy of replacing inpatient with outpatient care, and from the introduction of GP fundholding. Eleven Cornish general practices (out of 78) were listed as standard fundholding practices by 1995, covering some 30 per cent of Cornish residents, with another three practices planned to become fundholders in April 1996.[29] As yet (early 1996) there are no multifunds, community fundholders or total fundholders, although proposals for a pilot scheme for total purchasing fundholding at Saltash Health Centre are under discussion, and a group of non-fundholding GPs in south east Cornwall collaborate to influence the purchase of hospital services for their patients.

Doubtless, the recruitment of managers for Cornish NHS posts from a UK-wide labour market for NHS managers has assisted the centralizing process. When Treliske opened (1966) all its new managers were, as a matter of policy, recruited through UK-wide competition, with the great majority coming from outside Cornwall. Since then this tendency has spread upwards to Health Authority and Trust Board membership, with such matters becoming much more politicized during the 1980s. A recent Cornish *cause célèbre* was the controversial appointment and swift ousting of Abigail Kirby-Harris as chair of Cornwall Healthcare Trust. A striking feature of the out-of-court settlements made with both her and her predecessor is the Department of Health's apparent concern to keep Ministers out of the witness box and to silence any future public comment or criticism by either litigant.[30]

Whatever Cornish readers might think of this centralization, it has brought some concrete benefits to set against the loss of Cornish distinctiveness and autonomy in health policy. Outside Britain, the English model of general practice is generally regarded as advantageous, providing universal access to comparatively well-trained generalists who can manage most everyday presentations of ill-health; gatekeeping access to hospitals, preventing unnecessary use of specialists with concomitant higher levels of investigation, and as a consequence mantaining a relatively low cost of operation. Surveys taking Cornish and Devon GPs together suggest that their surgeries are quite well equipped and that these GPs are fairly enterprising: 80% offer minor operations, 33% manipulations, 10% homeopathy, 6% hypnosis and 5% acupuncture.[31] At hospital level, one NHS success has been to achieve a relatively even UK-wide distribution of good-quality hospital consultants. There is anecdotal evidence that those working in Cornwall are generally of fairly high calibre because Cornwall is an attractive place to live in, if not an easy base from which to pursue a medical-academic or research career. It is also worth noting that UK consultants' career patterns are extremely geographically stable; once appointed to a given post NHS consultants tend to stay in it for many years. Pre-1974 NHS practice of simply increasing past budgets slightly more than the rate of inflation, relatively disadvantaged Cornish hospital and community health services. But the reverse occurred after 1974 because the RAWP allocation formula and its successor, the capitation-based National Funding Formula, tend to favour health services in relatively underfunded parts of the UK. Cornwall was in this position until, in 1996, it came to within 1 per cent of its normative funding level under the formulae. By then, however, there were signs that Treliske was facing similar financial pressures to many of its English counterparts, especially in respect of nursing resources.[32] Above all, Cornwall shared in the NHS's greatest success: abolishing the market nexus between patients and health services, the biggest single obstacle to healthcare access in pre-NHS days, especially for working-class and lower-middle-class women and children.

Notwithstanding its standard English pattern of organization, the Cornish health system has still some distinctive public health issues and demographic patterns to cope with. These have, of course, a far bigger impact on population health than health services do.

As in the UK generally, occupational health services are under-developed. For Cornwall, the main occupations are of course mining, agriculture and tourism. Agriculture and tourism have extremely atomized workforces which resist organized occupational health measures; around half these enterprises occupy only one person so general practice has perforce to make the occupational health gap good. Tin mining still generates severe traumatic injuries of similar types as those recorded in earlier centuries (although no doubt fewer of them) as well as cases of silicosis and silicotuberculosis. Nowadays Cornish miners' exposure to underground radon is also thought to increase the more insidious risks of lung and stomach cancer, whilst china clay production has replaced tin-mining as the main source of such industrial illnesses as pneumoconiosis. The high quartz content in dust arising from china clay and its associated minerals also appears to be related to nodular fibrosis, whilst kaolinite seems to be associated with a risk of interstitial fibrosis and there is some evidence that it might be cytotoxic.[33]

The health effects of tourism are in general under-researched. However, there is nothing new either in the public health regulation of camping and caravan sites or in doctors seizing upon public health impacts when objecting to the less respectable forms of tourism:

> In recent years we have seen in Devon and Cornwall a less desirable type of itinerant holiday-maker. I refer to those people who either elect or are forced to spend their nights sleeping in cars on roadside verges or lay-bys. That this way of spending a holiday is uncomfortable and fatiguing is largely a matter for those who do it, although I can believe that the participants in a 'holiday' of this sort cannot be much of an asset to the organisation which employs them when they return to work. That they should cause the countryside adjacent to their halting places to become untidy, foul and insanitary from their own litter and dejecta is something we are all entitled to complain about. My own view of these people is that they are for the most part feckless and irresponsible by nature.[34]

So far as hospital managers are concerned, the summer workload in dealing with visitors' injuries and illness conveniently balances out the usual winter rise in demand for accident and emergency, orthopaedic and general medical services from local residents. Skin cancer incidence continues to increase in Cornwall, as might be expected given its position, climate and the influence of tourism on health behaviours.[35]

Tourism influences both the adequacy of water and sewerage services during the summer and the resulting water quality on beaches which the tourists use. During 1995 surfers' groups complained repeatedly about bathing water quality at some Cornish beaches. On land, the pollution of water supplies at Lowermoor (Camelford) with aluminium sulphate in 1988, although severe, was exceptional. It caused an increase in the use of hospital services by local residents, at least 480 of whom suffered such symptoms as aching joints or (among adults) impairment of information processing and memory. Local children do not seem to have been so severely affected and neither does the health of pregnant women or their children. The Wheal Jane pollution incident (1991) affected river rather than drinking or bathing water.[36]

Cornish environmental levels of gamma ray radiation, radon and arsenic are unusually high. Although radon in Cornish homes might appear to present a risk of myeloid leukaemia and other cancers, Grainger argues that any effects are likely to be at a genetic level or to result from sustained long-term exposure. However, a recent cluster of three leukaemia cases at Camelford has aroused speculation as to whether this view is too sanguine or whether (less plausibly) the cluster stems from the water pollution noted above. There appears little danger from the uranium also found in Cornwall. In general, cancers and circulatory diseases are the largest causes of death but in this Cornwall differs little from most developed countries.[37]

The health effects of poverty, unemployment, and poor housing are reasonably well known. In August 1993, for example, *The Times* observed that 'chronic ill-health is linked closely with poverty . . . in the North, inner cities and Cornwall, over a quarter of households contain at least one person suffering from long term illness'.[38] One would expect Cornwall to experience such conditions rather severely since Camborne-Redruth and Newquay are two of the four UK towns with the highest levels of unemployment, wages are lower than the UK average (especially in West Cornwall) and there is a chronic housing shortage. Cornwall's standardized mortality rate for suicide and self-injury is high at 141 (i.e. 41 per cent above the UK average, allowing for differences in the population profile). In recognition, Cornwall and Isles of Scilly Health Authority recently announced a 'Healthy Towns' initiative intended to focus health promotion on the present and former industrial bases—Camborne initially, then Falmouth, St Austell, other parts of the clay area and parts of Liskeard. Certainly, the position on some health behaviours seems to be worsening in the middle 1990s with lung cancers increasing (although smoking continues to decline), rising proportions of overweight people and relatively poor levels of child dental health.[38] While Cornish healthcare remains embedded within the highly centralized structures of the English NHS, rather than being determined as the health policy of one region of the European Union, these problems will continue to be addressed through England's somewhat limited *Health of the Nation* policy rather than the more ambitious and incisive *Health for All 2000* policy which both the World Health Organisation and European Union endorse more enthusiastically and actively than does the UK government.

CONCLUSION

This survey of Cornish healthcare and health suggests three conclusions: two concerning Cornish Studies as an area of academic activity, and one which also concerns health policy analysis.

Historically, the early nineteenth century represents for Cornwall a watershed in healthcare as in so many other spheres. This watershed was between a reliance on traditional medicine and on modern, scientific medicine; the former with strong, idiosyncratic residues of medieval Cornish and indeed older beliefs; the latter based on an increasingly internationalized body of scientific knowledge. Yet the contrast should not be overstated until certain medical-anthropological questions have been answered: Have 'modern' approaches to health and healthcare simply extinguished traditional beliefs and practice in Cornwall or instead overlain rather than replaced their predecessors? If 'overlain' rather than 'replaced', to what extent do traditional beliefs about health still animate the lay Cornish population and inform, for instance, their use of 'alternative' and 'complementary' medicine?

The watershed was not only in therapeutic beliefs and practice but also in organization; a watershed between essentially locally-organized healthcare and organization as a periphery of an increasingly centralized, state-dominated health system. Partly this peripheral role reflects Cornwall's size: by itself a population of 486,000 cannot sustain a medical school, a research infrastructure, healthworker training establishments and centres of clinical specialization, the conventional marks of a developed, more-or-less self-contained health system. Indeed, the latest (1996) centralizing act has been to combine midwifery and nursing training for Cornwall with that for Devon and Somerset under the aegis of the University of Plymouth.

This historical trend (for Cornwall) of combined centralization and peripheralization exposes two health policy problems:

1. For each type of health service, is there a *technically* optimal scale of provision? There is evidence, for instance, that the clinical outcome a surgeon achieves using a given surgical procedure improves, the more of them he or she performs each year.
2. If so, what is the corresponding *organizationally* optimal scale on which to organize each type of health service?

Suppose that the planners of, say, Treliske were right to assume that a catchment population of between quarter and half a million people is necessary for a modern hospital to operate at acceptable levels of clinical effectiveness and economic efficiency. Now suppose too that, following current health policy fashion, one intends to use competition between hospitals to stimulate cost control and innovation. Then whoever purchases hospital services for a given (here, the Cornish) population must have access to a healthcare system (whether an internal market or quasi-market, social market or conventional market) big enough to support at least two hospitals (since competition requires at least two competitors); that is, to a health system serving a population of around a million or more. 'Access', however, does not mean 'organizational integration' nor 'central control' nor 'playing a peripheral role'. In theory, it would be quite feasible for, say, Cornish local government to undertake this healthcare purchasing function more or less independently. The example of other small European countries such as Malta shows how such arrangements can work for health services which cannot, or as a matter of policy should not, be provided simply on a local scale. Neither does this larger health system need *a priori* to match the UK system alone. Early signs of a European Union-wide market for some health services are beginning to appear.[39]

Lastly, the survey of health and healthcare exposes a perhaps esoteric but not unexpected problem for Cornish Studies: that of defining Cornish nationality. Each year over a thousand East Cornish women give birth in Derriford, and a few even further afield, before returning to rear their children in Cornwall. Intuitively, one would regard these as the Cornish children of Cornish families. That implies a more sophisticated definition of 'Cornishness' than determination simply by birthplace. Here a new complex of problems about the relations between geographical place, social place, nationality, ethnicity and culture opens up. Indeed, Treliske Hospital has acknowledged that 'the term "Ethnic Group" legitimately and technically covers groups such as Cornish, Irish, Scottish, Welsh, English',[40] although in responding to the mandatory requirement that from 1 April 1995 it should record the ethnic origins of its patients, it is not at present making plans to actively seek details of Cornish ethnicity.

ACKNOWLEDGEMENTS

I gratefully acknowledge the help of: Elaine Fitzsimmons, Derriford Hospital; Kim Hitchins, Treliske Hospital; Graham Millard, Graham Millard Consultancy; John Pantall, HSMU Manchester University; Geoff Poxon, Cornwall CHC; Philip Payton, Institute of Cornish Studies, University of Exeter; Janet Rouse, Cornwall and Isles of Scilly Health Authority; Nigel Smith, Derriford Hospital; and the anonymous reviewer for *Cornish Studies*. However, the views expressed above do not necessarily represent the opinions either of these individuals or of the organizations for whom they work.

NOTES AND REFERENCES

1. Richard Carew, *Survey of Cornwall*, ed. F.E.Halliday, London, 1953, pp. 101, 168, 212.
2. J.G. Fraser, *The Golden Bough: A Study of Magic and Religion*, London, 1970, pp. 14–16, 18–22, 707–708, 712–716.
3. A.K. Hamilton Jenkin, *Cornwall and the Cornish*, Letchworth, 1933, p. 288.
4. Hamilton Jenkin, 1933, pp. 265–266; *West Briton*, 25 November 1897.
5. Hamilton Jenkin, 1933, p. 261.

6. *West Briton*, 4 November 1842; Hamilton Jenkin, 1933, pp. 295–299; A.K. Hamilton Jenkin, *Cornwall and its People*, Newton Abbot, 1970, p. 309.
7. Carew, 1953, p. 193
8. M. Focault, *Madness and Civilization: A History of Insanity in the Age of Reason*, London, 1971, p. 172; Hamilton Jenkin, 1970, p. 311.
9. Hamilton Jenkin, 1933, pp. 242–243, 245, 247, 265, 270, 275.
10. *West Briton*, 25 November 1897, 4 July 1845, 10 October 1845; Hamilton Jenkin, 1933, p. 281.
11. Hamilton Jenkin, 1970, p. 337; Carew, 1953, p. 140; C.T. Andrews, *The First Cornish Hospital*, Penzance, 1975, p. 48; John Hatcher, *Rural Society and Economy in the Duchy of Cornwall*, Cambridge, 1970, p. 14; James Whetter, *Cornwall in the Seventeenth Century: An Economic History of Kernow*, Padstow, 1974, p. 9.
12. John Rowe, *Cornwall in the Age of the Industrial Revolution*, Liverpool, 1953, repub. St Austell, 1993, pp. 26, 153–155, 312–313; Andrews, 1975, pp.1-2; R.Robins, 'An Old Cornish Hand', *Journal of Hand Surgery*, ix (2), June 1984.
13. Rowe, 1953 and 1993, pp. 32, 152, 312–313; *West Briton*, 26 February 1847, 25 May 1849, 3 March 1848.
14. *West Briton*, 5 October 1832, 27 July 1849, 31 August 1849; Hamilton Jenkin, 1970, p. 342; R.M.Barton (ed.), *Life in Cornwall at the End of the Nineteenth Century*, Truro, 1974, p. 233.
15. *West Briton*, 26 October 1849, 19 April 1833, 18 January 1822, 17 November 1892, 31 August 1849, 21 March 1851, 6 November 1890; Barton, 1974, pp. 9–10.
16. *West Briton*, 19 June 1899, 2 June 1837, 21 July 1887, 9 July 1888, 14 September 1893; Andrews, 1975, pp. 59–60; Carew, 1953, p. 195.
17. *West Briton*, 11 February 1853, 9 June 1853; Andrews, 1975, p. 60; Cornwall and Isles of Scilly Health Authority (CISHA), *Health of the Population 1995*, St Austell, 1995B, p. 7; A. Guthrie, *Cornwall in the Age of Steam*, Padstow, 1994, p. 184.
18. *West Briton*, 3 March 1879; Rowe, 1953 and 1993, pp. 153, 313–315; Guthrie, 1994, p. 73.
19. *West Briton*, 2 March 1810; 25 October 1811; 12 January 1827; 1 December 1815, 16 May 1823, 8 May 1812; T.McKeown, *The Role of Medicine: Dream, Mirage or Nemesis?*, London, 1976, pp. 7, 43–44, 72–74.
20. *West Briton*, 2 April 1842, 1 October 1830, 20 March 1812, 31 May 1816, 16 July 1852, 20 April 1849, 8 February 1811; Carew, 1953, p. 131; A.K. Hamilton Jenkin, *News From Cornwall*, London, 1951, p. 141.
21. *West Briton*, 21 July 1837; Rowe, 1953 and 1993, pp. 246–247.
22. *West Briton*, 22 May 1812, 1 June 1821; Barton, 1974, p. 85.
23. *West Briton*, 29 January 1819; P.J. Fox, *Liskeard Rural District Council: The Annual Report of the Medical Officer of Health for the Year 1959*, Liskeard, 1959, p. 2.
24. *West Briton*, 28 February 1817, 20 August 1819; Foucault, 1971, pp. 241–251.

25. *West Briton*, 24 August 1810, 9 April 1847; R.Rowe, 'Psychiatric Hospital Attendant', in J. Gillespie (ed.), *Good Health! Stories from the Lives of Pioneers in the Health Service*, Padstow, 1993, p. 84; P. Sedgwick, *Psycho Politics*, London, 1982, p. 232.
26. CHISHA, 1995B, p, 8.; J. Seabrook, 'Cornwall Gone West', *New Statesman & Society*, 7 August 1992.
27. Institute of Health Services Management (IHSM), *The Hospitals and Health Services Year Book 1996*, London, 1996; Cornwall Community Health Council (CCHC), *1994/1995 Annual Report*, Truro, 1995, p. 14.
28. A.Rouse, 'Effect of the Cornwall Helicopter Ambulance on Ambulance Service Emergency Response Time', *West of England Medical Journal*, cvi (3), September 1991; A. Rouse, 'The Effect of the Cornwall and Isles of Scilly Helicopter Ambulance Unit on the Ambulance Service's Ability to Deliver Acutely Traumatized Patients to Hospital', *Archives of Emergency Medicine*, ix (2), June 1992; J.P. Nicholl, N.R.Beeby and J.E. Brazier, 'A Comparison of the Costs and Performance of an Emergency Helicopter and Land Ambulances in a Rural Area', *Injury*, xxv (2), April 1994; N. Selwood, 'An Ambulance Helicopter for Emergency Calls', *Archives of Emergency Medicine*, ix (3), September 1992; Department of Health, *Press Release 94/401*, 12 September 1994.
29. IHSM, 1996; CISHA, *Health Matters*, St Austell, Summer 1995A.
30. D. Bence, 'All Over Bar the Shouting', *Health Services Journal*, 1 February 1996.
31. N. Bradley and S. Watkins, 'Survey of Equipment in General Practice', *British Medical Journal*, cclxxxxix (6696), 1989; N. Bradley and R. Gude, 'Survey of Services to Patients in General Practice', *West of England Medical Journal*, coil (1), 1992.
32. CCHC, 1995, p. 9.
33. Alan M. Williams, Gareth Shaw and J. Greenwood, 'From Tourist to Tourist Entrepreneur, from Consumption to Production: Evidence from Cornwall, England', *Environment and Planning A*, xxi, 1989; R.N. Jones, 'Crush Syndrome in a Cornish Tin Miner', *Injury*, xv (4), January 1984; A.J. Fox, P. Goldlbatt and L.J. Kinlen, 'A Study of the Mortality of Cornish Tin Miners', *British Journal of Industrial Medicine*, xxxviii (4), November 1981; R.D. Oldham, 'Pneumoconiosis in Cornish China Clay Workers', *British Journal of Industrial Medicine*, xxxx (2), 1995; J.C. Wagner, F.D. Pooley, A. Gibbs, J. Lyons, G. Sheers and C.B. Moncrieff, 'Inhalation of China Stone and China Clay Dusts: Relationship Between the Minerology of Dust Retained in the Lungs and Pathological changes', *Thorax*, xxxx (3), March 1986; R. Davies, 'Factors Involved in the Cytotoxicity of Kaolinite towards Macrophages in Vitro', *Environmental Health Perspectives*, li, September 1983.
34. Fox, 1959, p. 3.
35. CISHA, 1995B, p. 60.
36. P.J. Owen and D.P. Miles, 'A Review of Hospital Discharge Rates in a Population around Camelford in North Cornwall up to the Fifth

Anniversary of an Episode of Aluminium Sulphate Absorption', *Journal of Public Health Medicine*, xvii (2), June 1995.

37. N. Hawkes, 'Three Children in the Same Classroom contact Leukaemia', *The Times*, 17 May 1996; D.L. Henshaw, J.P. Eatough and R.B. Richardson, 'Radon as a Causative Factor in Induction of Myeloid Leukaemia and Other Cancers', *Lancet*, cccxxxv (8696), 28 April 1990; C.R. Grainger, 'Terrestial Gamma Ray Radiation in Cornwall', *Royal Society of Health Journal*, cvi (3), June 1986; C.R. Grainger, 'Geochemistry and Environmental Health', cviii (2), April 1988; C.R. Grainger, 'Geochemistry and Health: Arsenic in Cornwall', *Royal Society of Health Journal*, cviii (5), October 1988; C.R. Grainger, 'Geochemistry and Environmental Health: Uranium in Cornwall', *Royal Society of Health Journal*, cxiv (1), February 1994.

38. *The Times*, 10 August 1993, cited in Philip Payton (ed.), *Cornwall Since the War: The Contemporary History of a European Region*, Redruth, 1993, p. 233.

39. Seabrook, 1992; Carol Williams, 'Housing in Cornwall: A Two-Tier System?', in Philip Payton (ed.), *Cornish Studies: Three*, Exeter, 1995; CISHA, 1995B, p. 73; *West Briton*, 23 June 1994.

40. J. Hermesse and H. Lewalle, *L'acces aux Soins en Europe. Quelle mobilite du Patient?*, Louvain-la-Neuve, 1993.

41. Health Records Memorandum, Treliske Hospital, 1995.

RESEARCH NOTES

NEGATIVE PARTICLES IN CORNISH

Glanville Price

INTRODUCTION

French, Welsh and Breton have a common syntactic feature in that, whereas most other western European languages express negation of the verb by means of a negative adverb such as *not, nicht, no, non*, the languages in question are characterized by a discontinuous construction consisting of a preverbal negative element, French *ne*, Welsh *ni*, Breton *ne,* and a postverbal element that I shall term a 'negative particle' but which originally had a positive value, French *pas*, Welsh *dim/ddim*, Breton *ket*. To varying degrees in French and Welsh particularly, these particles have assumed a negative value to the point where, in speech, the original negative element, *ne* or *ni*, is frequently omitted, e.g.:

French *tu (ne) vois pas*
Welsh *(ni) weli di ddim*
Breton *ne welez ket*
'You do not see'.

There are differences of detail,[1] that I shall not go into here, in the syntax of the particles in the three languages but the basic construction is the same. Further, though the characteristic particle of Parisian and of literary French is *pas*, *point* also occurs and other particles such as (to name the most widespread) *mie* and *nient* are characteristic of other dialects.[2]

It is worthy of note (i) that, within the Romance-speaking area, the discontinuous negative construction is virtually restricted to languages (French, Occitan, northern Italian dialects, and Romansh dialects in Switzerland) spoken in territories where Gaulish and related dialects were spoken, (ii) that, in Celtic, the construction is characteristic of the Brittonic languages Welsh and Breton but not of the Gaelic languages, and (iii) that Gaulish and Brittonic were so closely related as to be considered by many scholars to have been dialects of the same language. On this basis, I argue elsewhere[3] that there is at least a prima-facie case for considering that the fact that the construction occurs in the Romance and Celtic vernaculars of the areas in question is more than coincidental and that, at some time during a period of Celtic/Romance bilingualism, Celtic-speakers carried it over into the Romance speech they were in the process of acquiring.

The purpose of this research note is to demonstrate that, whatever may be the reason for it, there is evidence to show that the discontinuous construction also occurred in Cornish. To be precise, I have identified a total of nineteen examples[4] involving four different particles, viz: *cam(an)* 'step', *banna* 'drop', *tam* 'bit', and (one example only) *poynt*. They occur in the 'Passion' poem (sometimes known as *Pascon agan Arluth*),[5] in the *Passio Domini*[6] (but apparently not in other sections of the *Ordinalia*), and in the *Creacion of the World*.[7] To the best of my knowledge, there are no examples in the 'Life of Meriasek' or later texts.

EXAMPLES

The Cornish examples I have noted are the following:

(i) *cam(an)* (literally 'step')—5 examples
     This occurs only in *Pascon agan Arluth:*
     gans gloteny ef pan welas cam na ylly y dolla (stanza 13) 'when he saw that by gluttony he could not deceive him'
     ny dayl thys cam y naghe (stanza 85) 'it is no use to you to deny it'
     camen Pylat pan welas na ylly Crist delyffre (stanza 150) 'when Pilate saw that he could not deliver Christ'
     i beyn o mar greff ha tyn caman na ylly bewe heb dascor y eneff gwyn (stanza 204) 'his pain was so strong and keen that he could not live without giving up his fair soul'
     caman na ylly gwythe war nans na bosse y ben (stanza 205) 'he could not keep his head from leaning downwards'

(ii) *banna, banne* (literally 'drop')—7 examples[8]
     gans queth y ben y quethens guelas banna na ylly (*Pascon*, stanza 96) 'they covered his head with a cloth so that he could not see'

dal o, ny wely banna (*Pascon*, stanza 217) 'he was blind, he could not see'
bythqueth whet tebel na mas ny wylys ganse banne (*Passio*, 397–98) 'never yet, bad or good, have I seen with them [i.e. with my eyes]'
ny clev banne (*Passio*, 2321) 'he does not hear'
kyyna wore hy cowse banna (*Creacion*, 507) 'though she does not know how to speak'
banna ny allaf gwellas (*Creacion*, 1621) 'I cannot see'
ha me ny wyllyn banna (*Creacion*, 1652) 'and I could not see'

(iii) *tam, tabm* 'a bit'—6 examples
ha gwythe tam na guskens (*Pascon*, stanza 241) 'and to take care they did not sleep'
tam vyth ny vyth cregys (*Creacion*, 627) 'it will not be believed ever'
ny wothyan tabm y naha (*Creacion*, 775) 'I knew not how to deny him'
neb na vyth tam lowena (*Creacion*, 2028) 'where there will be no joy'
han marbell tam consumys der thower ny vyth (*Creacion*, 2189–90) 'and the marble will not be worn away by water'
ha nynges tam amendya (*Creacion*, 2337) 'and there is no atonement'

(iv) *poynt*—1 example
me, ew heare, ny sensaf poynt (*Creacion*, 1135-36) 'I, who am heir, shall not mind'

EXPLANATIONS
While there can be no reasonable doubt that the discontinuous construction in Welsh and Breton is of indigenous origin, one has at least to envisage for Cornish two different historical explanations:

(a) Here too, it is indigenous and the fact that there are relatively few examples is to be attributed to the fact that our existing texts are all in verse, the syntax of which may not reflect accurately spoken usage; it is also the case that, in Old French, the use of particles is less widespread in many verse texts than it clearly must have been in the spoken language.[9]

(b) It is at least possible that the use of the construction in Cornish is a Gallicism, and that the direct source of it is the language of

Anglo-Norman or possibly (given the relatively late date of the Cornish texts) Continental French texts known to the composers of the Cornish texts. In favour of this are the following considerations:

(i) of the four particles we have identified, one, namely *poynt*, is French in origin (though, alternatively, it could have passed into Cornish from English);

(ii) two others, *cam* 'step' and *banna* 'drop' are the literal equivalents of French *pas* and *goute* (*gote*, *gute*) (= modern French *goutte*); furthermore, just as Old and Middle French *goute* occurs primarily with the verbs (to give them in modern orthography) *voir* 'to see' and *ouïr* 'to hear', so five of our seven examples of *banna* occur with *gueles* 'to see' and one with *clowas* 'to hear';[10]

(iii) *tam* 'bit', however, is not the precise equivalent of any of the French particles, though it could perhaps be equated with *mie* 'crumb'; alternatively, even if the discontinous construction is borrowed from French, this cannot exclude the possibility that a purely native element came to be used as one possible particle.

Against the hypothesis of a French origin are:

(1) the fact that, though the evidence is lacking to determine to what extent *ket* was characteristic of medieval Breton, the discontinuous construction was already well established in Welsh, where it is certainly not a Gallicism, some centuries before the date of the Cornish texts;

(2) the fact that there is no evidence of a comparable influence on English, which one might well have expected if the use of the discontinuous construction in Cornish is to be plausibly attributed to French influence.

NOTES AND REFERENCES

1. These include (i) the fact that, in Old French, the particle could also precede the verb, e.g. *ki pas ne fut produme* 'who was not a man of worth' (*Chanson de Roland*, line 1528), and (ii) the extent (much greater in Welsh than in French) to which, in the literary language, negation may be expressed by *ne* or *ni* alone, e.g. French *je n'ose le dire* 'I dare not say so', Welsh *ni sylweddolais* 'I did not realize'.

2. In Old French and, to some extent, up to the eighteenth century, *point* was used with partitive constructions, e.g. *il n'a point de pain* 'he has no bread', and *pas* elsewhere, e.g. *il ne vient pas* 'he is not coming'. On this, and on the dialectal distribution of different particles, see Glanville Price, 'The Negative Particles *pas, mie* and *point* in French', *Archivum*

Linguisticum, 14, 1962, and 'Negative Particles in French' (forthcoming in a Festschrift for William Rothwell).

3. Glanville Price, 'A Possible Celtic Influence in Romance Syntax', in Ronald Black, William Gillies and Roibeard O'Maolalaigh (eds), *Celtic Connections*, Tuckwell, Edinburgh, forthcoming 1997.

4. I have not counted the following example in which I am uncertain as to whether *malbew* 'at all' could properly be considered as a negative particle analogous to the others: *ny veas malbew serrys* (*Creacion*, 813) 'you would not be [at all] sorry'.

5. Quoted after the edition by Whitley Stokes, 'The Passion', *Transactions of the Philological Society, 1860–61*, Appendix, pp. 1–100.

6. Quoted after the edition by Edwin Norris, *The Ancient Cornish Drama*, Oxford, 1869.

7. Quoted after Paula Neuss, *The Creacion of the World: A Critical Edition and Translation*, New York and London, 1983; line references to this edition differ by at most two lines from those in the Whitley Stokes edition of 1864.

8. I have not counted the following two examples which also include the numeral 'one': *skant ny welaf un banna* (*Creacion*, 1459) 'I can scarcely see', *Iudus ny gozk un banne* (*Passio*, 1078) 'Judas does not sleep [at all]', or the following in which there is an implied negation carried over from the main clause: *nynges omma dean in wlase a greys thybm vanna* (*Creacion*, 2328–29) 'there is not a man in the country who will believe me' i.e. 'one will not believe me'

9. See the articles referred to in Note 2. above.

10. It had been widely claimed that the use of *goute* in Old French must have begun with the verb *boire* 'to drink' and then spread *par analogie de son* to *voir* and then to other verbs; this theory ignores the facts (i) there is little phonetic similarity between the Old French forms of *boire* and *voir* (e.g., to take only the infinitives, the early Old French forms are *beivre* and *vedeir*) and (b) that no examples at all of its use with *beivre* are attested. I have shown elsewhere (Glanville Price, 'The Origins and Syntax of *ne . . . goutte*', in John N. Green and Wendy Ayres-Bennett (eds), *Variation and Change in French*, London, 1990) that, in fact the construction must have originated with *voir* and that *goute* meant 'tear'; *je ne voi goute* therefore meant at first something like 'I am so blind (or: it is so dark) that I cannot even see the tears in my eyes'. Its use then spread to the other *verbum sentiendi, ouir*.

SECOND HOMES IN CORNWALL

Paul Thornton

INTRODUCTION

The subject of second homes in Cornwall has been under-researched, for two reasons: cost, and aggregation within a data set covering the whole of the South-West 'planning region'. Second homes are difficult to identify and define within existing data sets, such as the census of population. Time series analysis is particularly fraught with problems, relating to changes in definition between censuses; for example, chalet sites may be enumerated as 'holiday accommodation, unoccupied' in an earlier census and recorded differently in a later one. Therefore, data on second homes needs to be collected separately, making research expensive and time consuming. The last major exercise of this type to cover Cornwall was reported by the South West Economic Planning Council (SWEPC) in 1975. As well as being dated, this data source suffers, from the perspective of studying Cornwall, by aggregating all second homes into one region, potentially disguising sub-regional variations.

While cost may be a factor in explaining the lack of attention to quantifying second homes, it does not explain a further under-researched question: where does the demand for second homes comes from and what is the subsequent response of the 'local' population towards the incomers? This research note is based upon a study aimed at redressing this lack of attention.[1]

DISTRIBUTION OF SECOND HOMES

The SWEPC survey claimed, correctly, that it is not easy to draw a hard and fast line between second homes and other accommodation used for holiday letting.[2] Therefore, the survey took second homes to include those properties used predominantly by their owners, rather

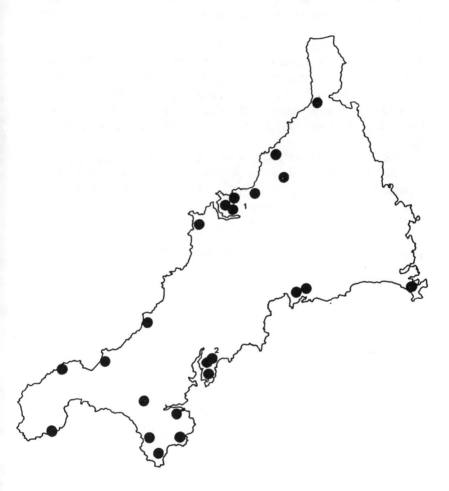

Figure 1: Communities in Cornwall with over 10% Second Homes.

than let out on a series of short tenancies. Thus second homes would have included chalets, houses, bungalows and flats used for recreation by their owners and in many cases also let for part of the year, homes bought for eventual use in retirement, and homes bought by those living in tied dwellings in other areas. Caravans were not included, but the approach remained broadbrushed. The study concluded there were approximately 3940 second homes in Cornwall and the Isles of Scilly in 1973, or 38 per cent of the total in the South West planning region.

More recent information is available from the 1991 Census of Population. Although the identification of second homes within this data is difficult, 4958 second residences are recorded in Cornwall.

According to the 1991 data, most second homes are found in North Cornwall, which also possesses the highest proportion of second homes to permanent residences of any of the Districts. Census of population data for 1991 was also used at a smaller scale to identify concentrations of second homes in Cornwall. It was found that 18 communities possessed more than 50 second homes. The greatest number of second residences were found to be in Polzeath (230 properties) and Rock (213). While this demonstrates the localized and concentrated nature of second homes, at the community scale it is the proportion of second homes to main homes that is crucial in determining social and economic impacts. Figure 1 marks the positions of the 24 communities with more than 10 per cent of their housing stock used as second homes. Particularly distinctive is the North Cornwall cluster (marked 1) and the Malpas to St Mawes area (marked 2).

In conclusion, the analysis of the 1991 census data set suggests second residences are spatially restricted and not a widespread phenomenon. At the District level only North Cornwall could be identified as significantly affected. Here, the popularity of second homes may derive from its position as one of the Districts closest to the rest of the United Kingdom and its reputation for having a coastline unspoilt by industry and tourism. All the high concentrations of second homes in Cornwall can be associated with proximity to the coast.

Without detailed local knowledge or a major interview survey, it is difficult to tell where second homes may be found within coastal communities. Fortunately, thanks to a study by Lee there is detailed information available for Port Isaac.[3] This demonstrated that few second-home owners are interested in purchasing modern properties away from the historic cores of coastal communities—even if this requires considerable investment in improving the property. For example, the cliff and quay areas of Port Isaac (the 'lower village') contained only 46 per cent permanently occupied properties. In contrast, the 'upper village' areas contained fewer seasonally occupied properties.

COMPARISON OF LOCAL AND SECOND HOME POPULATIONS

This study used a questionnaire survey in six coastal communities to examine the nature of the local and second-home populations and their perceptions of each other.

Occupational Backgrounds

There were clear differences in occupational background between the permanent and temporary populations: members of the local population were employed primarily in manual or clerical occupations, whilst the second home population held professional or managerial occupations. Unemployment was high in the local population and zero in the second-home population.

Social Distance

Other results were confusing, probably reflecting the situation in many communities. For example, there was evidence of 'social distance' between second home owners and local residents who held some resentment towards the former. But second home owners, in general, were unaware of this. Second homes are often accused of being disruptive of local communities, but second home owners were unsure whether they wanted to integrate themselves with the local community. Indeed, permanent residents were also unclear on whether they wanted integration.

Economic Impacts

Second home owners felt they made a contribution to the local economy through utilizing properties that might otherwise become derelict, and through increasing consumer expenditure in the local area. Local residents attitudes were bi-polarized between those who agreed with the second home owners and those who did not. The obvious inference is that those local residents whose jobs are in some way dependent on second home owners are unlikely to view them negatively. The majority of jobs created by second homes involved cleaning or caretaking.

Second Home Owners

Second homes were used for an average of 63.2 nights a year, although most second home owners used their properties for between 20 and 39 nights.

The survey showed little evidence of people retiring to their second homes. Second homes were purchased for use as recreational properties by their owners. Local estate agents were the primary source of information on potential second homes. However, holiday experiences in Cornwall were important, substantiating the view of tourism as a factor in increasing second home ownership in a local area. The tourism/second home link was similarly reflected in the regional origins of second home owners, which fairly closely matched those of tourists. London and the South East were dominant, accounting for 49.4 per cent of second home owners.

TERRITORIAL LEGITIMACY, MORAL GEOGRAPHIES AND POLICY IMPLICATIONS

The *Second Homes in Cornwall* study also examined the potential for conflict between second home owners and the permanently resident population. This was conceptualized through the theories of 'territorial legitimacy' and 'moral geographies'. A territorially legitimate population includes individuals who feel they have a right to control their local environment. A moral geography refers to the view or ideal they develop of how a landscape or environment should look and, crucially, be lived in. Historically, the territorial legitimate population was synonymous with the permanent local residents. However, more recently the scope and variety of legitimating processes over space have been increasing. The study concluded that second home owners perceive themselves to be a territorially legitimate population on the basis of their property ownership. Furthermore, their moral geography is based upon maximizing the utility function of the landscape towards recreation. This appears to contrast with the locally resident population, particularly the 'Cornish', who are more prepared to view the landscape as a means towards *production* rather than *consumption*. The creation of local employment opportunities does not feature highly in the second home owners' moral geographies, and may be incompatible with them. Given the relative affluence of second home owners, and the strength of their reactions to what they perceive as threats to the environment, the study concluded that the potential for conflict remains high. But given the spatial concentration of second homes and the evidence of past conflicts, any problems, although emotive, are likely to remain localized.

This research note is based upon *Competing for Cornwall: A Study of Second Home Owners and Permanent Residences in Coastal Communities*, produced by the Institute of Cornish Studies with the co-operation of the Information and Statistics Section of the Planning Department, Cornwall County Council.

NOTES AND REFERENCES

1. Paul Thornton, *Competing for Cornwall: A Study of Second Home Owners and Permanent Residences in Coastal Communities*, Redruth, 1996.
2. 'Second Homes in Cornwall: A Report on the South-West Economic Planning Council's Survey', *Cornwall County Structure Plan, Interim Reports of Survey*, Truro, September 1975, pp. 6A–6D.
3. M. Lee, personal communication.

REVIEW ARTICLES

FOOT IN THE MOUTH OR
FOOT IN THE DOOR?
EVALUATING CHAPMAN'S *THE CELTS*

Amy Hale

Malcolm Chapman, *The Celts: The Construction of a Myth*, Macmillan, London, 1992, xv pp. + 342 pp. ISBN 0-333-52088-2, £47.50.

Malcolm Chapman knew that his publication *The Celts: The Construction of a Myth* probably would not earn him any friends. The most scathing criticism has come from Celticists and Celtic activists who feel that Chapman is attempting to erase their subject matter, and deny their reality. In this essay I will not act as an apologist for Chapman, but I will, however, attempt to provide a greater understanding of his work by situating it within an historical academic context. Although Chapman's work, and that of the other Oxford social anthropologists, needs to be critically examined, it should not be dismissed. I propose that these studies offer new challenges for those in the field of Celtic Studies to explore how Celtic identities are shaped and constructed by actual people.

One of the more important aspects of Chapman's *The Celts* is that it is one of the first major works to address 'Celtic' as a category from an anthropological perspective, rather than a linguistic one. In the first chapter of the book, Chapman gives a brief account of the split between Celtic Studies and Anthropology in the twentieth century. He notes that early in the development of the social and humanistic sciences in the nineteenth century, the Indo-European hypothesis led to co-operation between many fields, as the primary academic enterprise of the day was the reconstruction of the languages and cultures that formed European civilization.[1] 'Celtic' was defined by language and the academic inquiry into Celtic matters focused on medieval literature and philology, mostly to assist in interpreting and reconstructing the cultures and beliefs of 'the Celts'. This is largely the project of Celtic Studies today. Yet, early anthropology quickly abandoned any European focus, and most research focused on non-Western cultures that were thought to be 'primitive' and more 'exotic'.

Generally, the standard 'classic' anthropological texts have not been studies of Celtic peoples. Curtain, Donnan and Wilson, commenting on anthropological portrayals of Ireland, note that 'With only one or two exceptions, Irish ethnography generally is barely known beyond the small body of scholars with a professional interest in the island'.[2] This is perhaps even more true of ethnography in the other Celtic nations. The anthropological projects carried out in Celtic regions have focused on the 'fringe' aspect. Celts have always been considered to be the 'primitive exotics' in the backyard of the English empire, those who retained the 'true folk culture' in the face of modernity. This approach has mostly resulted in a stereotypical approach to ethnography in Celtic areas, that in fact helps reinforce dominant images of Celtic peoples. 'Celtic' anthropology has been dominated by the concerns and research questions of early folklore research; how to capture a dying culture in its last phases. For this reason, ethnographic portraits of the Celtic peoples have often been as rural illiterate peasants, very religious, speaking a dying language, upholding a great oral tradition that must be documented before it disappears.

Significantly, most 'Celtic' anthropology does not refer to the ethnic category of 'Celtic' at all. To put it simply, anthropologists may go to study the Cornish, Welsh, or the Bretons, but they do not go study 'the Celts'. The term has pejorative and somewhat 'flakey' connotations within the field, and carries with it the weight of nineteenth-century 'bad anthropology' infused with ideologies of the Romantic movement. On the other hand, one can travel to any number of Celtic Studies conferences and never hear an anthropological perspective.

Yet it can be argued that the idea of 'Celtic' identity is of crucial importance to the project of anthropological inquiry in 'Celtic' areas, but until fairly recently it has never been tackled head-on. In 1975 Michael Hechter produced a ground-breaking sociological work *Internal Colonialism: The Celtic Fringe in British National Development 1536–1966*.[3] This was not ethnography, nor had Hechter ever carried out a field study in a Celtic area, but the notion of a shared 'Celtic' ethnicity is somehow central to his work, even though he does not attempt to define what 'Celtic' is. Hechter examined the lack of economic development and continuing poverty in the Celtic areas of Britain that occurred, he argued, as the result of an ethnic division of labour. Although Hechter has been firmly criticized for not recognizing the individual development of each Celtic area, for our purposes the fact that he did a sociological study of 'Celtic' peoples is significant and rare.

In the late 1970s and through the 1980s, several European anthropologists, most notably those who trained under Edward Ardener at the Oxford Institute of Social Anthropology, turned their studies inward to instigate a new anthropology of Europe.[4] Responding to criticisms that European anthropology had been too rural, 'tribal' and community-oriented, these anthropologists began exploring issues such as urbanity, political movements and identity. Chapman and Maryon McDonald, both of the Ardener school, chose 'Celtic' field sites for their initial studies, Chapman in the Scottish Highlands, and McDonald in Brittany where she investigated Breton nationalism. Through a series of published essays and larger works, by both McDonald and Chapman, clearly developed in tandem, we can chart the development of the theories that Chapman presents in his 1992 piece.

In Chapman's first major work, *The Gaelic Vision in Scottish Culture*, he proposed the metaphoric oppositional categories for Celtic/ Non-Celtic that we see more clearly articulated in his 1992 work.[5] In a 1982 essay, 'Semantics and the Celt', Chapman elaborates on early Classical constructions of 'Celtic', first suggesting that Celtic is an empty category only to be filled by the interpretations by observers from dominant cultures.[6]

Maryon McDonald's 1989 *We Are Not French!* concerns identity development among Breton nationalists. The work also contains a probing look at the history and ideologies of Celtic Studies and the interplay between the discipline and the Breton nationalist movement. In one crucial chapter, she explores how Celtic Studies informed the construction of Celtic identities. She states that the philological reconstruction of languages gives Celtic political movements their structure in that they assume a point of origin and historic, cultural continuity which is linked with language. This assumption is not always logical, and McDonald's critique is harsh:

> The asterisked form [of a common Celtic word reconstruction] is
> a theoretical utility, a formal emptiness in historical linguistics . . .

however, it is often accorded an implicit historical reality that is at once—in nineteenth century style—linguistic, political, cultural and racial. The asterisk could be seen, therefore, for the hollow unity, theoretical and abstract in origin, that is pursued by the Celtic enthusiast, and which he fills with words and deeds, with birth, copulation and death.[7]

These earlier works, among others, laid the foundation for the analysis in Chapman's 1992 *The Celts* in which he attempts to deconstruct a category that is defined differently by archaeologists and linguists, yet is also understood by people as a term for cultural identification, and connotes various styles, cultural complexes and belief systems.

Chapman's primary objective it seems, in *The Celts: The Construction of a Myth,* is to examine the construction of a category 'Celtic' that arose as the result of historical oppositional systems of meaning. He proposes that the cultural traits that are commonly attributed to Celtic peoples are actually a result of 'Celtic' being essentially a category for 'Otherness'.

First, Chapman provides a brief outline of intellectual developments in the eighteenth and nineteenth centuries that linked language, culture and nationalism. He discusses the development of the Indo-European hypothesis during a period of nation-building and the formation of theories about what a 'nation' actually is. Models of the nation as an organic entity, rather than an intellectual construct, linked nationality with language, culture and race in ways that had not previously been done.[8] This was concurrent with the rise of evolutionary theory into which peoples and societies were eventually fitted in a continuum from 'primitive' to 'modern'. Within this scheme, the unit of analysis became 'race', which was at this point almost synonymous with language group. Chapman summarizes the discourse surrounding the study of the Celts within a context of Indo-European studies, the goals of which partially were to establish an extended lineage for European cultures, but he also extracts the motives underlying the foundations of the social and humanistic sciences: to understand the development of humanity from its most 'primitive' origins.

Chapman then continues to discuss systems of naming across cultures. When 'others' meet, they refer to each other in terms of difference that can range from 'foreigner' to the equivalent of 'sub-human barbarian'. Chapman's point is that sometimes names for groups that later become terms of self-identification begin as externally imposed labels that reveal more about the world view of those doing the naming than those being named in the quest for group self-identification.

Building from these generalizations, Chapman continues with a detailed discussion of the origin of the term 'Celt', from the earliest usage of the Greek *keltoi* in the fifth century BC. He argues that Greek ethnocentrism was so strong that all non-Greek speakers were labeled 'barbarian' and were considered less than human, a point that seems rather well attested.[9] He then suggests that the term *keltoi* was used by Greek geographers to describe the specific category of non-Greek speaking barbarians to the north and west. It is thus a category that carries no specific cultural content—it is merely a derogatory epithet. He further maintains that *keltoi* was in use throughout the Byzantine Empire, having a very similar meaning—to refer to an unruly, uncivilized people.

It is this Greek categorical origin that forms the basis of his argument that follows:

> The Celts were like the stars of the Great Bear, coherently patterned from a limited and distant viewpoint, but made up of elements joined together by nothing other than that viewpoint, and otherwise disparate, and figuratively or literally, great distances apart.[50]

The cultural meaning of 'Celtic' has been created, defined and refined from a distant viewpoint, that of a dominant culture, and ultimately the cultural attributions were reified by the Celtic peoples themselves. Chapman maintains that from these Greek and later Roman classificatory systems an empty category was created that has been perpetually filled by the 'others' of Western culture.

Chapman continues by describing the Germanic labelling of 'others' during the 'barbarian' invasions of Britain. He chronicles the development of the term 'Welsh' from the Germanic word for 'foreigner'. It is in this section that he suggests that peripherality is one of the most dominant features of the definition of 'Celtic'.

Perhaps one of the most crucial aspects of Chapman's *The Celts* is his theory of how the category of 'Celtic' developed specific cultural traits that are considered to characterize a group of people. He argues that, in fact, all the traits that are popularly (and even academically) associated with the 'Celtic character' are simply a product of 'otherness'. Chapman states that this occurred as the result of three processes:

1. The elaboration of an opposition self/other, with the 'Celts' (under whatever title) figuring as the 'other' and with Greek/Keltoi, Roman/ Galli, Anglo-Saxon/Welsh and English/Celtic succeeding one another. Geographically and conceptually the second of each of

these pairs is peripheral, the content of the second is determined by the first.

2. The steady movement of fashions from a centre to a periphery, with new fashions appearing at the centre and steadily moving toward the periphery.
3. A systematic function of the meeting of incongruent category systems, causing the perceiving culture to construct the perceived as inconstant, unreliable, irrational, given to excess and inadequacy, and so on.
4. Romanticism; this glamorises the other created in processes 1 and 2 and introduces a complicated refraction into the observation of process 2.

Chapman then lists some of the specific traits that arose from these cultural processes. In the pre-Romantic phase, Chapman suggests that the oppositional categories may have looked like this:[11]

Self	*Other*
rule	disrule
order	disorder
culture	nature
human	animal
controlled	uncontrolled
lawful	lawless
clean	dirty
reason	unreason
intellect	emotion
constant	inconstant
modern	backward
progressive	regressive

He then lists how the Celts were perceived after the process of romanticization. The traits in parentheses show the traits before the new 'moral valuation':

Self	*Other*
constraint	freedom
predictable	unpredictable
artificial	natural
urban	rural
(culture)	(nature)
artificial	natural
(human)	(animal)

reserved	impulsive
formal	informal
conventional	creative
sterile	fertile
(clean)	(dirty)
calculation	imagination
(reason)	(unreason)
measurement	passion
(intellect)	(emotion)
Christian	Pagan
religion	superstition
rational	irrational

Chapman goes on to illustrate how these traits, or stereotypes, have been and still are reflected in contemporary writings and beliefs about the Celts. He refers to a number of sources, from Matthew Arnold's polemics about the sentimental Celts in *The Study of Celtic Literature* to the May 1977 edition of *National Geographic* which contained a popular and picturesque rendering of life and culture of the Celtic lands.

Chapman concludes by stating that those today who identify themselves as 'Celts' are only unified by their opposition to the establishment, whether that is England, France, modernity, pollution, or Christianity. Chapman notes that as, in his view, the Celts are poised to play the moral other, many left-wing movements of the sixties, seventies and eighties found sympathy and clarity within a Celtic metaphor. In his final thoughts, he states that although he may have deconstructed the Celts out of existence historically, this category does have real meaning for people and so their experiences should not be discounted.

So, how can we begin to evaluate this fully packed volume which addresses a wide range of subjects? In the end, the questions Chapman raises are much more significant than any solutions he proposes.

Chapman's critique of popularly held beliefs concerning connections between Celtic language usage, culture and artifact distribution are quite useful, even if they are not necessarily original. Chapman does, however, lay out the paradigm with reference to the Celts in clear and direct language. It is true that many people would like to believe in a 'Celtic civilization' that spanned prehistoric Europe and has in some sense continued in an unbroken line to the Celts of the present day. Unfortunately, this is impossible to prove, and Chapman does a commendable job of presenting the academic biases that have led to such inquiries. Linguistic and archaeological definitions of 'Celtic' are quite different and, as Megaw and Megaw note, the evidence for 'Celtic' languages and 'Celtic' artifacts in prehistory are nowhere near consistent.[13]

Furthermore, as many contemporary scholars of nationalism have pointed out, language, ethnicity and material culture do not exist as a one-to-one correlation, and are not naturally linked into organic units. Such an assertion has largely been the product of a modern nationalism that arose in tandem with the development of social scientific methodology.[14] Chapman's contribution lies in unpacking the discipline of Celtic Studies in this light. Chapman, like McDonald before him, critiques Celtic Studies as an enterprise of philology, mainly concerned with comparing words, reconstructing meanings, and recreating cultures, sometimes rather indiscriminately with 'results' sounding more like fantasy projection than proof. Celtic Studies *has* developed within a discourse of emergent nationalism; the same can be said for folkloristics and the many other 'ethnic' studies disciplines now coming into prominence. For a discipline to have an understanding of the agendas that form the basis of its methodology, is a healthy thing. The social and humanistic sciences have been facing this crisis for at least a decade, and it is time for Celtic Studies to follow suit.

But just as Celtic Studies has developed out of emergent nationalism, it has also developed out of colonialism. Thus, another significant contribution of Chapman's work is his explicit analysis of Celtic stereotyping, although he clearly did not intend for his work to be seen in this light. His description of how Celtic peoples have come to be known by these attributes is accurate. Chapman is certainly not the only one to suggest this condition, but he does outline the results most comprehensively. As noted above, he commences the discussion in his 1978 *The Gaelic Vision in Scottish Culture,* where he begins to outline these oppositional categories with respect to the Gaelic communities in Scotland. At this stage he refers to the 'feminization' of the Gael, noting the similarities between dominant conceptions of the Gael and women. Saunders in 1983 recognized the same tendency in depictions of the Celts in general:

> The image of the Celts, on the other hand, derives from late-eighteenth century interest in the Natural Man not yet entered into civil society. Is his state innocent or barbaric? . . . The Celt is seen as an emotional creature, childlike, and unskilled in commerce, industry and administration. He (sic) is much concerned by hearth and homestead, and is given to strong fits of religiosity. Nevertheless, his loyalty to his past experience is extremely strong, and that loyalty is equally firm when transferred

to a masterful lord. In short, the typical Celt appears to manifest those characteristics and to voice those concerns which a nineteenth-century middle class Frenchman or Englishman would have considered appropriate in his wife.[15]

In 1986 Patrick Sims-Willliams described what he termed the 'Visionary Celt', referring to the stereotype of the Celt as mystical poet that has been perpetuated by both Celtic enthusiasts and Celts themselves.[16] He chronicles the development of this theme through the writings of Gerald of Wales, Arnold and Renan, and more recent works like Richard Kearney's *Irish Mind* and Robert O'Driscoll's (ed.) *The Celtic Consciousness*.[17]

Sims-Williams and Saunders both suggest the notion of 'feedback' and 'co-conspiracy' whereby the population in question reify and identify with the stereotype:

> racial stereotypes of the Celts are not solely created and maintained by non-Celts in an imperialist context, important though this context has often been. A shared sense of Celtic 'otherness' can be exploited by Celtic individuals and groups working within or against the non-Celtic establishment, so it is not surprising that some Celts should have an interest in maintaining it.[18]

> Ernest Renan . . . and Matthew Arnold completed the forging of that Celtic image which now seems to have gained acceptance in the Celtic countries themselves.[19]

The acceptance of Celtic 'otherness' by the Celts is amply borne out. Chapman cites many textual and recorded examples, but others are not hard to find. Henry Jenner uses many of these stereotypical conventions in his essay 'Cornwall: A Celtic Nation:

> As for Celtic characteristics, who could deny them to the Cornish? The imaginative temperament, the poetic mind, the superstitions, if you like to call them so, the religious fervour, the generosity of heart, the kindly hospitality, the passionate nature, the absolute honesty, the thirst for knowledge, the clan spirit, the homing instinct, all these are there.[20]

An understanding of how these conventions have developed and subsequently have been employed by Celts in shaping their social realities is very valuable indeed. Chapman provides a detailed template that can be applied to textual analysis, and can also be field tested. We can see how these conceptions of the 'ideal' Celt influenced the political platform of Eamon DeValera and contributed to the visions underlying the formation of the Irish nation-state:

> That Ireland which we dreamed of would be the home of a people who valued material wealth only as a basis of right living, of a people who were satisfied with frugal comfort and devoted their leisure to things of the spirit; a land whose countryside would be bright and cozy homesteads, whose fields and villages would be joyous with sounds of industry, the romping of sturdy children, the contests of athletic youths, the laughter of comely maidens; whose firesides would be the forums of the wisdom of serene old age.[21]

This quote exemplifies De Valera's vision of Ireland as predominantly rural, where the development of the spirit would be more important than the development of industry. This perspective has radical implications for an analysis of the Celtic revival in Cornwall, where symbols of identity based in a successful industrial past compete with a construction of 'Celticity' based in stereotypes of rurality, and an emphasis on artistic and spiritual awareness, where technological and industrial advances are either devalued, or transcended.

Although Chapman's model is useful, the largest failing of this work is that he fails to recognize the roots of the paradigm. With his clearly anti-Marxist stance he refuses to admit to the fact that he is dealing with a discourse of oppression. He comes close at one point by stating that:

> There is a suggestion that the rule/misrule series of metaphors, so obviously attractive to the human imagination, may have had a sexual element for a very long period. The Anglo-Saxon/Celtic recension is, perhaps, only a footnote to a longer and more fundamental story.[22]

Yet this oppositional construction goes far beyond a 'sexual element', and what Chapman maintains is a 'dispassionate' view of the facts on his part, reads like a frighteningly Anglophilic revisionist fantasy.

Chapman provides ample textual examples of how the Celts have been viewed as 'other' by the 'central, dominant' population, but he downplays the fact that these characteristics of 'Otherness' were used as justifications for colonization, patriarchy and ethnocide. This is one of the reasons why characterizations of colonized peoples (Native Americans and Australians, Africans, women and so on) often look so similar. There are many scholars who have examined the nature of these Western metaphors. An early example is Sherry Ortner's 1974 essay 'Is Female to Male as Nature Is to Culture?', where she outlines the metaphorical connection between women and nature, as men with 'culture' have attempted to devalue, control and dominate them both.[23] Another prominent example is Said's *Orientalism,* concerning Western images of the East.[24] In effect, there seems to be an entire body of work concerning these very oppositions, that Chapman does not address.

Instead of acknowledging the role of colonialism in shaping attitudes toward Celtic peoples, Chapman attempts to empower the Celts by making them masters of their own destinies:

> As with my discussion of the language question, my aim is not to take sides, but primarily to show that the periphery is where responsibility for culture loss seems to lodge . . . the inadequacy of the 'external oppression' model is perhaps best demonstrated by the continued popular commitment to emigration and language change, after the perceived 'external oppression' has been removed. Proponents of this model are driven, at this stage, to arguing that the people have been so deceived and demoralized that they are eventually reduced to oppressing themselves. The patent absurdity of such arguments, and their implicit contempt for the wit and intelligence of the common people, should be their own condemnation.[25]

He states that the main cause of Highland depopulation is that people want to leave because they disliked the lifestyle. He even goes so far as to invoke the conventions of 'traditionality' to bolster his claims about Celtic language decline:

> Many intellectuals in recent years have tried to impose this responsibility [of preservation] upon the remaining speakers of Celtic languages. This effectively is to ask them to abandon the traditional and long standing practice of their culture, which is to seek replacement of the Celtic language by English, and to implement instead a radical novelty-attachment to their language for its own sake.[26]

It is at this point that the logic of his argument falls apart. Chapman claims that culture change in Celtic areas occurs from 'a desire to emulate things perceived as socially superior, coming from places perceived as centres of sophistication' and then goes on to call this an *'indigenous* structure of estimation'.[27] If the power to control trends and images lies at the centre, how can Chapman suddenly give so much decision making power to the periphery? With this argument he seems to be forgetting the entire centre/periphery dynamic that has been central to his model. If, in fact, this power relationship exists, the power lies in the centre, and it is this that causes the culture change.

Chapman's strength seems to be in challenging paradigms that have been considered 'natural'. Then why, one must ask, does he seem to treat the centre/periphery relationship as a 'natural' development? There was, presumably, a time when London was not the centre of Britain, either economically or culturally. It is the necessity of serving the needs of the centre that causes the economy and culture of the periphery to conform to more centrist conventions. The project of Celtic independence movements today is to shift this model and create new centres.

The Celts: The Construction of a Myth could benefit from some of the same critiques that followed Maryon McDonald's 1986 essay 'Celtic Ethnic Kinship and the Problem of Being English' in which she previewed some of the theories in *We Are Not French!*. Teresa San Roman eloquently summed up some of the main concerns:

> The past is a source not only of material for the elaboration of symbols but frequently also of explanations for existing structures . . . The question is not so much whether Breton is closer to French or to its hypothetical origin as, for example, what the social relations have been between those who speak it and the various central powers. . .Nationalist political movements that appeal to ethnicity might be said to correspond to effective divisions of historical roots, and it is precisely their tradition of difference and their history of opposition that endures, whatever their cultural content or their interpretation at any moment of their origin or culture.[28]

Likewise, Anthony P.Cohen notes:

> But it is less important for anthropologists to cast academic aspersions on the authenticity of a group's putative lineage than to attempt to understand why a distinctive and oppositional identity should be so compelling to its members (some of whom are only voluntary affiliates).[29]

It is this challenge that should engage us in the field of Cornish Studies.

NOTES AND REFERENCES

1. Malcolm Chapman, *The Celts: The Construction of a Myth*, London, 1992, p. 4.
2. C. Curtain, H. Donnan and T.M. Wilson, *Irish Urban Studies*, Belfast, 1993, p. 1.

3. Michael Hechter, *Internal Colonialism: The Cetic Fringe in British National Development 1536–1966*, London, 1975.
4. Sharon MacDonald, 'Identity Complexes in Western Europe: Social Anthropological Perspectives', in Sharon MacDonald (ed.), *Inside European Identities*, Oxford, 1993, p. 11.
5. Malcolm Chapman, *The Gaelic Vision in Scottish Culture*, London, 1978.
6. Malcolm Chapman, 'Semantics and the Celt', 1982.
7. Maryon McDonald, *We are Not French! Language, Culture and Identity in Brittany*, London, 1989.
8. Benedict Anderson, *Imagined Communities*, London, 1983; E.J. Hobsbawm, *Nations and Nationalism Since 1780: Programme, Myth, Reality*, Cambridge, 1990.
9. See Chapman, 1992, p. 31.
10. Chapman, 1992, p. 50.
11. Chapman, 1992, p. 211.
12. Chapman, 1992, pp. 212–213.
13. Ruth Megaw and Vincent Megaw, 'The Prehistoric Celts: Identity and Contextuality', in M.Kina and N.Venclova (eds), *Whither Archaeology?: Papers in Honour of Evzen Neustupny*, Prague, 1995, p. 238.
14. Richard Handler, *Nationalism and the Politics of Culture in Quebec*, Madison (Wisconsin), 1988, p. 8.
15. Tim Saunders, 'Cornish: Symbol and Substance', in Cathal O'Lvain (ed.) *For A Celtic Future*, Dublin, 1983, pp. 255–256.
16. Patrick Sims-Williams, 'The Visionary Celt: The Construction of and Ethnic Preconception', *Cambridge Medieval Studies*, 11, 1986, p. 78.
17. Cited in Sims-Williams, 1986, p. 75.
18. Sims-Williams, 1986, p. 77.
19. Saunders, 1983, p. 255.
20. Henry Jenner, 'Cornwall: A Celtic Nation', *Celtic Review*, Vol. 1, No. 1, 1904.
21. Cited in Michael O. Henry, 'Institutions for the Promotion of Indigenous Music: The Case for Ireland's *Comhaltas Ceoltoiri Eireann*', *Ethnomusicology*, Vol. 33, No. 1, p. 69.
22. Chapman, 1992, p. 217
23. Sherry B. Ortnor, 'Is Female to Male as Nature is to Culture' in Michelle Zimbalist Rosaldo and Loise Lamphere (eds), *Women, Culture and Society*, Stanford, 1974.
24. Edward Said, *Orientalism*, New York, 1978.
25. Chapman, 1992, p. 108.
26. Chapman, 1992, p. 99.
27. Chapman, 1992, p. 109.
28. Cited in McDonald, 1986, p. 343.
29. Cited in McDonald, 1986, p. 342.

CORNISH TODAY: A MODERN CORNISH PERSPECTIVE

Neil Kennedy

N.J.A. Williams, *Cornish Today: An Examination of the Revived Language*, Kernewek dre Lyther, Sutton Coldfield, 1995, 289 pp., £11.95.

The appearance of *Cornish Today* has added a new chapter to the debate about revived Cornish. For the first time since the great schism of the mid 1980s a professional Celtic linguist has come to the defence of Unified Cornish (UC), the standard form of the language which was devised by R.M.Nance and used by almost all learners of Cornish until 1985. In so doing, Williams makes suggestions for reform of UC, rather than its abandonment, and presents the reformed version as 'Unified Cornish Revised' (UCR). To the stalwart advocates of UC, Williams may thus be seen as a valuable champion whose intervention heralds better times and provides a way forward. Amongst other users of Cornish, however, his contribution has received a mixed, sometimes contradictory response. But whatever these individual views might be, Williams has succeeded in reinvigorating the discussion.

Williams subtitles *Cornish Today* 'an examination of the revived language'. He presents sections on each of the three generally-used forms of revived Cornish but, since others have had opportunities to reply from the standpoint of Kernewek Kemmyn ('Common' or 'phonemic' Cornish), I shall mainly confine my attention here to the sections on Modern Cornish (MC) and its revived form. Firstly, I should make the general observation that Williams seems to have little idea about what exactly Richard Gendall (the main mover behind the revival of MC) is promoting and almost no idea of who else is involved. Williams' deductions in this area are disappointingly based on supposition. Richard Gendall has been the principal researcher of MC but decisions about the direction of MC are made collectively through an active process of negotiation and consensus. There has been an input from a number of Cornish revivalists, Celtic Studies students and academic linguists. Williams seems to be unaware of this ongoing process or its results. He refers frequently to 'the proponents of modern Cornish' but, apart from references to Gendall himself, he refers only to articles written by two learners, one of them a member of my beginners' class in Redruth.

Williams has had no correspondence with the Cornish Language Council (founded in 1988) and does not refer to it. He refers only to the private publishing body Teere ha Tavaz. Perhaps this is why he does not refer to Gendall's work on pronunciation and seems unaware of it. Similarly, he makes no reference to any teaching materials and does not appear to have examined the magazine *An Garrack*, the main body of writing in Revived Modern Cornish (RMC). It is these materials which would have given a clear idea of what is being promoted. Instead, he has based his appraisal of RMC on a misunderting of the purpose of two source materials produced by Gendall at an earlier stage in his work. Williams assumes that Gendall's *A Student's Dictionary of Modern Cornish* (SDMC) (Menheniot, 1990) and *A Student's Grammar of Modern Cornish* (SGMC) (Menheniot, 1991) are intended as materials for the ordinary, grass-roots learner of the language and that the wide choice of textual spellings and examples contained in them represent the language being promoted and taught. He assumes that all of the tentative reconstructions proffered in the second volume have been accepted into the revived language. In fact, these two publications are foundation texts, showing part of the historical basis of RMC. They are a starting point, not an end and were produced to assist in the collective process of working towards an accurate reconstruction of MC. In basing his judgement solely on these works and articles written by two learners of Cornish, Williams has succeeded only in reviewing something that is not actively promoted by anyone.

RMC is based on the period beginning with the homilies of John Tregear (*c.* 1558) and ending with William Bodinar's letter (1776). In other words, it is centred on a hypothetical date between the years 1660 and 1670. From this date it is possible and quite legitimate to go back a century to take in Tregear and Jordan (1611), or forward a century to take in the younger Mount's Bay writers and William Bodinar. Williams evidently assumes the central target date of RMC to be nearer to 1750, and makes much of the scarcity of material from the eighteenth century and what he describes as 'the poor quality of late Cornish'. He is unaware of the extent to which RMC openly draws from the works of Tregear and Jordan, and in later sections he draws attention to the use of information from Jordan as though it were some dark secret. This fundamental misunderstanding ensures that many of Williams' thrusts at RMC miss their target. Spellings taken from Jordan often sit quite comfortably alongside those of William Rowe (b 1666), a Sancreed farmer and translator of scripture who is often held up as an example by champions of MC. It would seem that Rowe was not entirely ignorant of other Cornish writing. Rowe receives little attention in Williams' examination of MC. Instead, he focuses his attention on the worst available sources, namely the younger members of the Boson family. His objectivity in doing so has to be questioned. He seems to be seeking out the poorest examples of the latest Cornish writing in an attempt to discredit the whole.

Much is made of the fact that many features associated with MC were present at an early date. He argues that, since this is the case, we might just as well go back to Tudor Cornish, an argument that works both ways. He strengthens the case for using those features by demonstrating that they are a long established part of Cornish and not the 'corrupt' features of a language in terminal decline. This is most welcome.

Williams suggests that 'Gendall speaks of Late Cornish as if it were a completely different language from Middle Cornish'. However, Gendall has frequently drawn attention to the presence of features associated with MC in texts such as the play *Beunans Meriasek* (*c.* 1504).

The impression is given that RMC advocates complete individual freedom to choose from the spellings of the period. In fact the Cornish Language Council promotes a standard orthography, representing a careful selection from textually attested examples. Williams then draws attention to some proposals put forward by Gendall in the magazine *Carn* (87:18), incidentally assumming in the process that they are a collective statement from 'Gendall and his associates'. These proposals are not those which were subsequently adopted as a standard and they have no bearing on the eventual spelling of RMC. Williams suggests that there is a contradiction between the assertion, on the one hand, that RMC 'uses the spelling of the writers of Late Cornish' and, on the other, the statement that users of RMC are 'evolving a sounder spelling system'. We have indeed worked towards a sounder and more consistent orthography but have done so by selecting the spellings of individual words from the variety found in historical texts; a reasonable approach which is in keeping with the wish to be both historically accurate and practical. The Council only deviates from the use of attested spellings in standardizing common suffixes. To do otherwise would present unnecessary obstacles to learners of the language. When Gendall wrote of the spelling *evolving*, he was referring to the process by which native spellings were selected from the range available, the *evolution* being towards an orthography which hangs together and is practical.

Williams draws attention to the respelling of words taken from the work of the Welsh linguist Edward Lhuyd. Lhuyd visited Cornwall in 1700 and recorded thousands of words in a form of phonetic notatation resembling our modern IPA. The Cornish Language Council supports the respelling of this in accordance with MC conventions. To not do so would be absurd. Nevertheless, Williams objects to the respelling of Lhuyd's dh in the verb *methes*. Since Lhuyd's script is simply a form of phonetic notation, it would seem quite reasonable to respell it according to the practice of native writers. Elsewhere in *Cornish Today* Williams advances an unconvincing argument for the continued use of dh in UC, in which he demonstrates an unfamiliarity with the pronunciation of the place names *Baldhu* and *Poldhu*. In Baldhu <d> represents /d/ and in Poldhu it is /dʒ/.

Williams' section entitled 'The Morphology of Modern Cornish' shows an unawareness of current practice and an over-estimation of the need to reconstruct by conjecture which is again based on a misunderstanding of the target period. In discussing the future tense of *boaz* 'to be' Williams objects to the spelling veath 'will be', saying that a <ea> suggests /i:/ to the reader, rather than /e:/. However a <ea> commonly represents /e:/ in MC. My students, familiar with place names like *Carn Brea*, quickly grasp this. Although <ea> a is also frequently employed in words containing /ɛ/ or /ɛ:/ it is rarely used for /i:/. For this MC more frequently uses <ee>, often adding a final mute <e> for good measure.

Williams' discussion of the prepositional pronouns shows misunderstanding of the origins and nature of the paradigms used in RMC. Again he has reviewed tentative proposals made in 1991 rather than those subsequently adopted. This renders his discussion almost worthless as an observation of RMC. The paradigm of *thort* 'from' now used in RMC is, for example:

> *thurtam, thaworthas, thurta/thaworte, thaworthan, thort why, thoranz*

> Similarly, the paradigm of *war* 'on'used in RMC is, for the record:
> *waram, warnas, warnotha/warnothe, warnan, warno, warnans/ warnethe*

extended form:
wara ve, warnas che, war eve/hye, wara nye, wara why, war angye

Williams makes very heavy weather of the first person singular of *worth/orth/urt* 'on/at/about', criticizing Gendall for including the conjectural form *ortham* in SGMC. Gendall's recent publications do not give a simple inflected form for the first person singular. In teaching the following paradigm is used. All of the forms are attested:

urta ve/ortha ve, orthez, worto/(w)orty, orthin, ortho, worthan

If we were to use a simple inflected form, then *ortham* would seem to be the most likely candidate. The ending *-am* has routinely replaced the ending *-af* in Cornish written after Jordan, both in prepositions and verbs. We find *genam, rebbam, thurtam, theram, thom, ome, veam, reegam, madam/vadam, ellam, menjam* etc. The only examples in *-af* are from Lhuyd or the later dictionary writers. At the same time the final *-f* is absorbed when followed by the suffixed pronoun *ve* to give such forms as *urta ve, gena ve* etc. Williams similarly objects to the form *gennam* as the first person singular of *gen* 'with', yet this is taken from J. Boson and by analogy with the first person of verbs we can clearly see that it is typical of our central target period, however many examples of *genaf* there might be in the earlier sources of RMC. Clearly in reviving the language we have a simple choice between the *-af* ending used by Jordan and earlier writers and the *-am* ending which has replaced it in later writing. To mix the two would result in a false and anachronistic amalgam. Williams does not seem to understand the nature and necessity of this choice.

It is suggested that the entire paradigm of *dar/der/dreth* 'through' used in RMC is an invention. However, it is largely drawn from Jordan (WJ) and Tregear (JT) with one person supplied by Lhuyd. The first person singular, recorded as *drethaf* in Jordan, is safely respelt as *dretham*. The other parts of the paradigm are all attested as follows:

2. drethas (WJ), 3m. dretha (WJ)/tardha (Lh), 1pl. drethan (JT), 2pl. drethowhy (JT), 3pl. dretha (JT)

RMC uses the following paradigm:

1. dretham, 2. drethas, 3m. dretha/tartha, 3f. drethe, 1pl. drethan, 2pl. dretho, 3pl. dretha

Only the feminine third person singular has been supplied by conjecture. The basic preposition itself is supplied as *dar*(T.Boson), *der* (Jordan, Rowe, Lhuyd), *dur* (T.Tonkin), *dreath* (Rowe), *dreth* (N.Boson), *drethe* (Borlase) and *dreath* (Rowe). RMC uses *der/dreth*.

Williams claims that Gendall's paradigm of *en* 'in' is 'particularly interesting', stating that 'Gendall's entire paradigm is an invention'. He objects to a hypothetical paradigm containing <t> or <tt> which is to be found in SGMC. However, in giving a paradigm of attested forms Williams does not include, (2s.) *etta ge* (Godolphin motto) or (3pl.) *et angy* (J.Tonkin). He also fails to observe that the 3s. form *ena* is permitted in RMC as an alternative to *etna/etta* etc. What we have to draw on then, is an incomplete paradigm of later forms containing <t> supplemented by earlier forms without <t>:

> 1. *innove/innave/ynaf (JT)* 2. *etta ge,* 3m. *ena/etten/itna/it an/etta/ etna,* 3f. *inhy (JT)/yny/unhy (WJ),* 1pl. *innan/innan ny (JT),* 2pl. *inno why (JT)* 3pl. *ettanz/ittanz/ettans/et angye*

The standard paradigm in RMC does indeed include some con-jectural forms but not as many as suggested:

> 1. *ena ve/eta ve,* 2. *etta ge,* 3m. *ena/etta/etna/etten,* 3f. *ette* 1pl. *ettan,* 2pl. *etto/etto why,* 3pl. *ettans/et angye*

These *t*-forms are probably the result of pre-occlusion. Already in Jordan we have the form *ydn* which might easily be expected to develop into *etn/etten*. This seems more likely as an explanation than Williams' suggestion of reshaping by analogy with *orta* and *theworta*.

Williams does not make clear why he has misgivings about the feminine 3rd person singulars given by Gendall. I assume that it is because he has not understood that the final <e> in such forms as *hepthe* corresponds in pronunciation to <y> in his own listed paradigms. He has, I think, wrongly assumed that the final <e> is intended to be mute. Williams produces *warnedhy* and *drethy* by analogy with other preposi-tions. There is no real doubt that he is correct and the resulting pronunciation is exactly that of RMC. Indeed the paradigms of *reb* and *heb* suggested by Williams differ from those of RMC in spelling only, the exception being the first person singular which requires *-am* in RMC. What then is Williams casting doubt over? He has demon-strated himself that almost all of the persons required for the main prepositional pronouns are to found in sources written after 1550 and in producing his own paradigms has used the same amount of conjecture used in RMC. Indeed, his own proposals are almost identical.

Williams is surely seeking to pull the wool over our eyes when he compares the paradigm of the verb *boaz* in MC and UC. He offers the full paradigm in MC but only part of it in UC. The reader is presumably supposed to conclude that the MC is longer and more complex. A correct comparison would be as given below (UC in italics):

Particular:
yth -esof, yth esos, yma, yth-eson, yth-esough, ymons
theram, theze, (e)ma, theren, thero, mowns

Combined:
yth-esof ve, yth-esos ta, (y)ma ef/hy, yth-eson ny, yth-esough why, ymons y
thera ve, thesta, (e)ma e/hye, thera nye, thera why, ma'ngye

Simple:
esof, esos, usy / us, eson,esough, esons
eram, eze, igge / eze, eren, ero, iggans

Williams dismisses what Gendall terms the 'simplified present tense'. This tense is constructed by following a personal pronoun with a verbal noun, either directly or after the particle *a* (<earlier *ow*). Williams' dismissal of this construction as pidginized is unsound. The tense is well attested in MC from a number of writers and has come about because it is easy to use and serves a purpose. To dismiss it as 'not Cornish' is insufficient and illogical. Clearly, it is Cornish because it developed naturally in the mouths of Cornish speakers. Williams even gives a reasonable account of how it evolved from such constructions as *me ew ow credgy* > *me a credgy*. Other examples of the tense include:

Ny en gweel gun moyha: We will do it to our utmost (NB) (with infixed pronoun)
Me a moaz than venten: I am going to the spring (from the song: *Delkiow Sivy*)

In his discussion of Nicholas Boson's work, Williams gives an explanation of the word *fratier* which seems incredibly far-fetched. He would have us believe that it is derived from a hypothetical word *screffager* scribe < screffa 'to write'. The word is more plausibly a development or misreading of *pratier* : 'talker' derived from English *prate, prattle, prattler*.

Williams has not, it seems, examined Gendall's *The Pronunciation of Modern Cornish* or been privy to the mountain of discussion papers and correspondence generated. It is not surprising, therefore, that he has no clear idea about the recommended pronunciation of RMC. At one point he writes 'Gendall and his associates, however lacking any theoretical understanding of Cornish phonology . . .'; rather a bold and dismissive statement from one who (a) does not know who Gendall's associates are and (b) has not read all Gendall's own work.

He draws attention to Gendall's use of the English dialect of Penwith as a source for the phonology of Cornish and, like others who have no aquaintance with that dialect, he voices scepticism, saying that 'much more can be deduced . . . from Lhuyd and the surviving texts'. It should be understood that Gendall has examined the dialect of Penwith (or rather the former dialect) as only one line of enquiry and that the evidence so gained frequently corroborates evidence from written sources. The phonology of English previously spoken in West Penwith's fishing ports shows close correlation with the records of Lhuyd and the sounds deduced from the spelling of the late writers. Williams quotes M.F. Wakelin in dismissing dialect English as a source. In his *Language and History in Cornwall* (Leicester, 1975) Wakelin fails to identify the distinct dialect of the fishing ports and tells us that words which we hear everyday are no longer in use. Wakelin was able to get away with this because of the absence of informed and empowered, native peers who might disillusion or challenge him.

Other workers, such as David North (*Studies in Anglo-Cornish Phonology 2: Studies in the Phonology of West Penwith English*, Redruth, 1991) have similarly failed to identify the dialect of the fishing ports. In North's case he had no points of inquiry in West Penwith's ports. His work, although very informative, ignores the historical context of the area. In Penwith the inland areas have a very different dialect from Mount's Bay, the western coves and St Ives, almost certainly as a result of population mobility between Cornwall's mining areas.

Williams characterizes the orthography of MC as 'anglicized' or 'English-based' but does not acknowledge in making this point that the spelling of Middle Cornish reflects the contemporary orthography of English and French. MC has features of its own which reflect the writers efforts to show distinctive sounds in a graphic way. The use of <lh> and <llh> is one such example, common to a number of writers, including Tregear and Rowe.

Williams refers to difficulty in distinguishing between /e:/ and /i:/ in MC. It is not nearly as difficult as he suggests. In discussing his chosen example, Middle Cornish *bys* 'world', Williams ignores the spellings *beaze* (Rowe) and *beaz* (Gwavas). In reaching a standard for

RMC it is invariably possible to select attested spelling which minimize any potential confusion, yet Williams, having ignored recent work, refers only to SDMC.

Naturally, the author turns his attention to the lexicon of RMC. In what seems a rather nit-picking way, he draws attention to a number of words which have been taken from Middle Cornish or Lhuyd and respelt according to the principles generally used by writers such as William Rowe. It is, in reality, rarely necessary to draw from sources written before Tregear. Since no single period gives all of the answers, it would seem more logical for MC to draw from its past than for Middle Cornish to draw from its future. Williams also refers to 'The absence from MC of any mechanism for adopting new words'. RMC in fact uses a range of strategies for the adoption of neologisms. It resists, however, the wanton assembly of clumsy and improbable words which has sadly characterised the recent development of some forms of Cornish, to the derision of critics.

Williams stresses the use in RMC of words taken from dialect English. In doing so he draws his examples from SDMC, the purpose of which is, as stated, that of a source dictionary. The majority of dialect words listed by Williams have not found their way into RMC. Their presence in SDMC does not indicate that they have been adopted, it merely means that they are available for consideration. Most have subsequently been considered and rejected. Cornish did, nevertheless, draw from the English dialect of Cornwall. Tregear's *'unfitty'* is one such example. It remains legitimate to fill lexical gaps from dialect sources if the words in question would have been known to bilingual speakers of Cornish and English in the seventeenth and eighteenth centuries. Such words have a special place in Cornwall and the gaps do after all have to be filled. An example of this would be the word *frawk* 'a pullover'. In recent years UC (and subsequently Common Cornish) has come up with *gwlanek* from *gwlan/gwloan/gwlawn*: wool. *Frawk*, although from French via English, would seem to be more realistic, comfortable, and furthermore likely to have been understood by late Cornish speakers.

One of the most interesting parts of *Cornish Today* is the section entitled 'Cornish in Eastern Cornwall' in which the traditional view, of a Cornish language always in retreat, is challenged. The case is put strongly for a medieval resurgence of Cornish and the survival of the language in East Cornwall until a later date than commonly assumed. Willaims draws on historical references and place-name evidence to support his case. As Cornish enthusiasts we have to examine the evidence with extra care since these are things that we want to hear! In presenting a counter argument to balance his claim, Williams refers

to names in mid and West Cornwall in which *-nt* and *-d* have not become
-ns, -s, the normal development, giving this as evidence of early English
settlement and suggesting that the decendants of these settlers became
Cornish-speaking. Let's consider another aspect of this: *Penpont* (St
Mawgan in Pydar) is alternatively known as *Penpons*. Here the
existence, side by side, of two forms of the name is interesting. We can
perhaps suppose that one form was formerly used when speaking
English and the other when speaking Cornish. We can compare
Liskeard where English preserved an archaic form after the Cornish
name had developed into *Liskyrres*. Similarly *Cutparret* is recorded as
Cosparveth and *Bodmin* as *Bosvena*. The same phenomenon can be
seen in Brittany where the French forms of names often preserve an
older form eg.*Concarneau* for *Konkerne*. The existence of different
forms in English should not be a surprise. In some cases we even find
Cornish names translated eg. *Grampound* for *Ponsmur* and *Blackadon*
for *Menadue* (Cawsand).This last example is still alternatively known
by both names. We might also conclude from the persistence of certain
forms in *d* and *t*, that the shift of *-nt, -d > -ns, s* did not take place
uniformly. This would particularly seem to apply in the case of the
suffix *-dy* (house). We can find a few examples in Cornish writing of
words which have not developed in the expected way. An example
would be *hunt tho* 'beyond' (N.Boson). In this combination the
expected development to **hunz* (Jordan: *hans*) has not taken place.
Similarly, when looking at pre-occlusion we can see a pattern of
development that is not uniform.

The suggestions for the reform of UC are, in part, welcome and
would certainly narrow the gap between UC and RMC to the point
where it ceased to be a significant barrier to understanding and
co-operation. If, in addition to using the proposed spelling, grammar
and vocabulary of UCR, speakers were to regularly introduce pre-
occlusion into their spoken language, they would come very close
indeed to RMC. Indeed, it is interesting to note that Williams'
proposals seem to differ from RMC in little more than spelling, a factor
which creates new possiblities for dialogue. Nevertheless, by offering
a poorly informed review of RMC, Williams has made that dialogue
harder.

If it is to suit itself to the needs of the revival, it is clear that UC
requires a radical revision. Its progress to date has been characterised
by a high drop-out rate, poor achievement of the recommended
pronunciation and a failure to strike a chord with the public. In 1985,
after fifty years of existence, it had no more than fifty reasonably fluent
speakers.

It is evident that Williams, like others before him, does not appreciate the emotional pull of MC or its immediate familiarity to people raised amongst Cornish place-names, surnames and dialect survivals. My own experience of teaching and promoting RMC tells me that it is intrinsically better fitted to the purpose of developing a sense of ownership amongst people with that experience. Without that sense of ownership, no meaningful revival of Cornish is possible.

Cornish Today is useful in so far as it lays out, in a coherent way, a proposed reform of UC which has to be considered an improvement. Users of UC may indeed wish to adopt some of the proposals. In doing so they cannot fail to reduce the differences between Unified and Modern Cornish, and this can only benefit the language as a whole.

BOOK REVIEWS

Anne Duffin, *Faction and Faith: Politics and Religion of the Cornish Gentry before the Civil War*, University of Exeter Press, 1996, xvi pp. + 278 pp., ISBN 0 85989 435 5, £27.50

One of the most exciting developments in the writing of Cornish history in recent years has been a return to old themes by a new generation of younger scholars anxious to shed new light and to apply new perspectives. Nowhere is this trend more apparent than in the early modern period, where a vigorous reassessment of Tudor and (especially) seventeenth-century Cornwall is currently in progress. The Civil War, in particular, is attracting considerable attention, and the most recent contribution is Anne Duffin's examination of political and religious affiliations amongst the Cornish gentry in the years before the outbreak of hostilities.

Mary Coate's *Cornwall in the Great Civil War and Interregnum*, first published as long ago as 1933, was the first attempt to assess in detail the events of the conflict in Cornwall, and it has stood the test of time remarkably well. However, the renewed interest in the period, of which Dr Duffin's book is a part, has opened a stimulating historiographical debate about the way in which the history of seventeenth-century Cornwall is best understood and written. Dr Mark Stoyle, for example, has complained in his study of the Civil War in Devon (*Loyalty and Locality: Popular Allegiance in Devon during the English Civil War*, UEP, 1994) that, ever since Mary Coate's intervention, historians have tended to downplay and underestimate the strength of popular Royalist sentiment in Cornwall. Dr Duffin, in contrast, suggests that Coate over-estimated and over-simplified Cornish Royalist allegiance, and offers an alternative perspective which emphasizes Parliamentarian and Puritan sympathies, especially in South East Cornwall.

This apparent conflict of interpretation is resolved, at least in part, by a recognition that Mark Stoyle is concerned principally with popular opinion, the beliefs of ordinary people, while Anne Duffin has focused on the gentry. As Dr Stoyle has admitted graciously (in an article in the *English Historical Review*, Vol.CXI, 441, April 1996), 'The two approaches complement, rather than contradict each other, therefore'. Dr Duffin, equally graciously, concedes in her book that 'Stoyle's conclusion that religion was the primary influence upon popular allegiance in Cornwall is entirely convincing'.

However, this amicable papering over of the cracks is not entirely satisfactory. Mark Stoyle does indeed concentrate on the passions and motives of the ordinary Cornish (and Devon) folk, while Anne Duffin's book, as its subtitle makes plain, is interested principally in the gentry. Nonetheless, and this is where the debate is by no means resolved, Stoyle seeks to explain popular belief by pointing to the apparent strength of Cornish ethnic identity in the seventeenth century, while Duffin sets the Puritan sympathies that she identifies within a model that stresses the alleged relative weakness of Cornish ethnicity in that period.

Taking her cue from John Chynoweth's (in this reviewer's opinion, flawed) sketch of Cornish identity in his unpublished PhD 'The Gentry of Tudor Cornwall' (Exeter, 1994), Duffin cautions that this identity 'should not be over-emphasized', not least because 'by 1485 no more than half of the county's inhabitants could speak the [Cornish] language'. This perhaps conservative figure would certainly be disputed by some Cornish language scholars, not least N.J.A. Williams at Dublin, but even if it is correct it is not to be dismissed lightly. Ken George has estimated (*Cornish Studies*, 14, 1986) that in 1500 Cornish was spoken by some 33,000 people in an area over half the size of Cornwall. Although, by George's estimates, the number of speakers may have shrunk to 'only' 14,000 by 1650, that was still a considerable proportion of Cornwall's population of c.93,000, with the language still spoken in more than a quarter of the geographical area of Cornwall. Rather like the Welsh language in contemporary Wales, the Cornish language in the early modern period is not to be written-off that easily.

Moreover, language is often a poor or only partial indicator of the strength and nature of ethnic identity. As Anthony D. Smith has emphasized in his *The Ethnic Origin of Nations* (London, 1986, p. 181), the insistence on language as an essential marker of ethnic or national identity, 'leads to gross simplification and misunderstanding of both ancient and modern periods of ethnic community'. Any assessment of Cornish identity, therefore, is necessarily flawed if it restricts itself principally to a consideration of language, a point well understood by Stoyle in his examination of seventeenth-century Cornwall.

Ironically, it was hardly necessary for Duffin to downplay the strength of Cornish identity in order to establish the legitimacy of her new perspectives. There was indeed, as she demonstrates so well, a reservoir of Puritan and Parliamentarian sympathy amongst elements of the Cornish gentry. But this is best understood against the background of the increasing anglicization of that gentry, especially in South East Cornwall. A better starting-point for her study might have been a fresh look at Richard Carew and his *Survey of Cornwall* of 1602. In contrast to the tired and oft-repeated assessments of Carew as antiquarian observer or even as an 'authentic Cornish voice', he might be viewed more profitably as a window into the process of anglicization that was by then affecting the Cornish gentry. Carew needs to be seen as both 'insider' and 'outsider', a member of the anglicized Cornish gentry whose sympathies and connections were in one sense Cornish, and yet who wrote from the margins. This marginality was both geographical (Carew lived at Antony) and cultural, Carew presenting himself as a typical 'Englishman' of the Renaaisance, in contradistinction to the ordinary Cornish from whom he was greatly removed. The anglicization of the Cornish gentry was not a function of, and is not explained by, the relative weakness (or otherwise) of the popular Cornish identity.

This should not, however, be a stumbling block in our wider appreciation of Duffin's contribution. Her strength lies in her gift for research and in her attention to detail, the ability to prise telling facts from unlikely and obscure sources. She calculates that there were some 321 gentry families in Cornwall in the years leading up to the Civil War, a figure which does not include the more obscure lesser gentry (for whom few records survive) but which does cover a broad spectrum from minor country gentlemen, through newly-emergent merchant families (such as the Rashleighs of Fowey), to the new peers (Cornwall's first) created in 1625 and 1628 respectively—Richard, 1st Baron Robartes of Truro, and John, 1st Baron Mohun of Okehampton. Approximately one-third of this gentry constituted the ruling elite of Cornwall, according to Duffin's calculations, and about a quarter of the 'greater gentry' was concentrated in the Hundred of East (Wivelshire)—the territorial subdivision of South East Cornwall that lay between the Looe and Tamar rivers.

The concentration of the more significant (and anglicized) gentry in South East Cornwall was reflected in Cornish religious divisions, with Puritanism more strongly established there than elsewhere. By the late 1620s the anti-Calvinist 'Arminians' had gained the upper-hand in the Anglican Church, signalling the re-assertion of High Church theology and ritual. This no doubt grated amongst Puritans in Cornwall as it did elsewhere, and for the gentry it simply added to an already growing catalogue of complaints and discontents. Cornwall had suffered, probably disproportionately, from the effects of Charles I's war with France and Spain. Local men had been pressed into dubious military adventures that had gone badly wrong, coastal defences such as Pendennis and St Mawes had been neglected and ill-provisioned (at a time when 'Turkish' pirates from North Africa were an ever-present threat along the Cornish coast), and the Forced Loan of 1626 had required the inhabitants of Cornwall to pay some £2000. The latter prompted the stand of the Cornish 'loan refusers', its focus amongst the Puritan gentry of South East Cornwall—men such as Sir John Eliot of St Germans, Andrew Manaton of Trecarrel, and Nicholas Trefusis of Landue.

Such influences and events helped determine the political allegiances of Cornwall's ruling elite and its relationship with central government. Come the Civil War, Cornwall might indeed declare for the King, with Royalism a popular expression of Cornish particularism, but—as Anne Duffin shows—Cornish religious and political allegiance amongst the gentry was complex. *Faction and Faith* is a major contribution to our understanding of a particular section of Cornish society at an important point in Cornwall's history. Much remains to be done, however, before our reassessment of the era is complete. In constructing new perspectives and new interpretations, we should be careful to learn from new debates that have emerged elsewhere, and we should not be shy in glancing across disciplinary boundaries to see what anthropologists and others are saying about the nature of ethnicity and identity.

Philip Payton
Institute of Cornish Studies

Jack Clemo, *The Cured Arno*, Bloodaxe, Newcastle-upon-Tyne, 1995, 62 pp., ISBN 1 85224 326 0, £6.95.

In 'Voice From a White Silence' (*Cornish Studies: Three*, 1995) John Hurst documents the manuscripts of Jack Clemo. He demonstrates Clemo's working techniques as well as the development of his poetry from an early puritanical anti-nature to a later, mellower outlook. *The Cured Arno* is Clemo's final poetic collection, which he had only just completed at the time of his death in 1994. Of the collection, Clemo himself writes:

My Italian visits gave me a symbol that illuminated even those poems which have no connection with Italy. The cured Arno may represent the cured ego, and sometimes I only showed the situation that needed cure. Dante knew his river only in its sick state. It was later 'cured' of its erratic and treacherous behaviour, its destructive winter floods and the stench of its dry mud bed in summer. The river image was apt for my purpose, whether I wrote about the Titanic disaster, which cured an earlier generation of its blind trust in mechanical power as the key to a safe world, or about my later marriage which cured my warped and bleak isolationism.

This is not a new theme or direction for Clemo. Indeed, since his 'creed-embedded marriage' (referred to here as the 'mature pledge') his work has followed this notion of the 'cured ego'. Thus *The Cured Arno* is to *Approach to Murano* as *A Different Drummer* is to *Broad Autumn*. In effect, this volume is *Approach to Murano Part II*. For afficianados of Clemo's work—more specifically his Cornish work—on the surface there would seem to be a further mellowing of his brittle as bedrock voice, though like *Approach to Murano*, dig deeper, and despite his desire to escape his poetic roots, they continue to reach out, grabbing Clemo by the ankle and yanking him back. The picture is not always what we may want, however. His fame as a Cornish poet is somewhat unrelated to the reality; there is a pervading sense of loathing of the earlier landscape and culture and a fuller embracement of what the high culture, literature and history of Italy may offer him.

'Quenched', the first poem in the collection, was the last Clemo was to write. It was written in the last of the seven Silvine exercise books that contained the manuscript, but at the back and upside down after many blank pages. In so many ways, the piece is a fitting ending of Clemo's career as he documents his final visit to the small cottage at Goonamarris, but 'the hill-knot fantasy has been abolished . . . No current jabs at the clotting shadows/With strange hints of industrial magic'. This is familiar enough territory for Clemo—and though the final two lines are not exactly unexpected ('But I avoid the house now: Its dark night has no message for me')—there is an admission that in Clemo's poetic construct Cornwall has lost favour. In the next poem 'The Tower' we find him in Italy, 'South of the Arno', in 'sprawled Tuscan splendor', and these symbols are developed through many of the new poems here, culminating in the masterful 'Heretic in Florence'. The piece is typically late-period Clemo, with him balancing the painful youth of his past with the resounding wisdom, tenderness and spiritual shift of his latter years. As usual the literary icons of Clemo's youth

come to the surface, but in the volume Clemo seems happier to accept
his role:

> I'm a poet
> Of Calvin's trend, one of the sparse tribe
> From English Dissent who found this relaxed city,
> This soft fount of culture, a strange, split home.
> Milton came first, and then, at Casa Guidi,
> The Brownings fused aesthete and Puritan.

Clemo explains how once he 'shrank from Dante, but now with his
healed river as metaphor, he can stand without shirking away from
what needed to be confronted. In a remarkable final stanza Clemo
manages to knot his earlier questioning style with an optimism, which
leaves us recoiling from its terseness and sparsity mixed with a daunting
final statement. This is the very epitomy of Clemo's style:

> How far can God's grace move the beholder
> Of mere cold skill or twisted vision?
> I sense the fringe, an electing flow.
> Summer heat has sucked churches, galleries
> And the river bridge I stand on,
> But there's no whimpering trickle, no silent bed:
> The cured Arno sings in freedom.

Historical portraiture has always generated some of Clemo's finest
work (witness 'Alfred Wallis' in *The Echoing Tip* (1971) and 'Virginia
Woolf Remembers St. Ives' from *A Different Drummer* (1986)). Here
Clemo turns his attention to George Müller, a lecherous German
student before his conversion, who became one of the most remarkable
Christian philanthropists of the nineteenth century. Müller is a figure
Clemo identifies with, relying as he did on faith and prayer, never
advertising or appealing for funds. Thus the powerful ending: 'The
saints' way of emptiness, blind trust in God. Its vindication is historic:
It bred no melancholy art'. Anne Brontë, sister to Charlotte and Emily,
is given similar treatment:

> There was irony: she returned to the hymn- scorning
> Shelter of the impious Emily,
> Stoic, unshocked by evil,
> Though this was only another form
> Of uncured ego, and disillusion came
> Before Branwell died and her defiance
> Lay hacked and unbreathing
> On the prosaic-sofa.

Anne Brontë became a governess at the home of the genteel Robinsons. One of her pupils disgraced the family by an elopement and a disastrous marriage. Anne's brother Branwell, a tutor in the same household, added further scandal by having a love affair with Mrs Robinson.

Clemo's construction of Cornwall has always been a problematical one. In this collection, it is a tourist Clemo that we are witnessing, the poet noticing how the landscape and culture have changed and what the place means to him now. Dorset is considered in a similar way, yet the Cornish poems have an edge since they are frighteningly melancholic. Only 'Delabole Quarry' succeeds on another level. The quarry is portrayed as a 'gaunt crater', Delabole is a 'foreign climate'. The slate can be used as roofing or as posts, yet the stone is also fine enough to take engraving. Clemo reflect on how when the slate is sliced, the craftsman is unsure of its properties. Clemo uses this as a metaphor for the poetic process, yet his art 'works on warmer material'.

In 'Cloud over Bugle' a more political Clemo emerges, where he writes a response to the news in 1980 that a clay district site had been chosen for the building of a nuclear power station. It is perfect subject matter. Do we need another layer of pollution the poem asks?—'We know pollution in these parts . . . Must we taste, besides clay, the freaks of science/In new ways of maiming the unborn/Planting cancer through the radioactive air'. Presumably this is an older piece and it perhaps regretful that Clemo did not pursue any further this kind of ideologically more dangerous poetic.

'Village Carnival (St Stephen, August 1928)' is a beautiful reflection on an earlier era. As usual, Clemo is the observer. He senses the 'receding swagger of a brass band' and 'panted old tunes in the twilight'. But Clemo chooses not to laugh, not because the poet was miserable, more because he senses the 'unbearable poignancy' of the village trying so hard to escape the reality of living.

The Cured Arno is not a volume that will please everyone; indeed the way in which Cornwall is negated and seen as a place he no longer wishes to know is particularly shocking, yet one needs to keep in mind the necessary progression of any poet. Clemo's lasting contribution to world literature transcends Cornwall and this needs to be voiced. However, his clear actualities remind us that a wish to bear faithful witness to such biographical upheavals and enchantments is often where poetry begins.

Alan M. Kent
University of Exeter

NOTES ON CONTRIBUTORS

Bernard Deacon is Associate Lecturer in Social Sciences at the Open University and tutor in Local and Regional History and in Cornish Studies at the University of Exeter's Department of Continuing and Adult Education in Truro. He has written widely on Cornish Studies, and is especially interested in identity formation in eighteenth and nineteenth-century Cornwall. His most recent publication is 'Industrial Civilization: Images of Cornwall Between West Barbary and Delectable Duchy' in Ella Westland (ed.), *Cornwall: The Cultural Construction of Place* (1996).

Amy Hale is a PhD student in Folklore at the University of California, Los Angeles, with a specialism in Celtic Studies. Current research is on contemporary Celtic identities in Cornwall. Recent publications include an essay on Celtic tourism in the *Proceedings of the 1995 Harvard Celtic Colloquium*. She resides in Cornwall.

Neil Kennedy is secretary of the Cornish Language Council and has worked closely with Richard Gendall (Honorary Research Fellow in the University of Exeter) on the revival of Modern Cornish. He edits the magazine *An Garrack*, and is part-time tutor in Cornish Language Studies in the University of Exeter's Department of Continuing and Adult Education in Truro.

Alan M. Kent is poet, novelist and a PhD student in the Institute of Cornish Studies and the School of English and American Studies at the University of Exeter, researching tradition and nationalism in Cornish literature. Recent academic publications include chapters in Ian A. Bell (ed.), *Peripheral Visions: Images of Nationhood in Contemporary British Fiction* (1995), and Ella Westland (ed.), *Cornwall: The Romantic Construction of Place*.

Brian Murdoch is Professor of German at the University of Stirling. His most recent book is *The Germanic Hero* (1996), based on his 1994 Waynflete Lectures at Magdalen College, Oxford. He has also written widely on Cornish texts, and his *Cornish Literature* appeared in 1993.

Philip Payton is Reader in Cornish Studies and Director of the Institute of Cornish Studies at the University of Exeter. Amongst his recent books are *The Making of Modern Cornwall: Historical Experience and the Persistence of 'Difference'* (1992), *Cornwall Since the War: The Contemporary History of a European Region* (editor, 1993), and *Cornwall* (1996).

Glanville Price is Emeritus Professor of French at the University of Wales Aberystwyth. His publications include *The French Language, Present and Past* (1971), *The Languages of Britain* (1984), *The Celtic Connection* (editor, 1992), and *A Comprehensive French Grammar* (4th edition, 1993). He is currently editing an *Encyclopedia of European Languages*.

Rod Sheaff is Fellow in the Health Services Management Unit at the University of Manchester, and is interested chiefly in health policy, social markets, and Eastern European health systems. Among his publications are *Marketing for Health Services* (1991) and *The Need for Healthcare* (1996).

Mark Stoyle is Lecturer in Early Modern History at the University of Southampton. He is author of *Loyalty and Locality: Popular Allegiance in Devon During the English Civil War* (1994) and *From Deliverance to Destruction: Rebellion and Civil War in an English City* (1995).

Paul Thornton is Assistant Director of the Institute of Cornish Studies at the University of Exeter. His research interests include the geography of tourism, on which he has written extensively, especially in its Cornish context. He has contributed regularly to the series *Cornish Studies*. In collaboration with Cornwall County Council, he has recently completed a major survey of second homes in Cornwall.

N.J.A. Williams is Lecturer in Irish at University College Dublin, and has also taught Celtic Studies at Queen's University Belfast and in the University of Liverpool. He taught himself Cornish while still at school and was elected Bard of the Cornish Gorsedd at the age of 19 for proficiency in the Cornish language. Amongst his recent publications is *Cornish Today* (1995).